P9-AQV-810

1-64

Examples of Gregorian Chant
and
Other Sacred Music of the 16th Century

Examples of Gregorian Chant and Other Sacred Music of the 16th Century

Compiled by

GUSTAVE FREDRIC SODERLUND

and

SAMUEL H. SCOTT

North Texas State University

APPLETON-CENTURY-CROFTS

Educational Division

MEREDITH CORPORATION

780-1

Library of Congress Card Number: 70-129090

PRINTED IN THE UNITED STATES OF AMERICA

390-82969-2

FOREWORD

This collection was conceived primarily as an organized body of material to be used in classes in 16th century counterpoint. Since the basis for mastery of the technique lies in the ability to understand and to write in two and three voices, we have included 26 examples of two voice writing and 27 examples of three voice writing. For more advanced students examples of four and five voice writing have been included as well as larger, multi-movement Masses.

In the belief that there is a common body of techniques employed by the great composers of the period, examples from five different composers have been included. It is interesting to note that the basic similarities among them far outnumber the differences with which each composer stamps his work with his own personality.

The examples have been designated systematically by number in order to aid in ready and specific classroom reference. The first digit indicates the number of voices in the composition, and the second number simply indicates the position of the example in the series. Example 3-14, then, is the fourteenth example in the group of three voice compositions.

Identification of sources, commentary and translations are provided at the end of the collection.

The two and three voice examples have been barred in such a way as to facilitate the study of the rhythmic-metric techniques of the period. No attempt has been made to use the half note as the inevitable pulse unit, for the student should develop the ability to recognize the proper pulse unit in spite of the conventional alla breve meter signature at the beginning of compositions.

Samuel Scott

Denton, Texas
July, 1970

CONTENTS

EXAMPLES OF GREGORIAN CHANT

EXAMPLES OF TWO VOICE COUNTERPOINT

Examples of Gregorian Chant
and
Other Sacred Music of the 16th Century

Gregorian Chant.
(Alme Pater.)
I. (Dorian)
M.M. ♪ = 138
XI c.
Ky- ri- e e- lé- i- son Ký- ri- e e- lé- i- son,
Ký- ri- e e- lé- i- son. Chri ste e- lé- i- son.
Chri- ste e- lé- i- son. Christe e- lé- i- son.
Ký-ri-e e- lé- i- son. Ký- ri- e e- le- i- son.
Ký-ri- e ** e- le-i-son
I. (Dorian) Alleluia.
M.M ♪=160
Alle- lú- ia. *
V. Jú- stus ger- mi- ná- bit. sic-ut lí- li- um: et flo- ré- -bit
in ae- tér- num * ante Dó- mi- num.

I (Dorian) Communion.
M.M. ♪=160
Pás ser * invé- nit sí- bi dó- mum, et túr- túr ní- dum, u- bi re- pó- nat púl-
-los sú- os: al- tá- ri- a tú- a Dó- mi- ne. vir- tú- tum, Rex mé- us,
et Dé- us mé- us: be- á- ti qui há- bi- tant in dó- mo
tú- a, in saé- cu- lum saé- cu- li lau- dá- bunt te.
II. (Hypodorian) Offertory.
M.M. ♪=144
Ad te Dó- mi- ne * le- vá- ri á-
nimam mé- am: Dé- us mé- us, in te con- fí- do, non e- ru-
bé- scam: ne- que ir- rí- de- ant me in- i- mí- ci mé- i:
ét- e- nim u- ni- vér- si qui te exspé- ctant, non con- fun- dén- tur.
III. (Phrygian) Kyrie.
M.M. ♪=144
XI-XIII C
Ký- ri- e * e- lé- i- son. iij. Christe e- lé- i- son. iij Ký- ri- e e- lé- i- son. ij.
Ký- ri- e * e- lé i- son.

III. (Phrygian) Sanctus.
M.M. ♪ = 132
XI c.
Sánctus, * Sán-ctus, Sanctus Dómi-nus Dé-us Sá-ba-oth. Pléni sunt cae-li
et tér-ra gló-ri-a tú-a. Ho-sánna in ex-cél-sis.
Be-ne-dictus qui vé-nit in nó-mi-ne Dó-mi-ni. Ho-
sánna in ex-cel-sis
III. (Phrygian) Kýrie fons bonitatis.
M.M. ♪ = 132
X. c.
Ký-ri-e * e-lé-i-son. iij.
Chrí-ste e-
lé-i-son iij Ký-ri-e e-lé-i-son. ij
Ký-ri-e ** e-lé-i-son.
III (Phrygian) Alleluia.
M.M. ♪ = 160
Al-le-lú-ia. * ij.
℣. Ve-ni, Dó-mi-ne, et nó-

-li tar- dá- re: re- lá- xa fa- cí-
no- ra * plé- bis tú- ae.

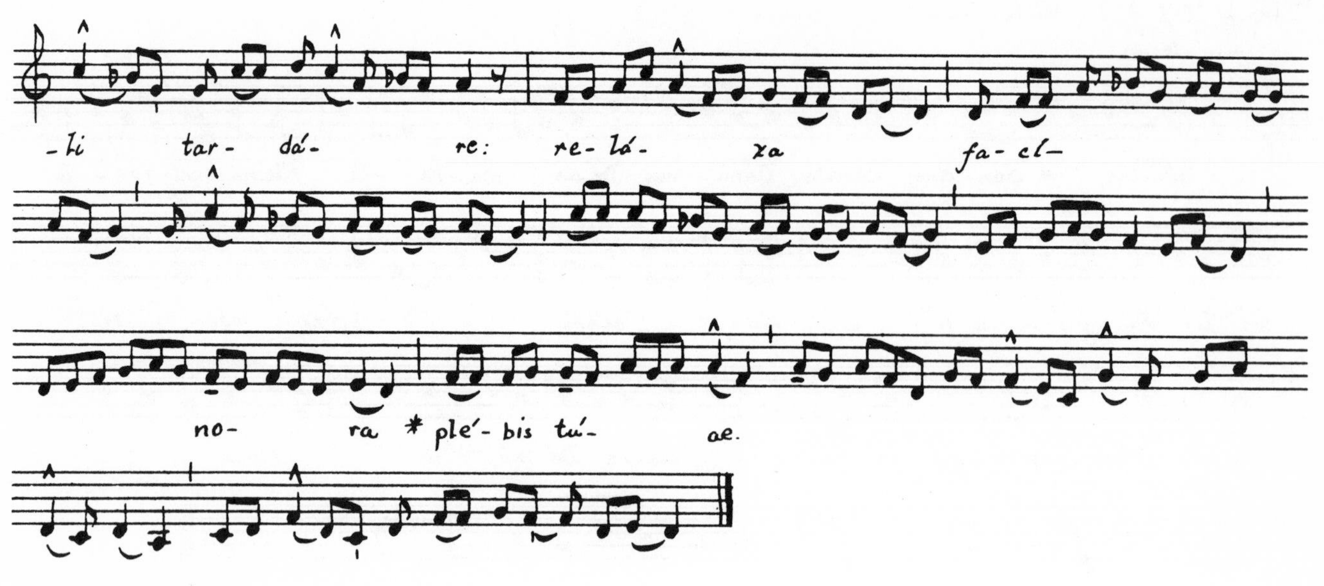

IV. (Hypophrygian) Response.

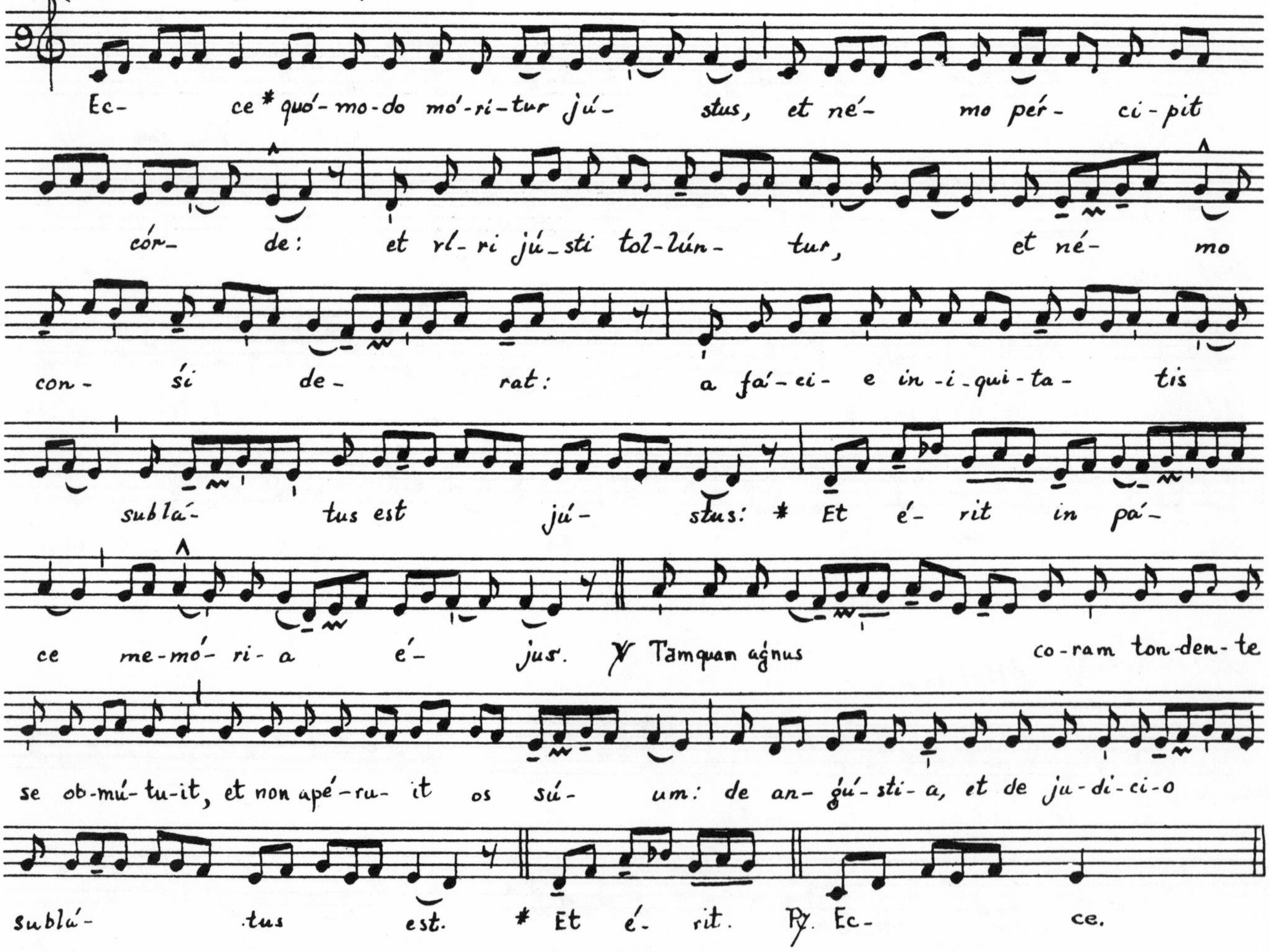
Ec- ce * quó- mo- do mó- ri- tur jú- stus, et né- mo pér- ci- pit
cór- de: et vi- ri jú- sti tol- lún- tur, et né- mo
con- sí de- rat: a fá- ci- e in- i- qui- ta- tis
sublá- tus est jú- stus: * Et é- rit in pá-
ce me- mó- ri- a é- jus. ℣ Tamquam agnus co- ram ton- den- te
se ob- mú- tu- it, et non apé- ru- it os sú- um: de an- gú- sti- a, et de ju- di- ci- o
sublá- tus est. * Et é- rit. ℟ Ec- ce.

V. (Lydian) Sanctus.
M.M. ♪=116
XIV c.
10
Sán- ctus, * Sánctus, Sán- ctus Dóminus De- us Sá-
ba- oth. Pléni sunt caéli et tér- ra glóri- a tú- a. Ho- sán- na in excél-
sis. Be- ne- dí- ctus qui vé- nit in nó- mi- ne Dó- mi- ni. Ho-
sán- na in ex- cél- sis.

V (Lydian) Agnus Dei.
M.M. ♪=132
(X) XIII c.
11
Ag- nus Dé- i, * qui tól- lis pec- cá- ta mún- di: mi-
se- ré re nó- bis: Ag- nus Dé- i, * qui tól- lis peccá- ta mún- di:
mi- se- ré- re nó- bis: Ag- nus Dé- i, * qui tól- lis peccá- ta
mún- di: dó- na nó- bis pá- cem.

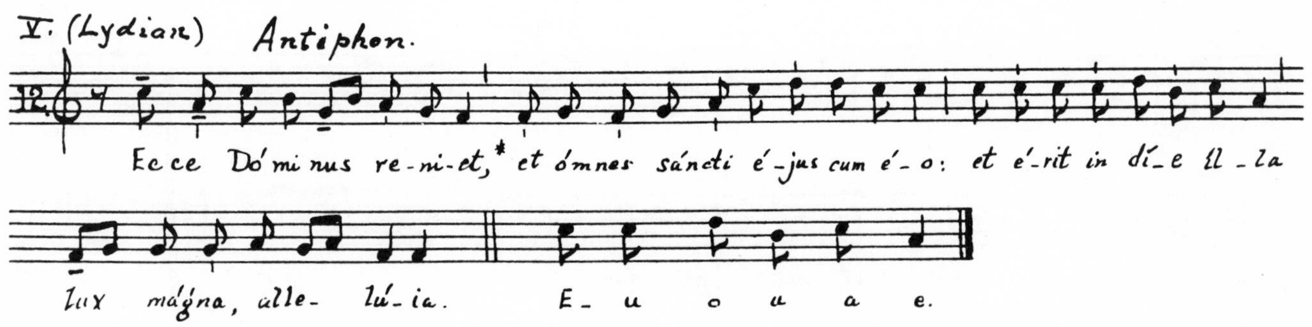
V. (Lydian) Antiphon.
12
Ecce Dóminus ve- ni- et, * et ómnes sáncti é- jus cum é- o: et é- rit in dí- e íl- la
lux mágna, alle- lú- ia. E- u o u a e.

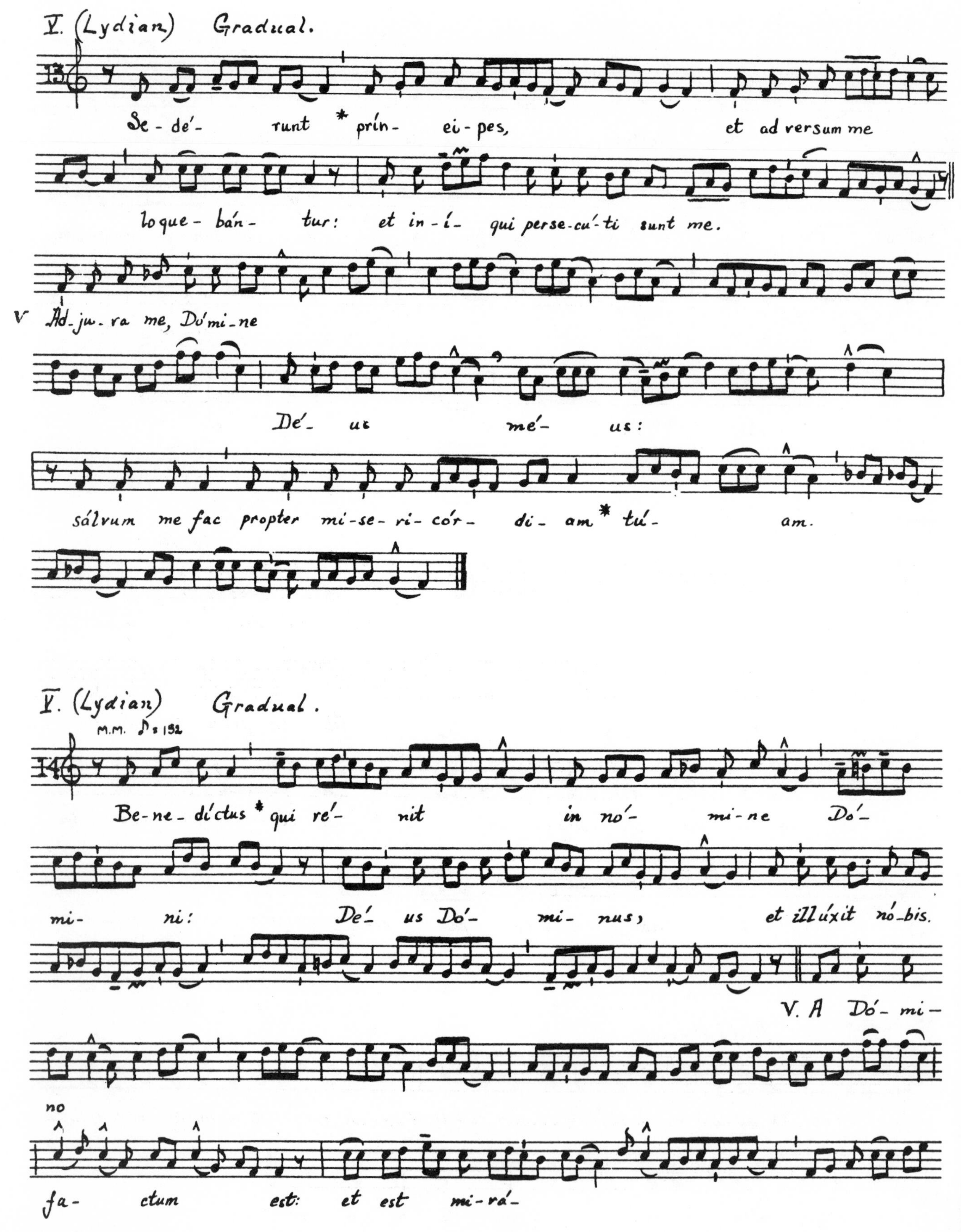
V. (Lydian) Gradual.
13
Se-dé- runt * prín- ci-pes, et adversum me
loque-bán- tur: et in-í- qui perse-cú-ti sunt me.
V Ad-ju-ra me, Dómi-ne
Dé- us mé- us:
sálvum me fac propter mi-se-ri-cór- di- am * tú- am.
V. (Lydian) Gradual.
M.M. ♪ = 132
14
Be-ne-díctus * qui vé- nit in nó- mi-ne Dó-
mi- ni: Dé- us Dó- mi- nus, et illúxit nó-bis.
V. A Dó-mi-
no
fa- ctum est: et est mi-rá-

VI. (Hypolydian) Communion.

VII. (Mixolydian) Antiphon.

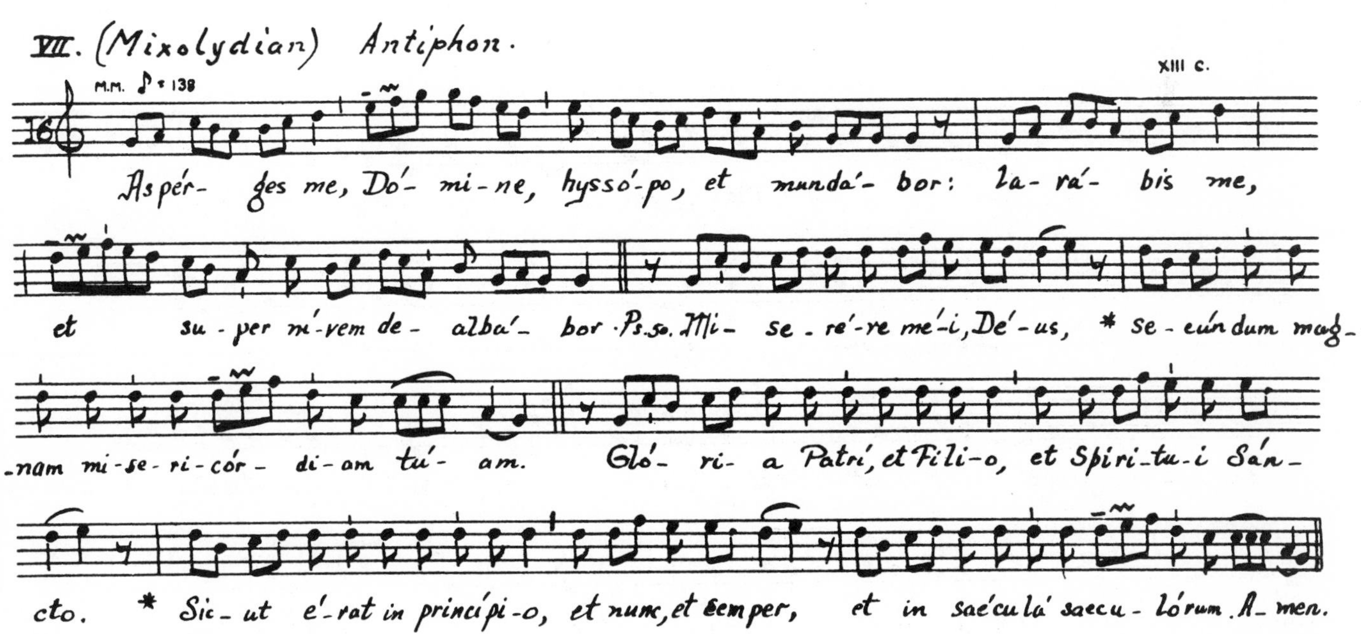

VII. (Mixolydian) Gradual.
M.M. ♪ = 152
17
Qui se-des, Dó-mi- ne *su- per Ché- ru-bim,
éx- ci- ta pot én- ti- am tu'am, et
ve'- ni. V. Qui ré-
gis Is- ra- el, in tén- de: qui
de - du'- cis vel- ut ó- vem *Jó seph.
VIII. (Hypomixolydian) Offertory.
M.M. ♪ = 144
18
Pre- cá- tus est * Mó- y - ses in con spé- ctu Dó-
mi- ni Dé- i sú- i, et dí- xit.
Pre- cá- tus est Mó y- ses in con spé- ctu Dó
mi- ni Dé- i sú- i, et dí- xit: Qua- re, Dó-
mi- ne, i- rá sce- ris in pó- pulo tu'-

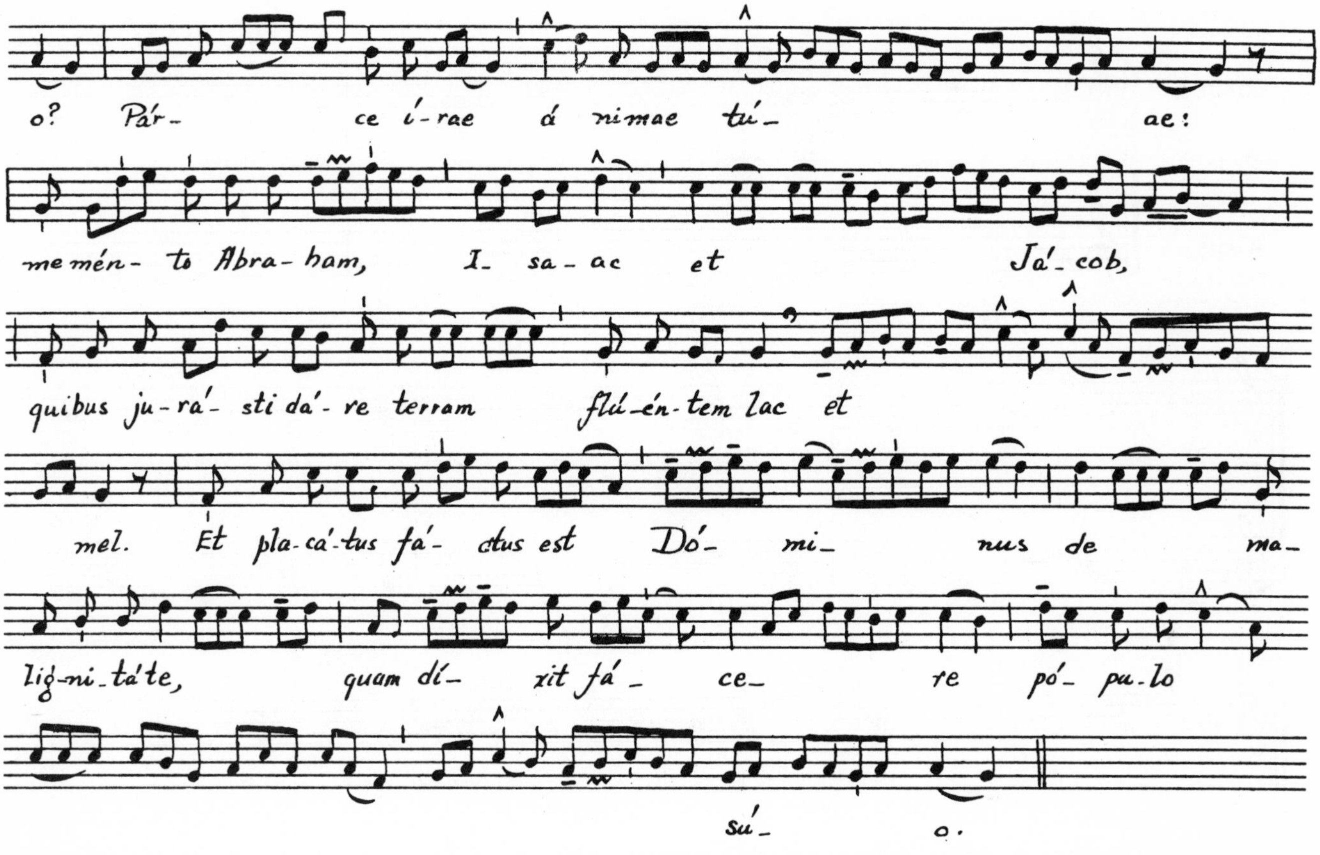

o? Pár- ce í-rae á nimae tú- ae:
meménto Abra-ham, I- sa-ac et Já-cob,
quibus ju-rá-sti dá-re terram flú-én-tem lac et
mel. Et pla-cá-tus fá- ctus est Dó- mi- nus de ma-
lig-ni-tá-te, quam dí- xit fá- ce- re pó- pu-lo
sú- o.

VIII. (Hypomixolydian) Introit.

19
Spí-ri - tus Dómi - - - ni * re - plé - vit ór-bem ter - rá-rum, al-le-
- - - lú - ia: et hoc quod cón- - ti - - net ó- - mni-a, sci-én-ti- am
- há-bet vó- cis, al-le - lú - - ia, al - le-lú - ia, al-le-lú-ia.
Ps. Ex-sur-gat Dé-us, et dis-si-péntur in-i- mí-ci é- jus: * et fú - gi-ant, qui o-dé-runt é-um,
a fá - ci - e é-jus. Gló-ri-a Pá-tri. E u o u a e.

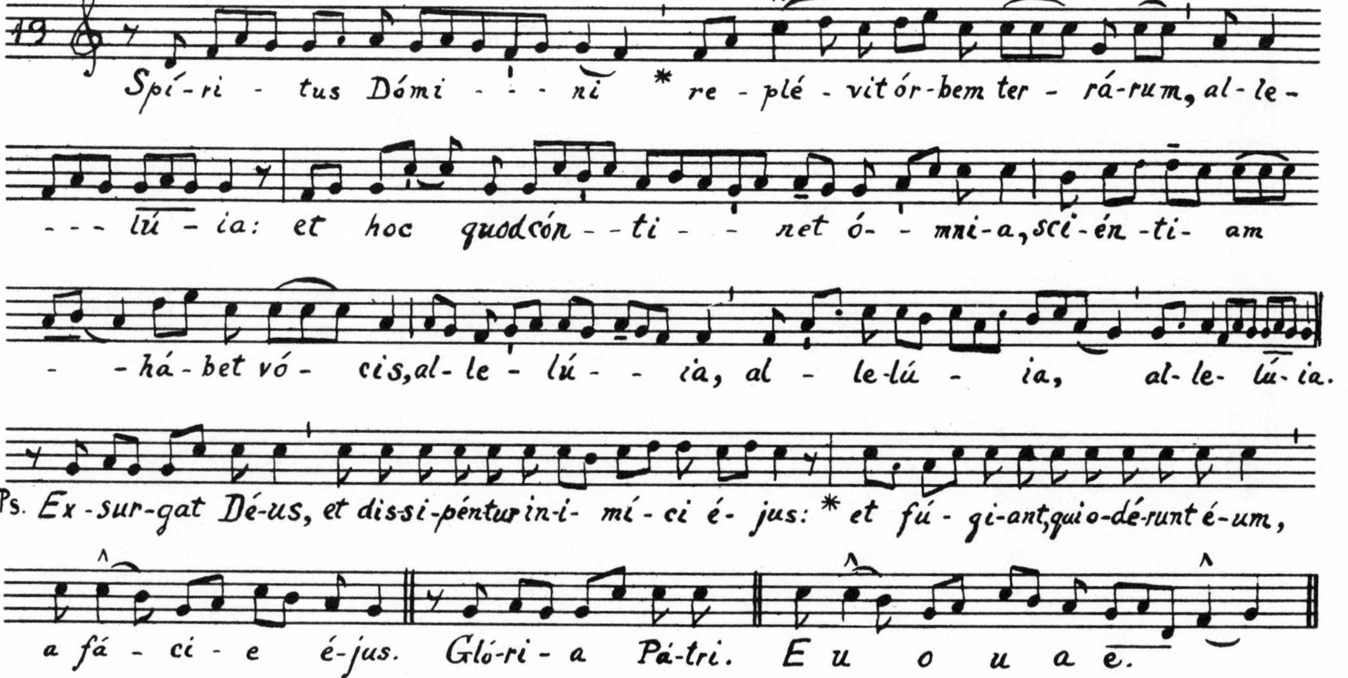

Cantiones duarum vocum

Lassus

-ta - bi-tur, et in sen - su ____ co -
- - - - - bi - tur, et in sen - su co -
-gi - ta - - - - - - bit cir - cum-spe - - cti -
- - gi - ta - - - - - - - bit cir - cum - spe -
- o - - nem De - - - - - - - - - - - - i,
- - cti - o - nem ____ De - - - - - - -
cir - cum - spe - - cti - o - - nem De - - - - - -
- i, cir - cum - spe - - cti - o - nem De - - - -
- - - - - - - - - - - - - - - - - - i.
- - - - - - - - - - - - - - - - - - - i.

Cantus
2 – 2
Altus
Be - - - a - tus, be - a - tus
Be - - - a - tus, be - a - tus ho - - - - -
ho - - mo, qui in - ve - nit,
- mo, qui in - ve - nit, qui
qui in - ve - - - - nit sa -
in - ve - - - - nit sa - - - - - - - - pi -
- pi - en - ti - am, et qui af - - -
- en - - - - - - - - - - ti - am, et
- flu - it pru - - - - den - ti - a me -
qui af - - flu - it pru - - den - ti - a me - li -

- - li - or, me - li - or est ac - qui - si - ti - o ___
- or, me - - li - or est ac - - qui - si - ti - o

___ e - - - - - - jus ne - go - ti -
e - - - - - - - - - - - - - - - - jus ne -

- a - ti - o - - ne ar - gen - - - ti et au - - - -
- go - ti - a - ti - o - - ne ar - gen - - - - ti et au - -

- - ri pri - - - mi et ___ pu - - -
- - - - - - ri pri - mi et ___ pu -

- - - ris - - - - - - - - - - - - - - - si - - mi.
- - - - - - ris - - - - - - - - - - - - - - si - - mi.

Cantus
2-3
Altus
O - - cu - lus non vi - - - - - - dit,
O - - - - cu - lus non
nec au - - - - - ris au - - -
vi - - - - - - dit, nec au - -
- di - - - - - - - - - - - - - vit, nec
- - - ris au - - - - - - - - di - - - vit,
in cor ho - - mi - nis a - - - scen - - - -
nec in cor ho - mi - nis a - - - - - scen - - -
- - - - - - - - - - - - - dit quae
- - - - - - - - - - - - - - - dit quae prae - - -

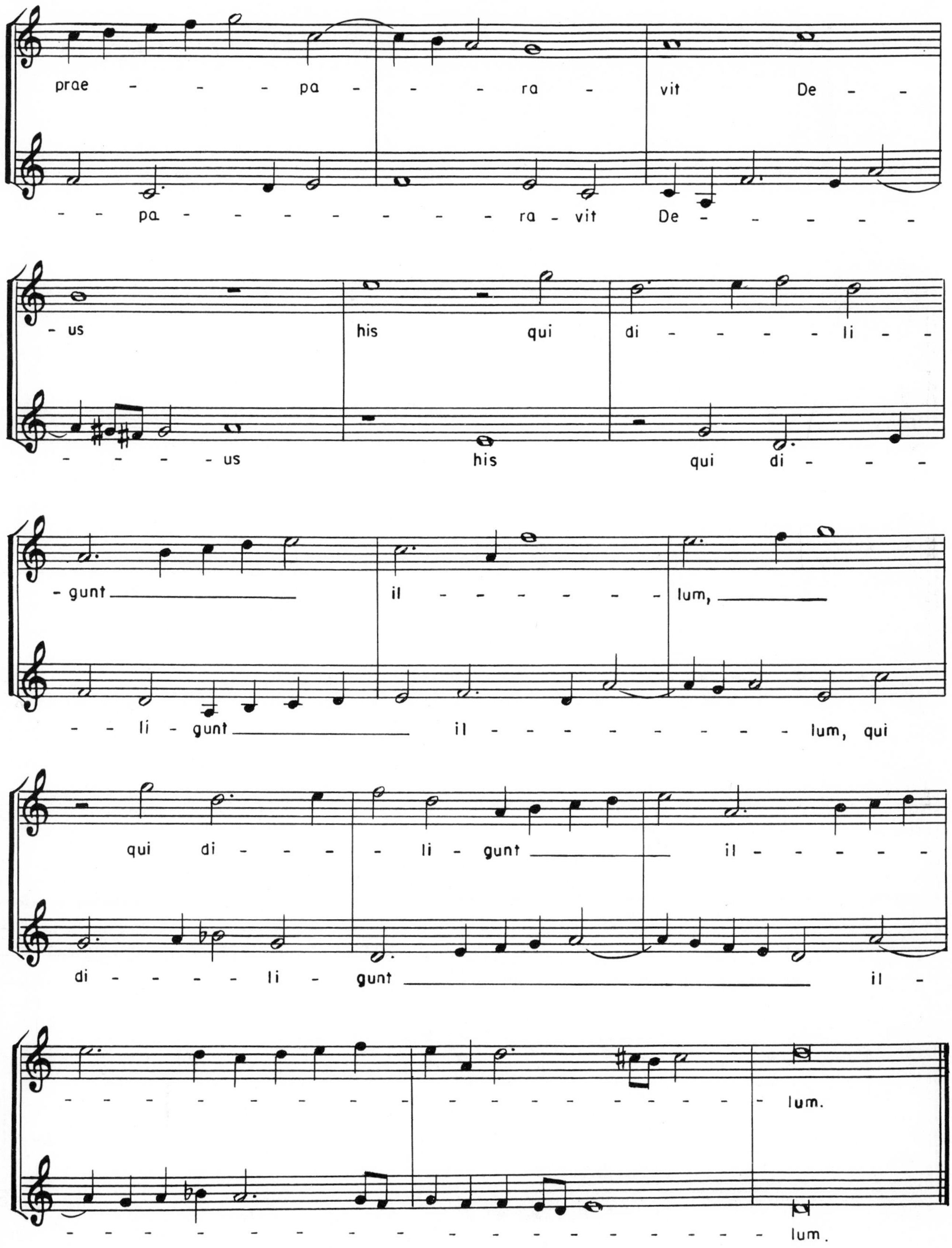
prae - - - pa - - - ra - vit De - -
- - pa - - - - - - - ra - vit De - - - - - -
- us his qui di - - - - - li - -
- - - - us his qui di - - -
- gunt il - - - - - - - lum,
- - li - gunt il - - - - - - - - - lum, qui
qui di - - - - li - gunt il - - - - - -
di - - - - - li - gunt il -
- lum.
- lum.

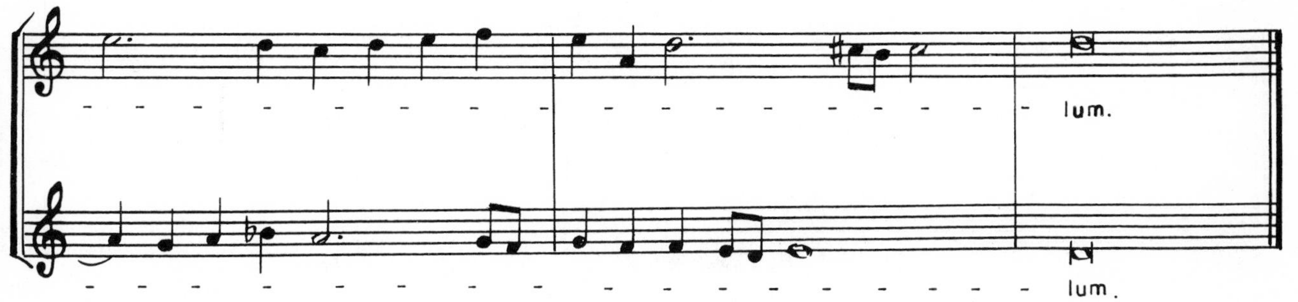

Cantus
2 – 4
Altus
Ju – – stus cor su – – – um tra –
Ju – – – stus cor su – –
– – – det ad vi – gi – lan – dum di – – – – – – – –
– – um tra – – – – det ad vi – gi – lan – dum di –
– lu – – – – – – – – – – – – – – – – – cu – lo
– – – – – – – – – lu – – – – – – – – – – – – cu – lo
ad Do – – – – – – – – – – – mi – num, ad
ad Do – – – – – – – – – – – – mi – num,
Do – – – – – – – – – – – – mi – num qui fe – cit il – lum,
ad Do – – – – – – – – – – – – mi – num qui fe – cit

et in con - spe - - - - - - - - - - ctu al - - -
il - lum, et in con - spe - - - - - - - - - - - - ctu
- - - - - - - - - - - - - - - tis - - - - - - si - mi
al - - - - - - - - - - - tis - - - - - - si - mi de -
de - - - - - - - pre - - ca - - - - - - bi - tur, de - -
- - - - - - - - - pre - ca - - - - - - - - - - - bi - tur,
- pre - ca - - - - - - - - - - - - - - - - - bi - tur,
de - - - - - - - - pre - - - - - ca - - - - - - - bi - tur,
de - pre - ca - - - - - - - - - - - - - - bi - tur.
de - - - - - - - - pre - - - - ca - - - - - - bi - - tur.

Cantus
2 – 5
Altus
Ex - - spec - ta - ti - o jus - to - -
Ex - spec - ta - ti - o jus - to - - - - - - rum lae -
- - - - rum lae - ti - - - - - - - - - - -
- ti - - - - - - - - - - - - - - ti - a, spes
- - ti - a, spes au - - - - - - - - - -
au - - - - - - - - - - - - - - tem im - pi - o - -
- - tem im - pi - o - - - - - - rum per - - -
- - - - rum per - - - - - - - - - - -
- - - - i - - - - - bit; for - ti - tu - do
- - - - - - - - i - - bit; for - - ti - tu - -

sim - - - - - - - - - - - - - - pli - cis ri - - - -

-do sim - - - - - - - - - - - - - - pli - cis ri - - - - - - -

-a Do - - - - - mi - ni, et pa - - - -

- - - - - - - a ——— Do - - mi - ni,

- - - vor his, qui o - pe - ran - - - tur, qui o - pe -

et pa - - - - - - - vor his, qui o - pe - ran - - - tur,

-ran - tur ma -

qui o - pe - ran - - - - tur ma - - - - - - - -

- lum.

- lum.

20.
Cantus
2-6
Altus
Qui se - - qui-tur me, qui se - qui-tur me,
Qui se - qui-tur me, qui se - qui-tur
qui se - - qui-tur me non
me, qui se - - - qui-tur me
am - - bu - lat, non am - - bu - lat in
non am - - - - bu - lat, non am - - bu - lat in
te - - - - - - - - ne - bris,
te - ne - bris, sed
sed ha - be - - - - - - - bit,
ha - be - - - - - - - - - - - bit, sed ha - be -

sed ha - be - bit lu -
bit lu -

men vi -
men vi -

tae: di - cit Do - mi -
tae: di - cit Do -

nus, di - cit Do -
mi - nus, di - cit Do -

mi - nus.
mi - nus.

Altus
2 - 7
Bassus
Ju - - - - - sti tu - le - runt spo - li - a
Ju - - - - - - - sti tu - le - runt
im - - pi - o - rum, im - - pi - o - rum,
spo - li - a im - - pi - o - rum, im - pi -
et can - - - - - ta - ve - - - - - runt, Do -
- o - - rum, et can - - - - - - ta - ve - - -
- - mi - ne, no - - men san - - - - - ctum
- runt, Do - mi - ne, no - men san - - - - ctum
tu - - - - - - - - um, et vic - tri - -
tu - - - - um, et vic - tri - - cem

- - cem ma - - - - - - - - num tu - - - um lau -
ma - - - - - - - - - - - - - - num tu - um
- da - ve - - - - - - - - runt pa - - - - - - - - ri -
lau - - - - da - ve - - - - - - - - - - runt pa - ri -
- ter, Do - - - - mi - ne De - - - -
- ter, Do - - mi - ne De - - - - - us,
- - - us, De - - - - - - - - - - - - - -
De - - - - - - - - - - - - - us
- - - us no - - - - - ster.
no - - - - - - - - - - - - - - - ster.

Tenor
2 - 8
Bassus
San - - - - - cti me - - i,
San - - - - - - - - - - - cti me - - -
san - - - - - - - - - - cti me - - - - - -
- - i, san - - - - - cti me - - i, qui
- i, qui in i - - sto
in i - - - sto
sae - - - - - cu - lo cer - ta - - - - - - - - -
saecu - lo cer - ta - - - - - - - - men ha -
- men ha - - - - - - - bu - i - - - stis, mer - ce - -
- - - - - - - - - - - bu - i - - - - - - stis, mer -

-dem la - bo - - - - rum ves - - tro - - - - - - - -
- ce - - - dem la - bo - - - rum ves - tro - - - -
- - - rum e - go red - dam vo - - -
- - - rum e - go red - dam vo - - - - - - - - - - -
- - - bis, e - go red - dam vo - - -
- - - - - - - bis, e - - go red - dam
- - - - - - - - - - - - - - - - bis, e - - go
vo - - - - - - - - - - - - - - bis, e - - - go, e -
red - - dam vo - - - - - - - - - - - - bis.
- go red - dam vo - - - - - - - - - - - - - bis.

Tenor
2 - 9
Bassus
Qui vult ve - ni - - re post
Qui vult ve - ni - - re post me,
me, ve - ni - re post me, ve - ni - - re
ve - ni - - re post me, ve - ni - - re post
— post me, ab - ne - get se - met
me, ab - ne - get se -
i - psum, ab - ne - get se - met i - psum, et tol - let cru - - -
- met i - psum, ab - ne - get se - met i - psum, et
- - - - - cem su - - am, et tol - let cru - - - cem
tol - let cru - - - cem su - - am, et tol - let cru - - -

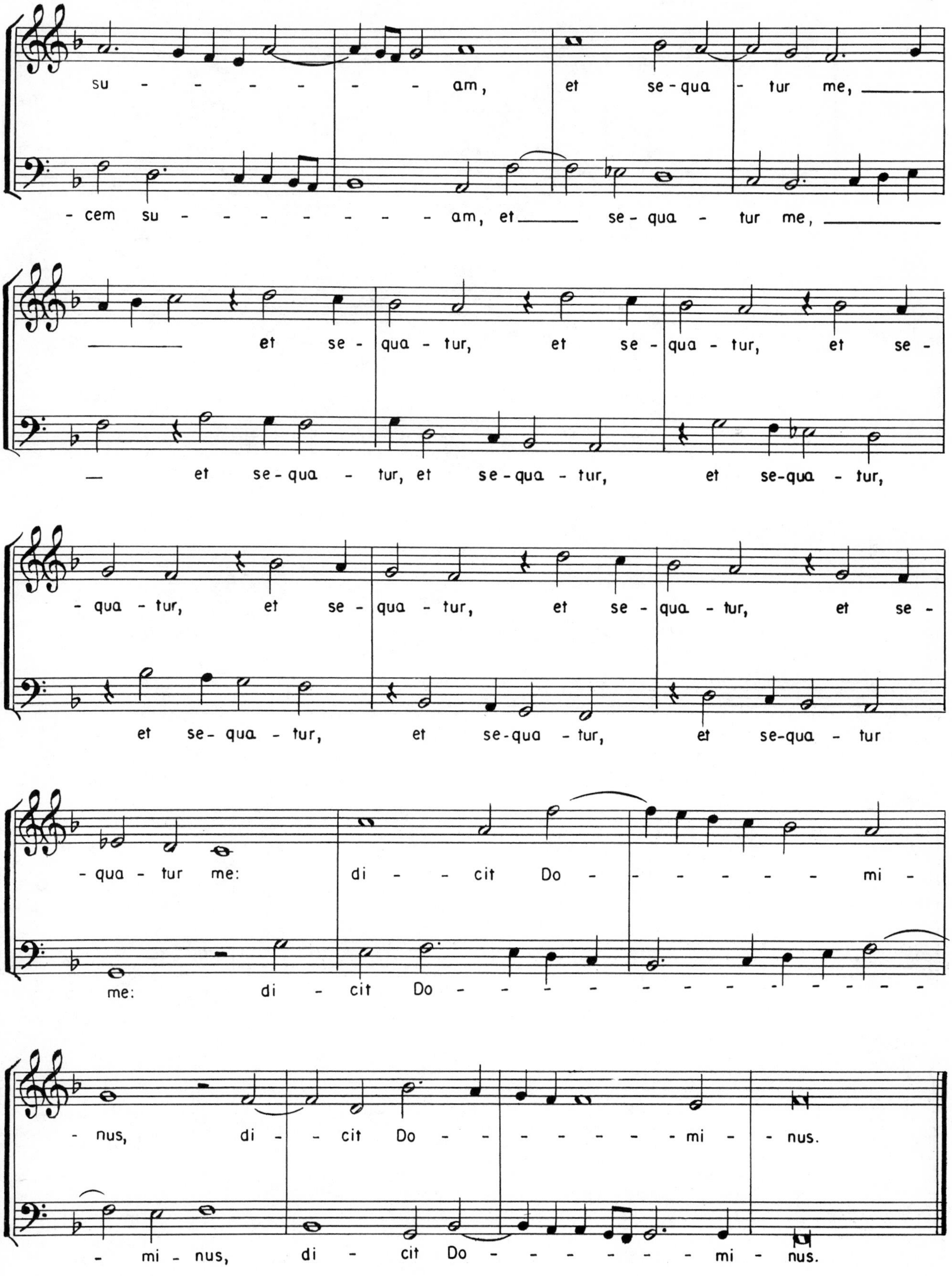
su - - - - - - am, et se-qua - tur me,
-cem su - - - - - - - - - am, et se-qua - tur me,
et se - qua - tur, et se - qua - tur, et se -
et se-qua - tur, et se-qua - tur, et se-qua - tur,
-qua - tur, et se - qua - tur, et se - qua - tur, et se -
et se-qua - tur, et se-qua - tur, et se-qua - tur
-qua - tur me: di - - cit Do - - - - - - - - mi -
me: di - cit Do - - - - - - - - - - - - - -
- nus, di - - cit Do - - - - - - - - mi - - nus.
- mi - nus, di - cit Do - - - - - - - - mi - nus.

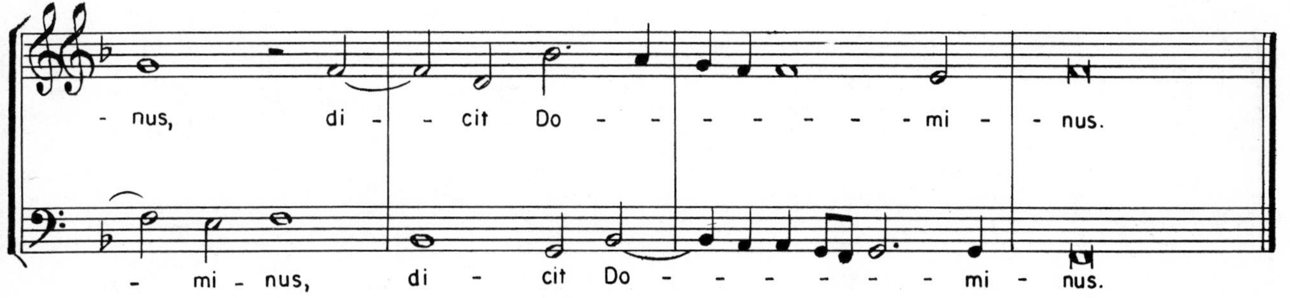

28.
Altus
2-10
Bassus
Ser - ve bo - ne et fi - de - - - - - - - - - - - - - - - - - - lis, qui - a in pau - - - - - - ca fu - i - sti fi - de - - - - - lis, fu - i - sti fi - de - - - lis, su - - - - - pra mul - - - - ta
Ser - - ve bo - ne et fi - de - - lis, qui - a in pau - - - - - - ca fu - i - sti fi - de - - - - - - lis, fu - i - sti fi - de - - - - lis, su - - - - pra mul - - - - - - ta te con -

te con - sti - tu - am, con - sti - tu - am
-sti - tu - am, con - sti - tu - am in -
in - tra, in - tra in qua - di - um
- tra, in - - tra in qua - di - um Do - -
Do - mi - ni, in qua - di - um, in qua - di - um
- mi - ni, in qua - di - um, in qua - di - um
Do - mi - ni De - - - -
Do - - mi - ni De - - - -
- i tu - - - i.
- - i tu - - - - i.

Tenor
2-11
Bassus
Ful - ge - bunt ju - - - - - - - - sti sic -
Ful - - ge - bunt ju - - - - - -
- ut li - li - um, ful - ge - bunt ju - - - - - - -
- - sti sic - ut li - li - um, ful - ge - bunt
- - - - - - - - - - - - - - sti sic - ut li - li - um
ju - sti sic - ut
et sic - ut ro - - - - sa in Je - ri - cho flo -
li - li - um et sic - ut ro - - - - sa in Je - ri -
- re - - - - - bunt, flo - re - - - - - bunt, flo -
- cho flo - re - - - - - - bunt, flo - re - - - - -

- re - - - - - bunt an - - - - - - - te Do - - - - -

- bunt, flo - re - - - - - - - bunt an - - - - - - - - -

- - - - - - - mi - num, an - - - - - - - - - - - te

- te Do - - - - - - - - - mi - num, an -

Do - - - - - - - - mi - num, an -

- - - - - - - te Do - - - - - - - - - - - - - - - - mi -

- - - - - - te Do - - - - - - - - - - - - - - - -

num, an - - - - - - - - - - - - - - - - - te

- - - - - - mi - num.

Do - - - - - - mi - num, an - - - - - - - te Do - mi - num.

Tenor
2 - 12
Bassus
Sic - - - - - - - - - - - ut ro - - - - - - -
Sic - - ut ro - - - - - - - - - - - - sa,
sa, sic - - ut ro - - - - - - - - - - - sa
sic - - - - - - - - - - - - - - ut ro - - - - - - - -
in - - - - - - ter spi - - nas il - las ad - dit spe -
- sa in - - - - ter spi - - - - - nas il - las
- - - - - - - - - - - - ci - em, sic re -
ad - - dit spe - - - - - - - - - ci - em,
- nu - stat su - - - - - - - am Vir - - go Ma -
sic re - nu - - stat su - - - - - - - - am

-ri - a pro - - ge - - - ni - em, Ma - ri - a pro - ge - - -
Vir - go Ma - ri - a pro - - ge - ni - em, Ma - ri - a
- - - - - - - - ni - em: ger - mi - na - vit e - -
pro - - ge - ni - em: ger - mi - na - vit e - nim flo -
- nim flo - - - - - - - - - - - - - - - - rem,
- rem, qui
qui vi - ta - - - lem dat o - do - - - - - rem, qui
vi - ta - - - lem dat o - do - - - - - - - - rem, qui vi - ta -
vi - ta - - - - lem dat o - - do - - - - - - - rem.
- - lem dat o - do - - - - - - - - - - - rem.

Missa ad imitationem moduli Puis que i'ay perdu : Gloria

Missa ad imitationem moduli O passi sparsi: Gloria

Missa super Frere Thibault: Credo

Missa ad imitationem moduli Doulce memoire: Credo

Tenor
2-16b
Bassus
Et i - te-rum ven - tu - rus est cum glo - ri - a ju - di - ca - re vi - vos et mor - tu - os: cu - jus re - gni non e - rit fi - nis.
Et i - te - rum ven - tu - rus est cum glo - ri - a ju - di - ca - re vi - vos et mor - tu - os: cu - jus re - gni non e - rit fi - nis.

Missa Da pacem: Credo

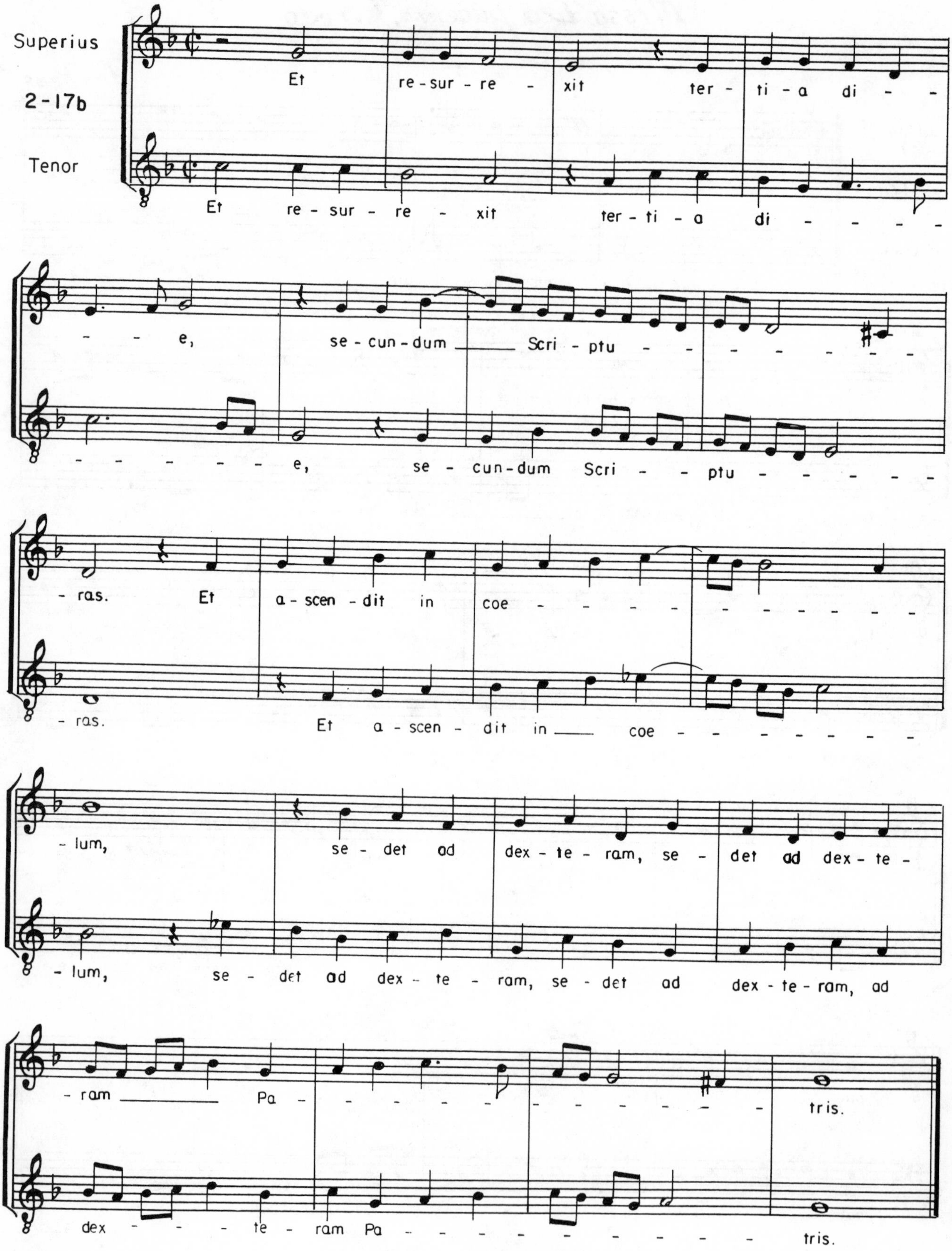
Superius
2-17b
Tenor
Et re-sur-re - xit ter - ti-a di - - - - e, se-cun-dum Scri-ptu - - - - - - - - - - - ras. Et a-scen-dit in coe - - - - - - - - - - - lum, se - det ad dex-te-ram, se - det ad dex-te - ram Pa - - - - - - - - - - - - - tris.
Et re-sur-re - xit ter-ti-a di - - - - - - - - - - - - e, se-cun-dum Scri - - ptu - - - - - - ras. Et a-scen-dit in coe - - - - - - - - - lum, se - det ad dex-te-ram, se-det ad dex-te-ram, ad dex - - - te-ram Pa - - - - - - - - - - - - tris.

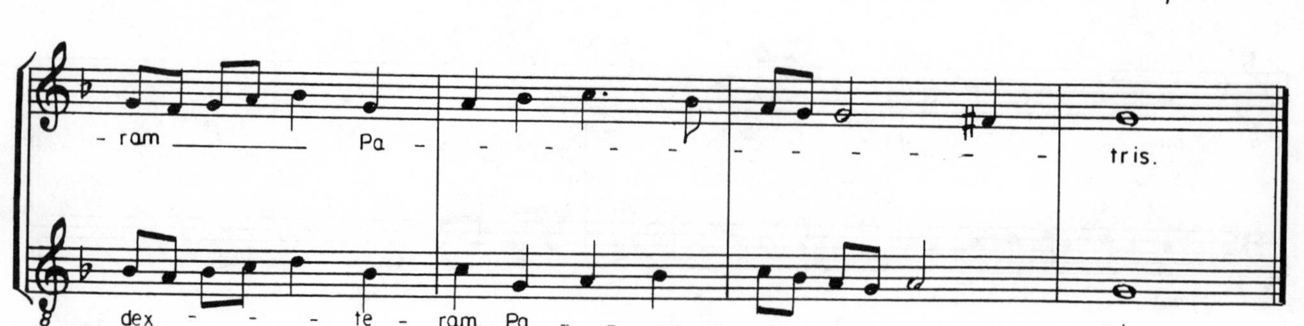

Missa Mater Patris: Sanctus

ter - - - - - - - - - - - ra, ple - ni ___ sunt coe -
- - - - - - - - ra, ple - ni ___ sunt coe - li et
- li et ter - - - - - - - ra glo - - -
ter - - - - - - - - ra glo - - - - ri - -
- - ri - a, glo - ri - a tu - a, glo - ri - a tu -
- a, glo - ri - a tu - a, glo - ri - a tu - a, glo -
- a, glo - ri - a tu - - - - - - a, glo - ri - a tu - a, glo -
- ri - a tu - - - - - - - - - a, glo - ri - a tu - a, glo - - ri - a
- - ri - a tu - - - - - - - - - a.
tu - - - - - - - - - - - - - - a.

Missa Super Frere Thibault: Benedictus

Missa l'homme armé: Benedictus

des Pres

nit, qui
ve nit, qui
ve nit.
ve nit.
Superius
2 - 20c
Superius
In no mi ne
In no - mi - ne Do
Do
mi - ni, Do mi - ni,
mi - ni, Do
in no mi - ne, in no
mi ni.
mi - ne Do - mi - ni.

Missa ad fugam: Benedictus

des Pres

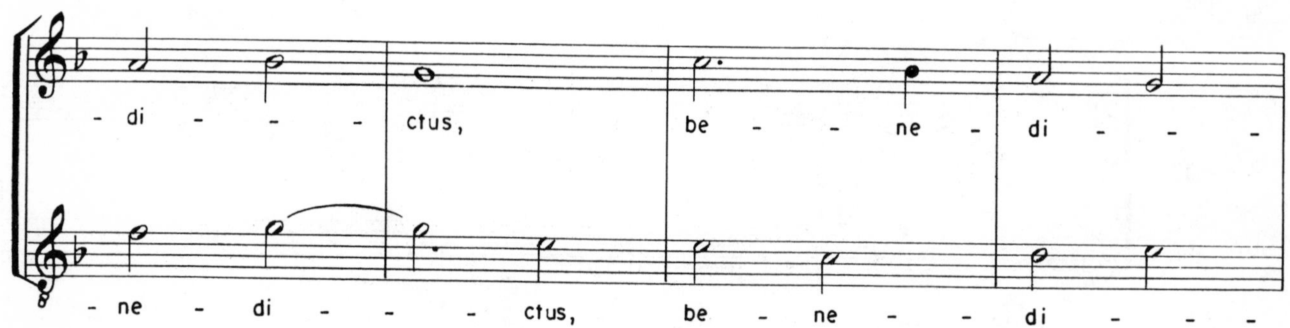

Altus
2 - 21b
Bassus
Qui ve - nit,
Qui ve - nit, qui ve - - -
qui ve - - - - - - - - - - - - - - - - -
- - - - - - - - - - - - - - - - - - - -
- nit in no - mi - ne, in no -
- - - nit in no - - - - - - - -
- - - - - - - - - mi - ne Do - - - - - - - - -
- - - - mi - - ne Do - - - - - - - - -
- - - - - - - - - - - - - - - - - mi - ni.
- - - - - - - - - - - - - - mi - - - - - ni.

Missa Mater Patris: Benedictus

- mi - ne Do - mi - ni, in no - mi - ne Do - - - - - - -
in no - mi - ne Do - - mi - ni, in no - mi - ne Do - - - -
- mi - ni, in no - mi - ne, in no - mi - ne, in no -
- - - - - mi - ni, in no - mi - ne, in no - mi - ne,
- mi - ne, in no - mi - ne, in no - - - - -
in no - mi - ne, in no - mi - ne, in no - -
- - mi - ne Do - - - - - - - - - - - - - - -
- - - - - - mi - ne Do - - - - - - - - - - - -
- - - - - - - - - - - - - mi - ni.
- - - - - - - - - - - - - mi - - ni.

Missa Di dadi : Benedictus

des Pres

- - san - - - na, ho - - san - - - - - na in
- na, ho - - san - - na, ho - san - - - - na in ex -
ex - cel - - - - - sis, in ex - cel - - - - - - - -
- cel - - - - - - - sis, in ex - cel - - - - - - - - -
- - - - - sis, in ex - cel - sis, in ex - cel - - - - -
- - - - - sis, in ex - cel - sis, in ex - cel - - - - - - -
- - - - sis, in ex -
- - sis, in ex -
- cel - - - - sis, in ex - cel - - - - sis, in
- cel - - - - - - - - - - - - sis, in
ex - - cel - - - - - sis.
ex - cel - - - - - - - - - - sis.

Missa La sol fa re mi: Agnus Dei

Missa Mater Patris: Agnus Dei

mi - se - re - - - - - re no - - - - -
- - re no - - - - - - - bis, mi - - - - se - re -
- bis, mi - - se - re - re no - - bis, mi -
- re no - bis, mi - - - se - re - - - - - - - -
- se - re - - - - - - - - - re no - bis, mi - -
- - - - re no - bis, mi - - - - se - re - - re no - - -
- se - re - - re no - - - - - - - - - - - - - -
- -
- - - - - - - - - - - - bis.
- bis, no - - - - - - - - - - - bis.

Missa de Beata Virgine: Agnus Dei

- - - - - - di, mi - se - re -
- - - - - - - - di, mi - se - re -
- - - - - - - - re no - - - - - - - - -
- - - - - - - - re no - - - - - - - - - - -
- - - - - - - - - - - - - bis, mi - - se -
- - - - - - - - - - - - - - bis, mi - - se - re - re
- re - re no - - - - - - - - - - - - - -
no - - - - - - - - - - - - - - - - - -
- - - - - - - - - - - - - - bis, mi -
- - - - bis, mi - se - re - re no - - - - - - - - bis, mi - -
- se - - re - - re no - - - - - bis.
- se - re - re no - - - - - - - - - - bis.

Magnificat Primi Toni: Et misericordia

es, in pro - ge - - - - - - - - - - - -
— pro - ge - - ni - es, in pro - ge - - - - - - - -
- es, in pro - ge - - ni -
- ni es ti - men - - ti - bus
- ni - es ti - men - ti - bus e - - -
- es ti - men - - ti - bus e - - -
e - - - - - - - - - - um, ti - men - ti -
- - - - - - - um, ti - men - ti - bus e -
- - - - - - - - - - - - um, ti - men - - ti - bus e -
- bus e - - - - - - - - - um.
- - - - - - - - - - - um.
- - - - - - - - - - - - - um.

Magnificat Tertii Toni : Et misericordia

— in — pro - ge - - - - - - - - - ni -
- ni - es, — in — pro - - - - ge - ni - es
— pro - ge - - - - - ni - es, in pro - ge - ni - es —

- es ti - men - - ti - bus e -
ti - men - ti - bus e - - - - - - - - - - - -
— ti - men - ti - bus e - - - - - - - um,

- um. —
um, ti - men - ti - bus — e - - um.
ti - men - - ti - bus — e - - - um.

Magnificat Quinti Toni: Et misericordia

Palestrina

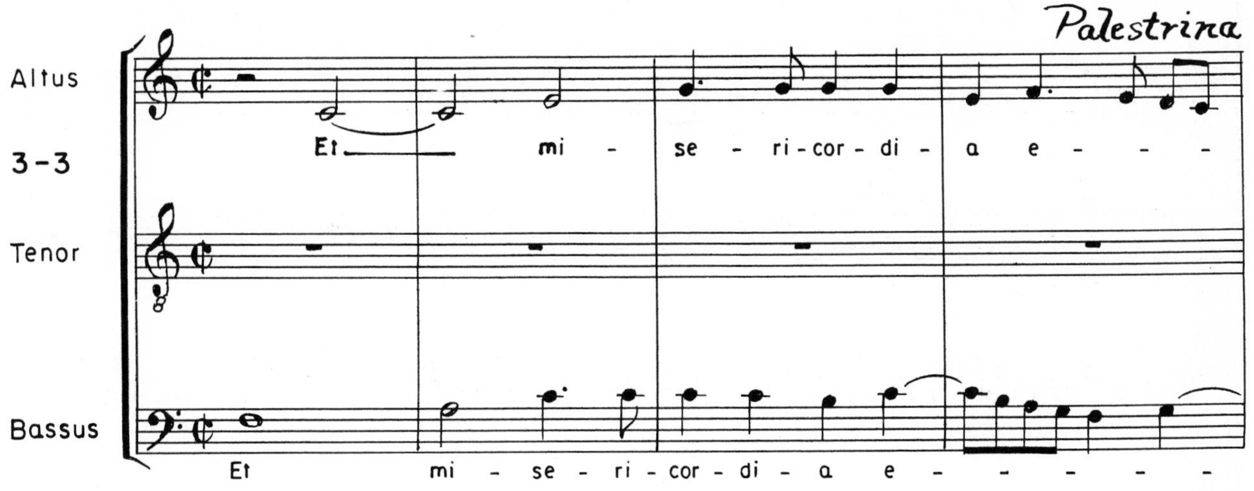

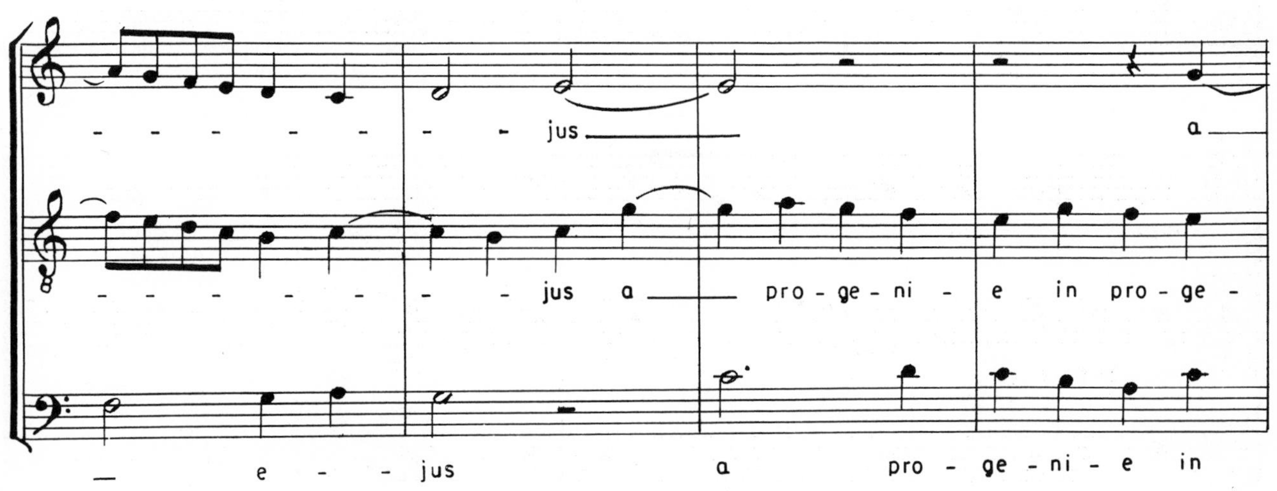

— pro - ge - ni - e in pro - ge - ni - es ——— ti -
- - - - - - - - - - - - - ni - es ti - men -
pro - ge - - - - - - - - - - ni - es ti - men - ti - bus

- men - ti - bus e - um, ti - men - ti - bus e -
- ti - bus e - um, ti - men - ti - bus e - um,
e - um, ti - men - ti - bus e - um, ti - men - ti - bus

- um, ——— ti - men - ti - bus e - um, ti -
ti - men - - ti - bus e - - um, ti - men -
e - um, ti - men - ti - bus e - um, ti -

- men - ti - bus e - - - - - - - um. ———
- ti - bus e - - - - - - - - - - - - um.
- men - ti - bus e - - - - - - - - um. ———

Magnificat Sexti Toni : Et misericordia

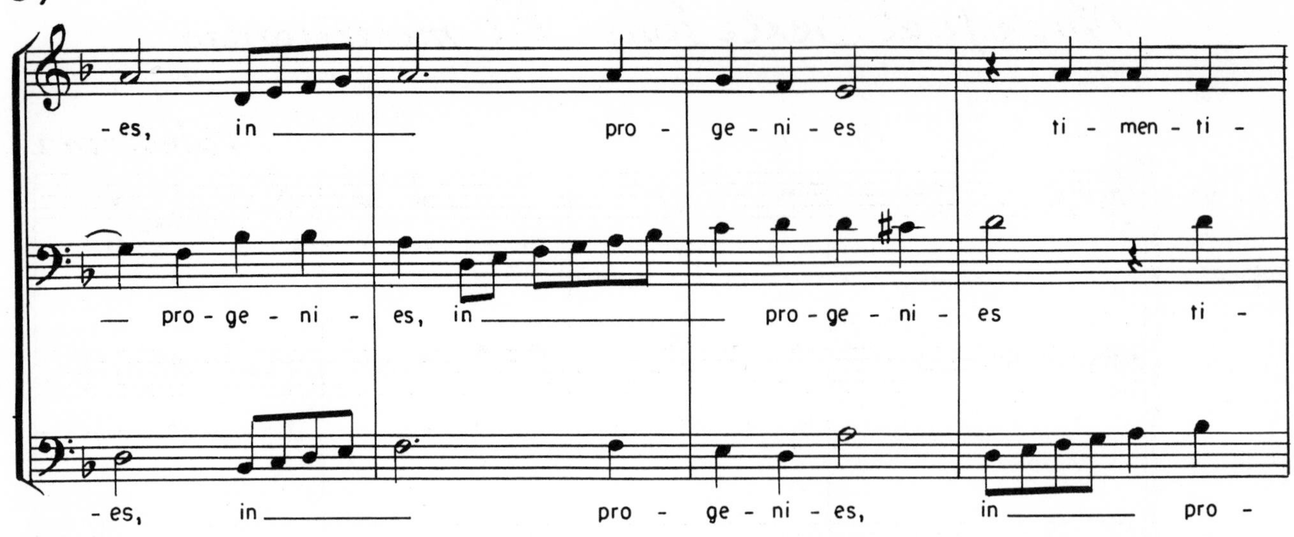
-es, in pro - ge - ni - es ti - men - ti -
— pro - ge - ni - es, in pro - ge - ni - es ti -
- es, in pro - ge - ni - es, in pro -

- bus e - - - - - - - - - - - - - um, ti -
men - ti - bus e - - - - - - - - - - - - um,
- ge - ni - es ti - men - ti - bus e - -

- men - ti - bus e - - - - - - - - - - - - um.
ti - men - ti - bus e - - - - - - - um.
- um.

Magnificat Tertii Toni : Et misericordia

Victoria

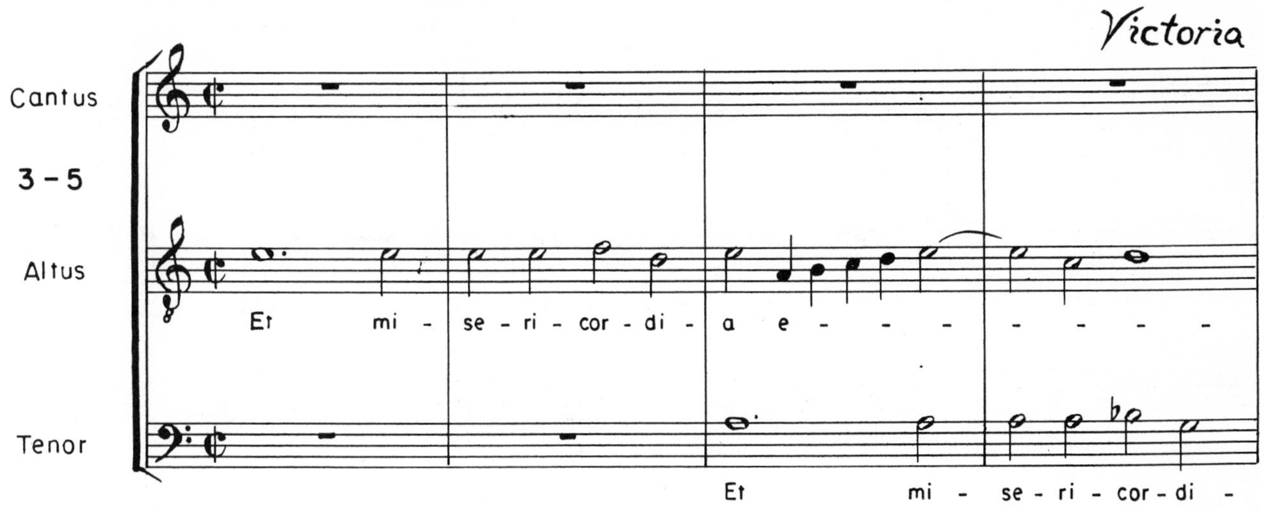

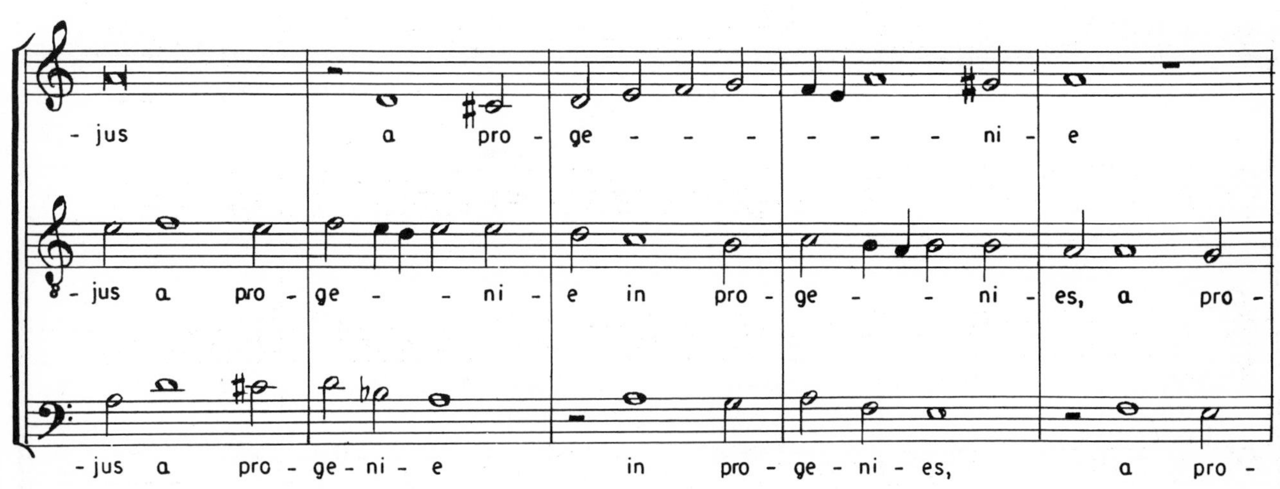

in pro - ge - - - - - ni - es

ge - - ni - e in pro - ge - - ni - es ti - men - ti -

ge - ni - e in pro - ge - ni - es ti - men - ti - bus e -

ti - men - ti - bus e - - - - - -

bus e - um, ti - men - - ti - - bus e - -

- - - - - um, ti - men - ti - bus

- - - - - - - - um, ti - men - ti - bus e - - - -

um, ti - men - ti - bus e -

e - - - - - - - - um, ti - men - ti - bus

Magnificat Secundi Toni: De posuit potentes

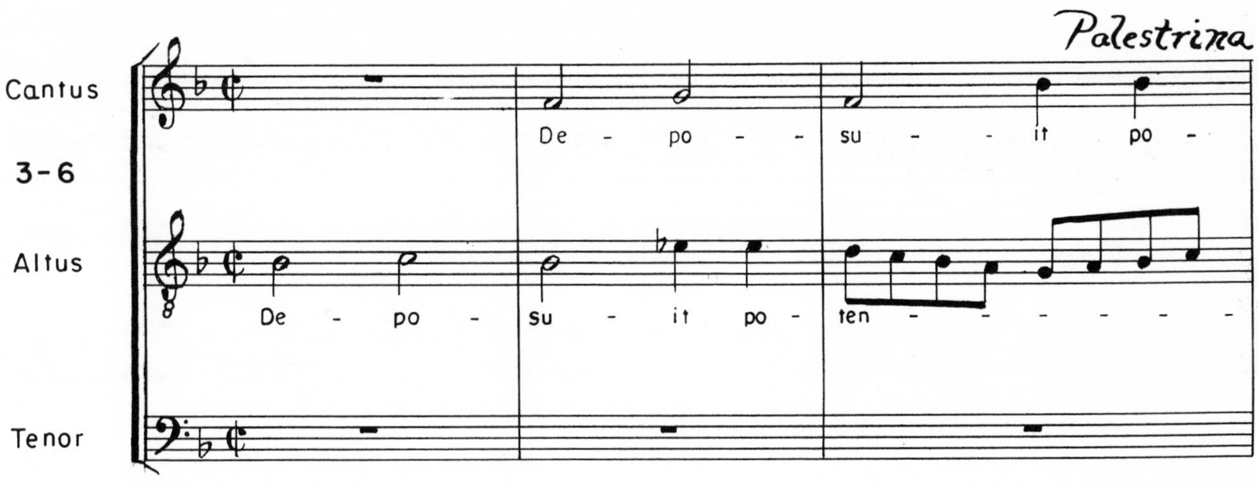

- - de, et ex - al - ta - - vit hu - - - - mi -
- - de, ___ et ex - al - ta - vit ___ hu -
- de, et ex - al - ta - - vit ___ hu - - - - - - -

- les, et ex - al - ta - - vit ___
- - - - - - mi - les, ___ et ex - al -
- - - - - - mi - les, et ex - al - ta - - -

___ hu - - - - - - - - mi - les.
- ta - vit hu - - - - - - - - - - - - - mi - les.
- vit hu - - - - mi - les. ___

Magnificat Quarti Toni: De posuit potentes

-vit hu - - - - - mi - les, et ex - al - ta - vit
et ex - al - ta - vit hu - - - - mi - les,
-ta - vit hu - mi - les, et ex - al - ta - vit

hu mi les, et ex - al -
hu - - - - - mi - les, et ex - al - ta - vit
hu - mi - les, et ex - al - ta - vit hu - mi -

-ta - vit hu - - mi - les, hu - mi - les.
hu - mi - les, hu - - mi - les, hu - - mi - les.
- les, et ex - al - ta - vit hu - mi - les.

Magnificat Octavi Toni: Deposuit potentes

et ex - al - ta - vit hu - mi - les, et ex - al - ta - vit
ex - al - ta - vit hu - mi - les, et ex - al - ta - vit hu - mi -
- ta - vit hu - mi - les, hu - mi - les,

hu - - - - - - - - - - mi - les,
les, hu - - - - - mi - les, et ex - al -
et ex - al - ta - vit hu - mi - les, et ex - al - ta - vit

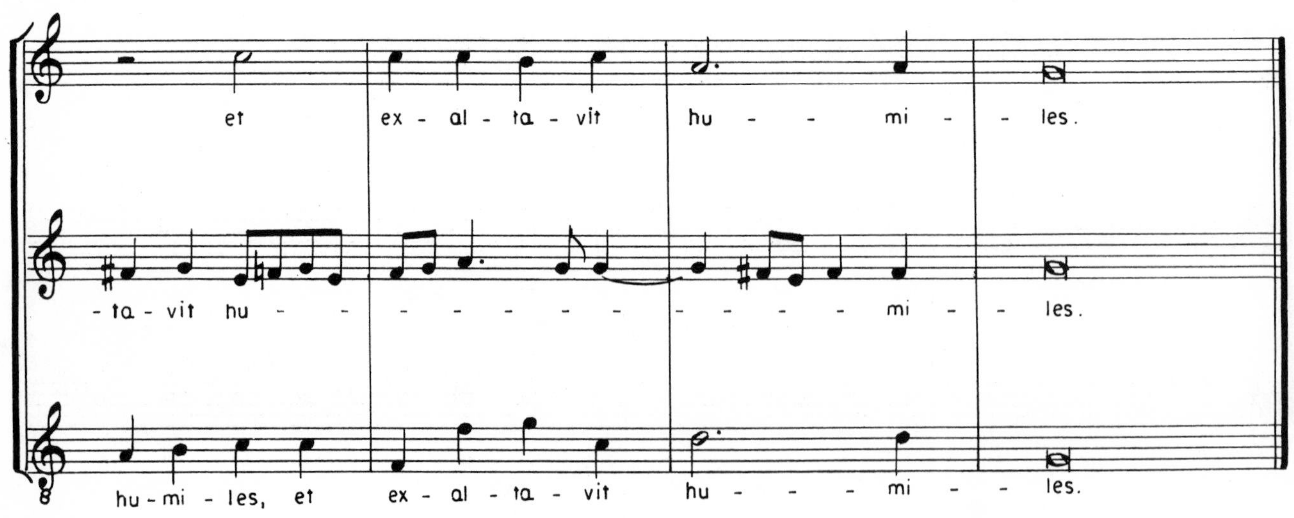
et ex - al - ta - vit hu - - mi - - les.
- ta - vit hu - - - - - - - - - - mi - - les.
hu - mi - les, et ex - al - ta - vit hu - - - mi - - les.

Magnificat Secundi Toni: Deposuit potentes

Victoria

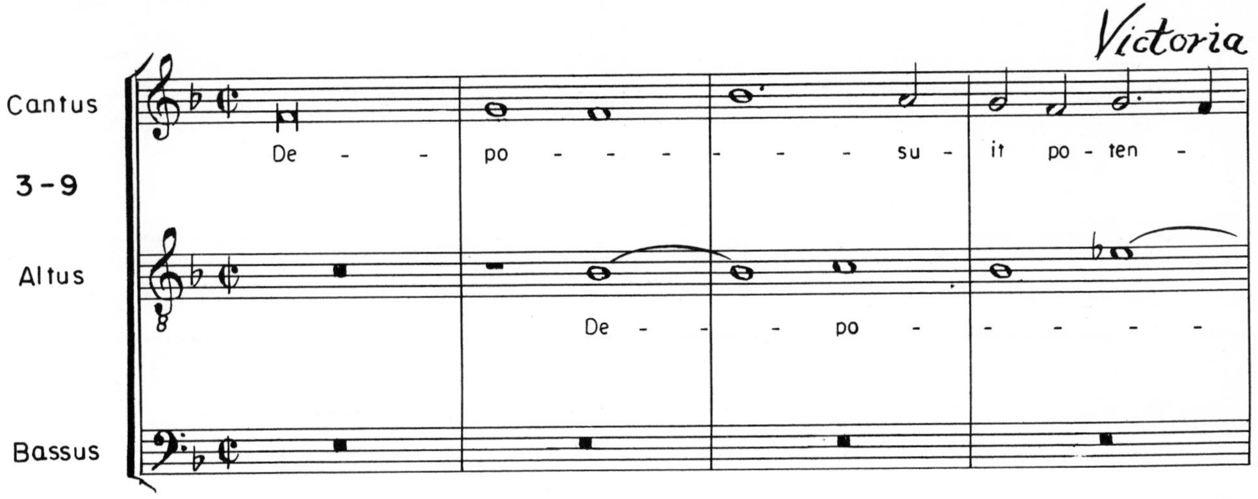

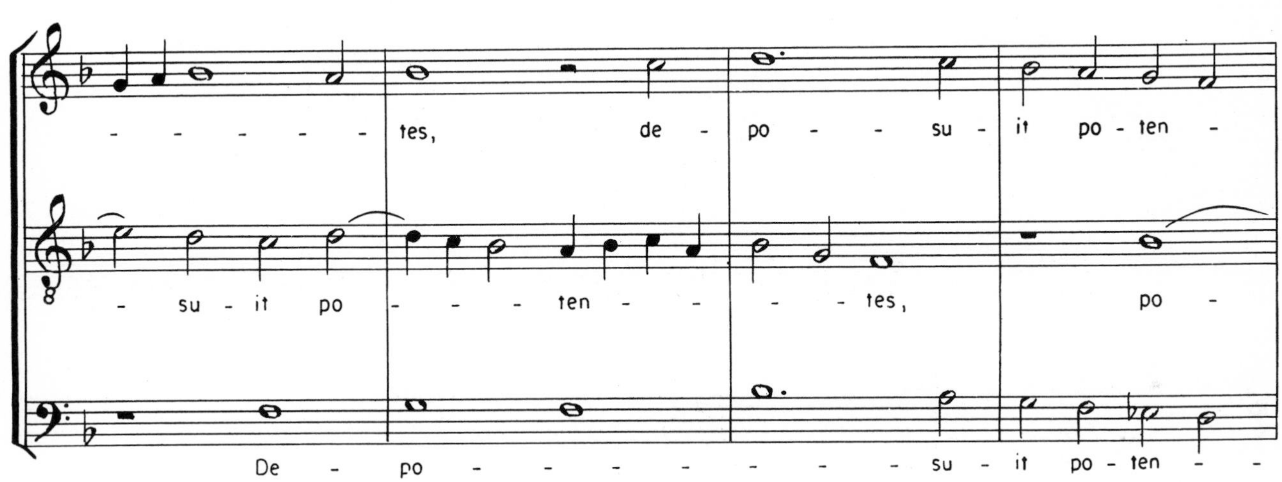

ex - al - ta - vit hu - - - - - - - - - - - - mi -
et ex - al - ta - vit hu - - - - - - - - - - mi -
ex - al - ta - vit hu - - - - - - - - - - - - - mi -
- les, et ex - al - ta - - vit hu - mi - les, et
les, et ex - al - ta - - vit hu - - - - - - mi - les,
- les et ex - al - ta - - vit hu - - - - mi - les, et
ex - al - ta - - vit hu - - - - - - - mi - les, et ex - al -
et ex - al - ta - vit hu - - - - - mi - - les, et
ex - al - ta - - vit hu - - - - - - - mi - les, et ex - al -
- ta - - - - - vit hu - - - - mi - les.
ex - al - ta - - - vit hu - - - - mi - les.
- ta - - - - - - vit hu - - - - - - mi - - les.

Magnificat Septimi Toni: Deposuit potentes

Victoria

hu - - - - mi - les, et ex - al - ta - - vit hu -
- vit hu - - mi - les, et ex - al - ta - vit
- vit hu - - mi - les, et ex - al - ta - vit

- - - mi - les, et ex - al - ta - - - - - vit
hu - mi - les, et ex - al - ta - - vit hu - -
hu - mi - les, et ex - al - ta - vit

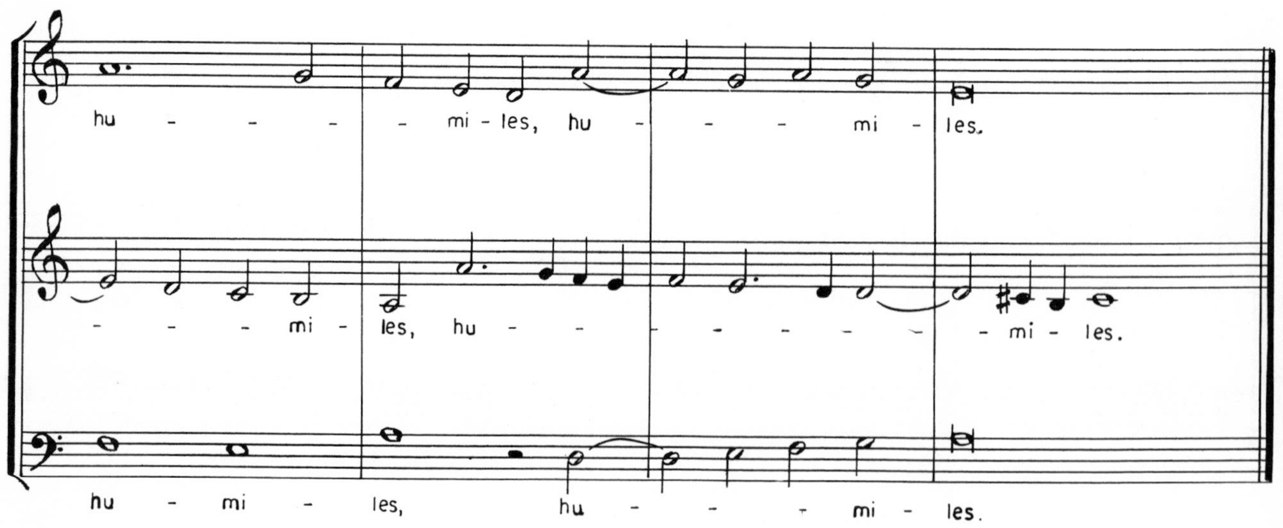
hu - - - - mi - les, hu - - - mi - les.
- - - mi - les, hu - - - - - - - mi - les.
hu - mi - les, hu - - - - mi - les.

Missa Jam Christus astra ascenderat: Credo

Palestrina

se - pul - tus est. Et re - sur - re - xit ter - - ti - a
et se - pul - tus est. Et re - sur - re - xit ter - ti - a di - e, ter -
- sus et se - pul - tus est. Et re - sur - re - xit
di - - e.
se - cun -
- - ti - a di - e se - cun - dum Scrip - tu - - - - -
ter - ti - a di - e se-cun-dum Scrip - - - - - - tu -
- dum Scrip - tu - ras. Et a - scen - dit in
- ras. Et a - scen - dit in coe - - - - - lum,
- ras. Et a - scen -
coe - - - - - - - - - - - - lum: se -
et a - scen - dit in coe - lum:
- dit in coe - lum: se - det ad dex - te -

- det ad dex - te - ram Pa - - - - - - - tris.
se - det ad dex - te - ram Pa - - tris. Et i - te
- ram Pa - - tris, ad dex - te - ram Pa - tris. Et i - te - rum ven -
Et i - te - rum ven - tu - rus est cum glo - ri - a ju - di - ca - re vi -
- rum ven - tu - rus est cum glo - ri - a ju - di - ca - re vi -
- tu - rus est cum glo - ri - a ju - di - ca - - - re vi - vos
- vos et mor - tu - os: cu - jus re - gni non e -
- vos et mor - tu - os: cu - jus re - gni non e - rit,
et mor - tu - os: cu - jus re - gni non
- rit fi - - nis, non e - rit fi - - nis.
non e - rit fi - - nis.
e - rit fi - - - - - - nis, non e - rit fi - nis.

Missa Spem in alium: Credo

Palestrina

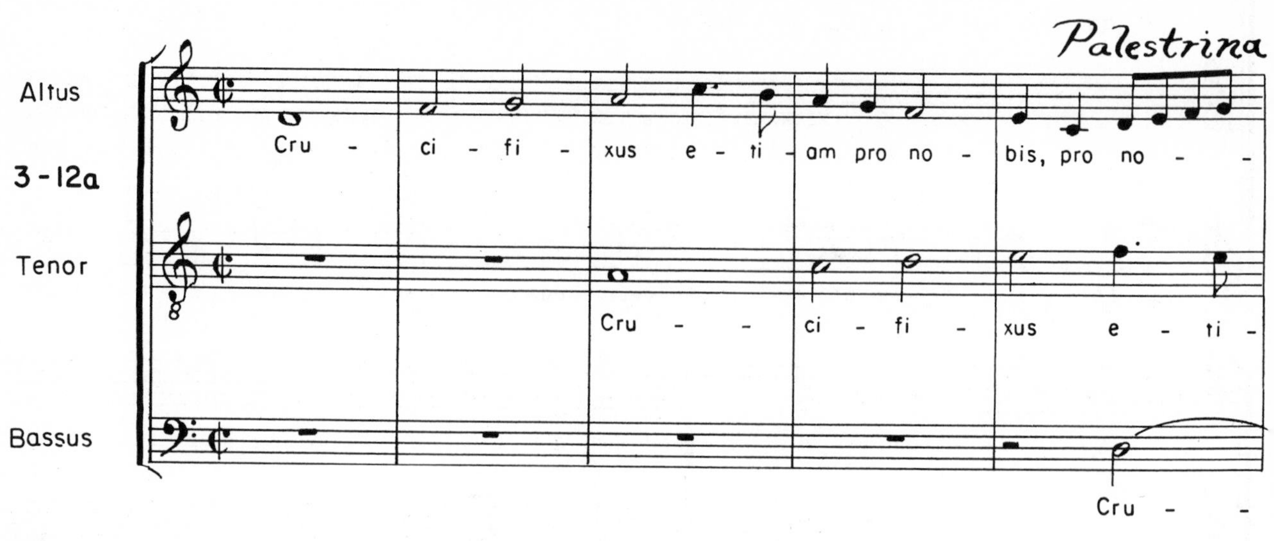

sub Pon-ti - o Pi - la - - - - - - - - - to pas -
- to, sub Pon - ti - o Pi - la - - - - - - to pas -
Pon - ti - o Pi - la - - - - - - - - - - - - to
- sus, pas - sus et se -
- sus et se - pul - - tus est,
pas - sus et se - pul - tus est, pas - -
- pul - tus est.
pas - sus et se - pul - tus est. Et re - sur -
- sus et se - pul - - tus est. Et re - sur - re - xit
Et re - sur - re - xit ter - - ti - a di - e,
- re - xit ter - ti - a di - - - - e, ter - ti - a di - - e
ter - ti - a di - - - - - - e, ter - ti - a di - e

di - - - - - e
se - cun - dum Scrip-tu -
se - cun - dum Scip - tu - - - - - - - - - - - -
se - cun - - dum Scrip-tu - - - - - - - - - -
- - - - - - - - - - - - - - - - - - ras,
- - - - - ras, se - cun - dum Scrip-tu - -
- - - - - ras, se - cun - dum
se - cun - dum Scrip-tu - - - - ras, se - cun -
- - ras, se - cun-dum Scrip - tu - - - - - ras,
Scrip - tu - - - - - - - - - - - - - - ras.
- dum Scrip - tu - - - - - - - - - - ras.
se - - cun - dum Scrip - tu - - - - - ras.

Cantus
3-12b
Altus
Bassus
Et a - scen - dit in coe - - - - - - - - - - - - - lum, et a - scen - dit in coe - - lum, in coe - - - - -
Et a - scen - dit in coe - - - - - - - - - - lum, et a - scen - dit in coe lum, et a scen - - - dit in coe -
Et a - scen - dit in coe - - - - - - - lum, et a - scen - dit in

- - - lum: se - det ad dex - te - ram
- - - lum: se - det ad dex - te - ram Pa -
coe - - - lum:
Pa - - - tris, se - det ad
- - - tris, se - det ad dex - te - ram Pa -
se - det ad dex - te - ram Pa - - -
dex - te - ram Pa - - - tris.
- - - tris. Et i -
- - - tris. Et i - te - rum
Et i - te - rum ven -
- te - rum ven - tu - rus est cum glo - ri - a,
ven - tu - rus est cum glo - ri - a,

-tu - rus est cum glo - - - - -
et i - - te - rum ven - tu - rus est cum
et i - te - rum ven - tu - rus est cum glo - -
- - - ri - a ju - di -
glo - ri - a ju - di - ca - re vi - vos et
- - - ri - a ju - di - ca - re vi - vos,
- ca - re vi - vos et mor - - tu - os,
mor - tu - os, ju - - di - ca - re vi - - -
ju - di -
vi - vos et mor - - tu - os:
- - - vos et mor - - tu - os: cu -
- ca - re vi - vos et mor - - tu - os: cu - jus

cu - jus re - gni non e - -
- jus re - gni non e - rit fi - - - - nis, cu - jus
re - gni non e - rit fi - - - - - - - - nis,

- rit fi - - - - - nis, cu - - jus
re - gni non e - rit fi - - - - - - - - - - -
cu - jus re - gni non e - - rit

re - gni non e - - rit fi - - - - - nis,
- - nis, cu - jus re - gni non
fi - nis, non e - rit fi - nis, cu -

non e - - - - - rit fi - - - nis.
e - rit, non e - rit fi - - - nis.
- jus re - - gni non e - rit fi - - - - nis.

Missa Repleatur os meum laude: Credo

Palestrina

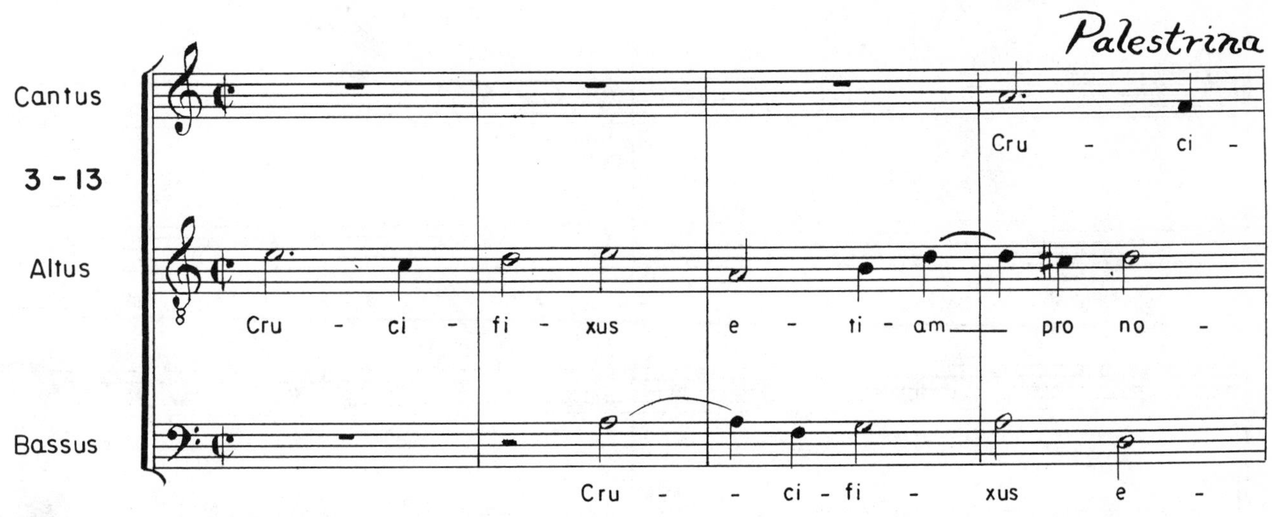

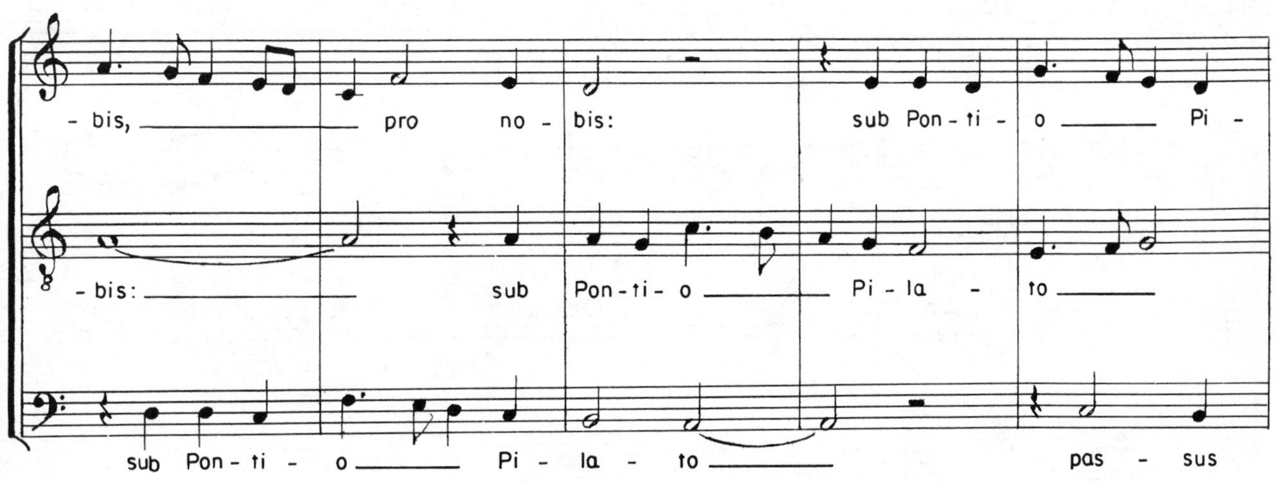

-la - - to pas - sus et se - pul - tus est.
pas - sus et se - pul - - - tus est.
et se - pul - tus est, et se - pul - tus est.
Et re - sur - re - xit ter - ti - a di - e, di -
Et re - sur - re - xit ter - ti - a
- - - - - - - - - - - - - e.
di - e se - cun - dum Scrip - tu - -
Et re - sur - re - xit ter - ti - a di - e, di - - - - - - -
se - cun - dum Scrip - tu - ras, Scrip - - - - -
- ras, se - cun - dum Scrip - - - - - - - tu -
- - - - e se - cun - dum Scrip -

- tu - ras. Et a - scen - dit in coe - -
- - - ras. Et a - scen - dit in coe - -
- tu - ras.
- - - - - - lum:
- - - - - - lum: se - det ad
Et a - scen - dit in coe - - - - -
se - det ad dex - te - ram Pa - - - - - - -
dex - te - ram Pa - - tris. Et i - te - rum ven - tu - rus
- lum: se - det ad dex - - te - ram Pa - tris. Et i -
tris. cum glo - ri - a ju - di - ca - re vi -
est cum glo - ri - a ju - di - ca -
- te - rum ven - tu - rus est cum glo - ri - a ju - di - ca -

- vos et mor - - - - tu - os:
- re vi - vos, vi - vos et mor - - - tu -
- re vi - vos et mor - - tu - os:
cu - jus re - gni non e - rit fi - - -
os: cu - jus re - gni non e - rit
cu - jus re - gni non e - rit fi - nis, non e - rit fi - - -
- nis, cu - jus re - gni non e - rit fi - nis,
fi - nis, fi - - - - - nis, cu - jus re - gni non e - rit
- - - - - - - nis, cu - jus re - gni non
cu - jus re - gni non e - rit fi - - - nis.
fi - - - - - - - - nis, non e - rit fi - nis.
e - rit fi - nis, non e - rit fi - - - nis.

Missa Inviolata: Credo

Palestrina

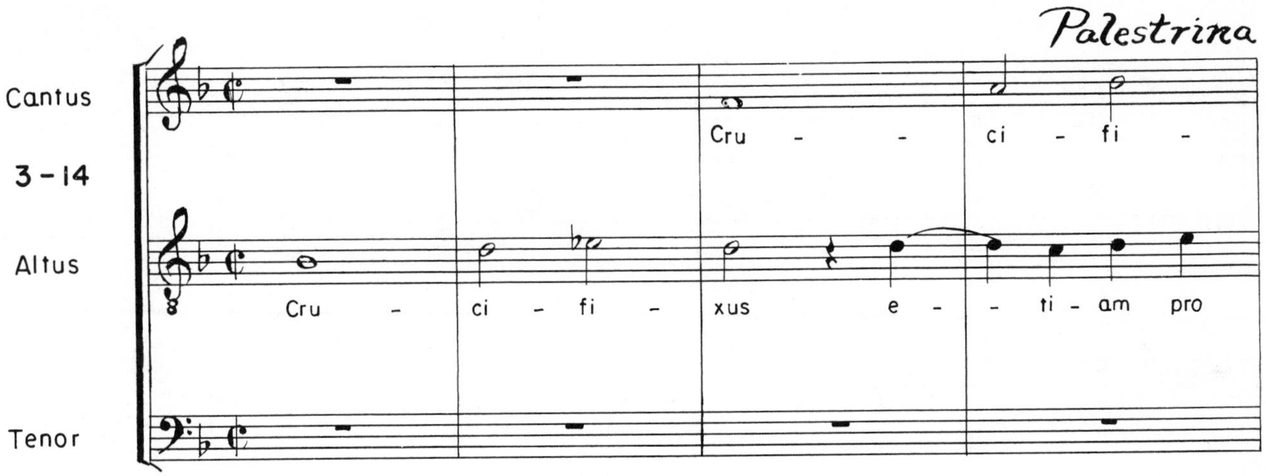

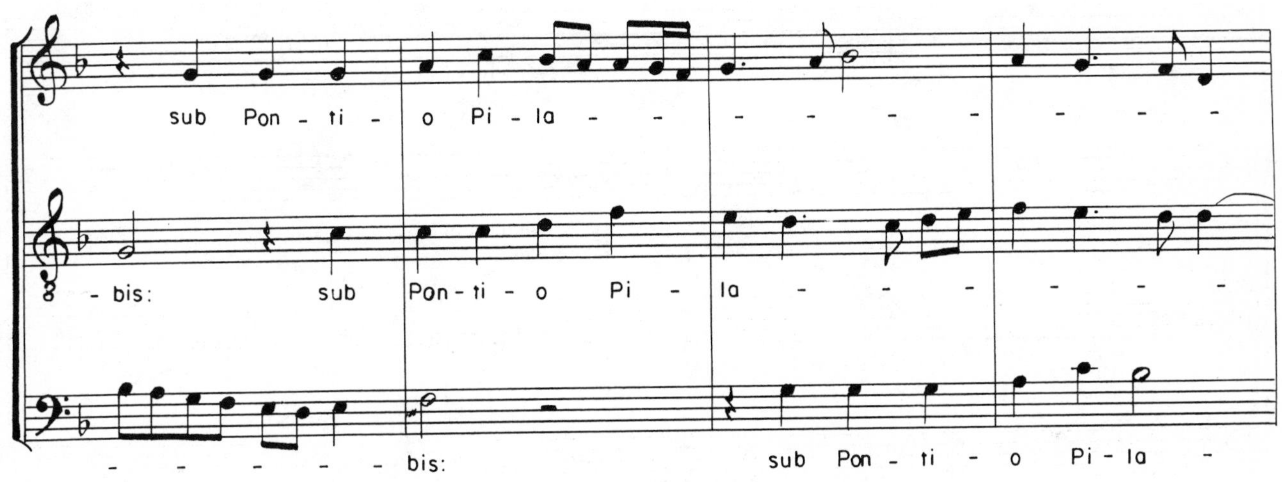

- - - to, Pi - - la - to pas - sus et
- - - - to pas - sus et se - pul - tus est, pas -
- to pas - sus et se - pul - tus est,
se - pul - tus est, et se - pul - - - tus est. Et
- sus et se - pul - tus est. Et re - sur - re - xit,
pas - sus et se - pul - tus est. Et re - sur - re -
re - sur - re - xit ter - ti - a di - - - - - - -
et re - sur - re - xit ter - ti - a di - - e
- xit ter - ti - a di - - - - - e, ter - ti - a di - - - - - -
- e se - cun - dum Scrip - tu - - - -
se - cun - dum Scrip - tu - - ras, Scrip - -
- - - - - - - e se -

- - - - - - - - - - ras. Et a - scen - dit in
- tu - - - - - - - - ras. Et a - scen -
- cun - dum Scrip - tu - - ras, Scrip - - - tu - ras.
coe - - - - - - - - lum: se - det ad dex - te-ram Pa -
- dit in coe - - - lum, in coe - lum: se - det ad
Et a - scen - dit in coe - - lum, in coe - - lum:
- - - tris, se - det ad dex - te-ram Pa - - tris,
dex - te-ram Pa - - - - - tris, se - det ad dex - te-ram Pa -
se - det ad dex - te-ram Pa - - - tris, se - det ad
se - det ad dex - te-ram Pa - - tris.
- - - - - - - tris, Pa - - - - tris.
dex - te-ram Pa - - - - - tris, Pa - - tris.

Missa ad imitationem moduli Susanne un iour: Credo

- tu - ras . Et a - scen - dit in coe - lum: se - det ad dex -
- - ras. Et a - scen - - dit in coe - - lum: se - det
Et a - scen - dit in coe - lum, et a - scen - dit in coe -
- - - - - - te - ram Pa - tris,
ad dex - te - ram, se - det ad dex - te - ram Pa -
- lum: se - det ad dex - te - ram Pa - - -
se - det ad dex - te - ram Pa - - - - tris,
- tris, se - - - det ad dex - te - ram, se - det
- - tris, se - det ad dex - te -
se - det ad dex - - - - te - ram Pa - tris.
ad dex - te - ram Pa - - - tris, ad dex - te - ram Pa - - tris.
- ram Pa - tris, se - det ad dex - te - ram Pa - tris.

Missa super Le Berger et la Bergere: Credo

Lassus

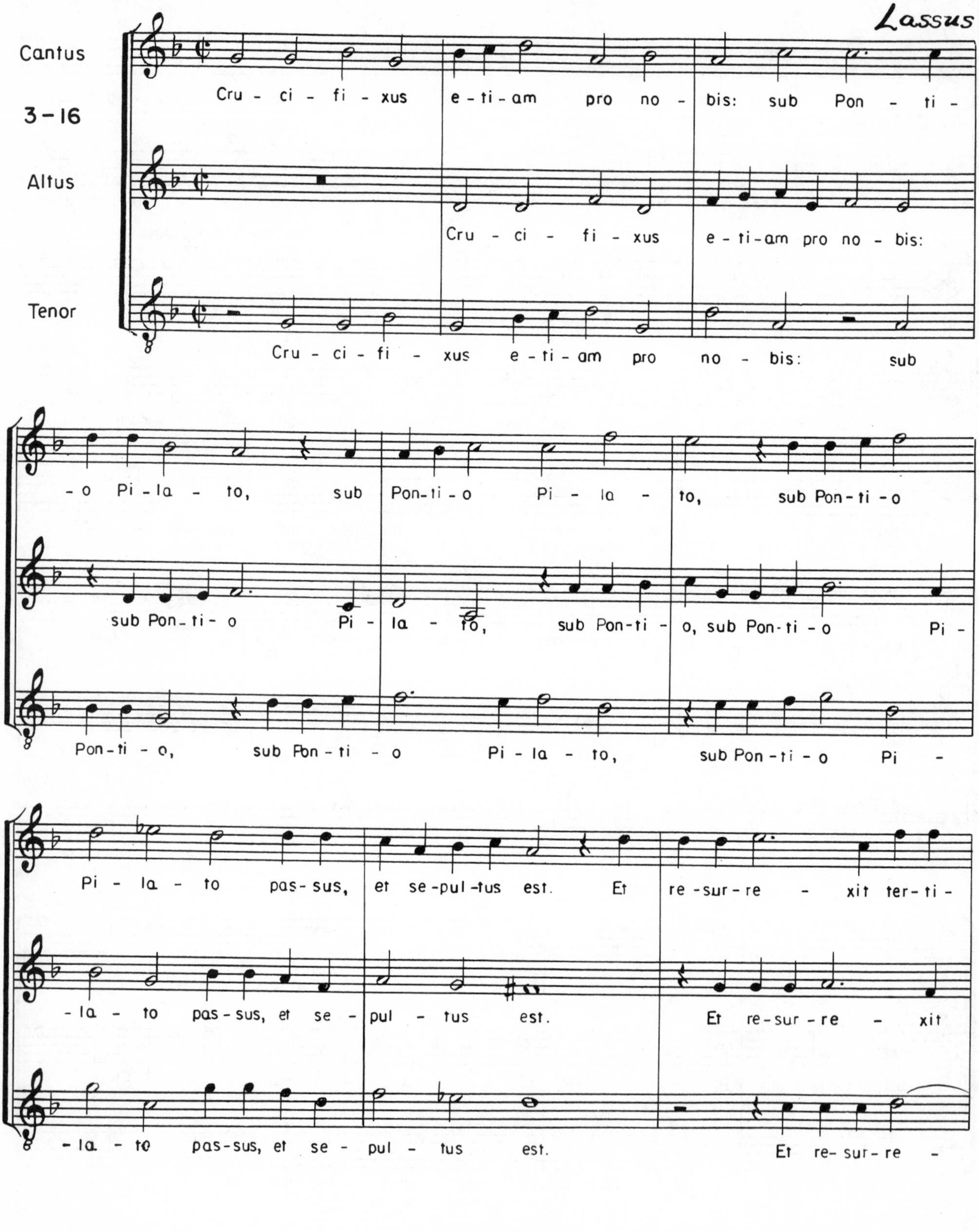

Cantus

3–16

Cru - ci - fi - xus e - ti - am pro no - bis: sub Pon - ti -

Altus

Cru - ci - fi - xus e - ti - am pro no - bis:

Tenor

Cru - ci - fi - xus e - ti - am pro no - bis: sub

- o Pi - la - to, sub Pon - ti - o Pi - la - to, sub Pon - ti - o

sub Pon - ti - o Pi - la - to, sub Pon - ti - o, sub Pon - ti - o Pi -

Pon - ti - o, sub Pon - ti - o Pi - la - to, sub Pon - ti - o Pi -

- a di - e se - cun - dum, se - cun - dum Scrip - tu - ras.
ter - ti - a di - e se - cun - dum Scrip - tu - - - ras. Et a -
- xit ter - ti - a di - e se - cun - dum Scrip - tu - ras.
Et a - scen - dit in coe - lum: se - det ad dex - te - ram Pa -
- scen - dit, et a - scen - dit in coe - lum: se - det ad dex - te - ram Pa -
Et a - scen - dit in coe - lum: se - det ad dex - te - ram
- - tris. Et i - te - rum ven - tu - rus est cum glo - ri - a ju - di -
- - tris. Et i - te - rum ven - tu - rus est cum glo - ri - a ju - di -
Pa - tris. Et i - te - rum ven - tu - rus est cum glo - ri - a ju - di -

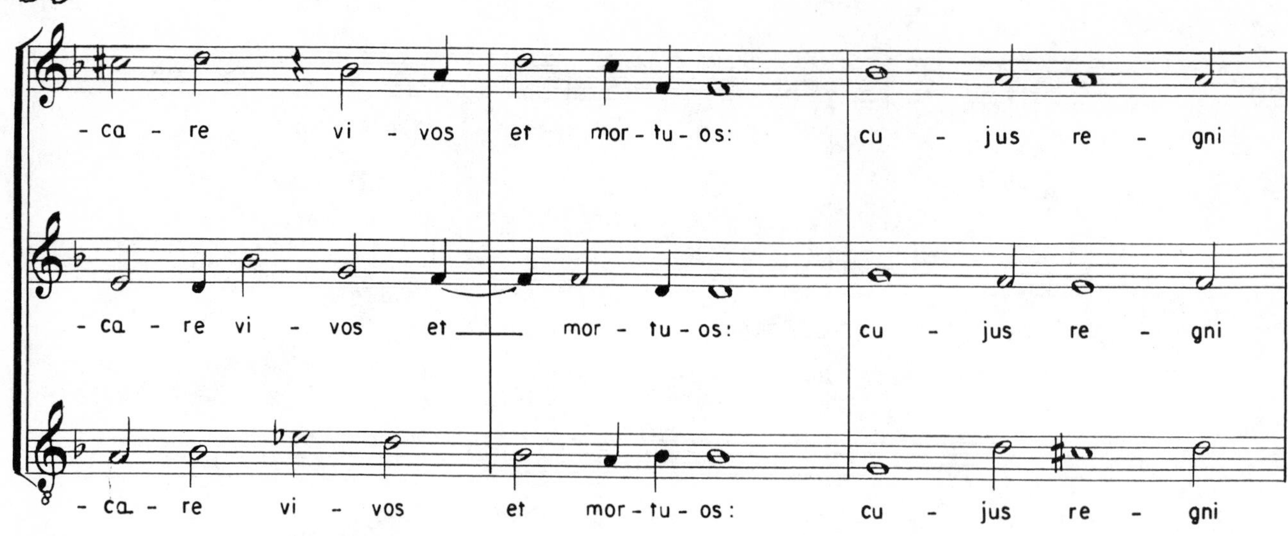
-ca - re vi - vos et mor-tu-os: cu - jus re - gni
-ca - re vi - vos et mor - tu-os: cu - jus re - gni
-ca - re vi - vos et mor-tu-os: cu - jus re - gni

non e-rit fi - nis, non e-rit fi - nis, non e-rit fi - nis,
non e-rit fi - nis, non e-rit fi - nis, non e-rit fi - -
non e-rit fi - - - nis, non e-rit fi - nis,

non e-rit fi - - - nis, non e-rit fi - - nis.
-nis, non e-rit fi - nis, non e-rit fi - - nis.
non e-rit fi - - - nis, non e-rit fi - - nis.

Missa de Beata Virgine: Credo

Morales

- - tus est. Et re-sur-re-xit ter-ti-a di - - - e
- tus est. Et re-sur-re - xit ter -
- pul-tus est. Et re-sur-re-xit ter-ti-a di - - - - -
se - cun - - - - dum Scrip - tu - - ras.
- ti - a di - e se - - cun - - dum Scrip - - tu - -
- - - - e se - cun - - dum Scrip-tu - - - -
Et a - scen - dit in coe - lum: se - det ad dex - te -
- ras. Et a-scen-dit in coe-lum:
- ras. Et a-scen - dit in coe - - - - - - - - lum:
- ram Pa - - - - - - - - tris. Et
se - - det ad dex - - te - ram Pa - - - tris.
se - det ad dex - te - ram Pa - - - - - tris.

— i - te - rum ven - tu - - rus est cum — glo - - - ri - a
Et — i - te - rum ven - tu - rus est cum
Et — i - te - rum ven - tu - rus est cum glo - - - ri - a
ju - di - ca - - re, ju - di - ca - re vi - vos —
glo - ri - a — ju - di - ca - re —
ju - di - ca - - - - re vi - vos et
— et — mor - - - - - tu - - os: cu - jus — re - gni
vi - - - vos et mor - tu - - os:
mor - - - - - - - - - tu - os: cu - jus re -
non e - rit fi - - - - - - - nis.
cu - jus re - gni non e - rit — fi - - nis.
- gni non e - rit fi - - - - - - - - - - nis.

Missa de Beata Virgine: Sanctus

- ra glo - - ri - a
- ra glo - ri - a tu - - - -
glo - ri - a tu - - - - - - - - - - - - a, glo -
tu - - - - - - - - - - - - a,
- a, glo - - ri - a tu - - - - - a,
- ri - a tu - - a, glo - ri -
glo - - - - - - - ri - a
glo - - - ri - a tu - - - - a, glo -
- a tu - - - - - - - - - - a, glo - ri -
tu - - - - - - - a, glo - ri - a tu - - a.
- ri - a tu - a, glo - ri - a tu - - a.
- a tu - a, glo - - ri - a tu - - a.

Missa ad fugam: Sanctus

-ra glo - ri - a tu - - - - - a,
-ri - a tu - - - - a, glo- ri - a
tu - - - - - - - a, glo - ri - a tu - -
glo - ri - a tu - - - - - - - - -
tu - - - - - - - - - - - a, glo -
- - - - - - - - - - - - - a, glo - ri -
-a, glo - ri - a tu - a.
- ri - a tu - a.
-a tu - a, tu - - - - - - - a.

Missa Aspice Domine: Sanctus

coe - li et ter - - - - - -
- - ra, ple - ni sunt coe - li et
ple - ni sunt coe - li et
- - - - ra glo - ri - a
ter - - ra glo - ri - a tu - -
ter - ra glo - ri - a tu - - -
tu - - - - - - - - - - - -
- - a, glo - ri - a tu - a,
- - a, glo - ri - a tu - - - - - -

- a, glo - ri - a tu - a,
glo - ri - a tu - - a,
- - - - a, glo - ri - a
glo - ri - a tu - - - - -
glo - - ri - a tu - - a, glo - ri - a tu -
tu - - - - a, glo - ri - a
- - - a, glo - ri - a tu - - a.
- - - a, glo - ri - a tu - - a.
tu - a, glo - ri - a tu - - a.

Missa ad fugam: Sanctus

des Pres

Superius

3-21

Tenor

Bassus

Superius: Ple - - - - - - - - - - - - - - ni
Tenor: Ple - - - - - - - - - -
Bassus: Ple - - - - - - - - ni sunt

Superius: sunt coe - - - li, ple - - - - - - - - -
Tenor: - - - ni sunt coe - - - - li, ple -
Bassus: coe - - - - - - - - - - - - li, ple - - - -

Superius: - ni sunt coe - - - - - li, ple -
Tenor: - - - - - - - ni sunt coe - - - - -
Bassus: - - ni sunt coe - li, coe - - - - -

Superius: - ni sunt coe - - - - - - - - - - - li
Tenor: - li, ple - ni sunt coe - - - - - - - - - -
Bassus: - li, coe - - - - - - li et ter - -

— et ter - - - ra glo - - - - - - - - -
- li — et ter - - - - ra glo - - -
- - - - - - ra glo - - ri - a — tu - - -
- ri-a tu - - - - - a, glo - - - - -
- - - - - - ri-a tu - - - - a,
- a, glo - ri - a tu - - - - - - - -
- ri - a tu - - - a, glo - - - - -
glo - - - - - ri - a tu - - a,
- a, glo - ri - a tu - - - - - - a, glo - ri - a
- - - - ri - a tu - - - - - - a. —
glo - - - - - ri - a tu - a. —
tu - - a, tu - - - - - - - - a. —

Missa Brevis: Benedictus

ve - - - - - - - - - - - - nit,
- - - - - - - - - - - - - nit, qui ve - -
be - - - - ne - di - ctus qui

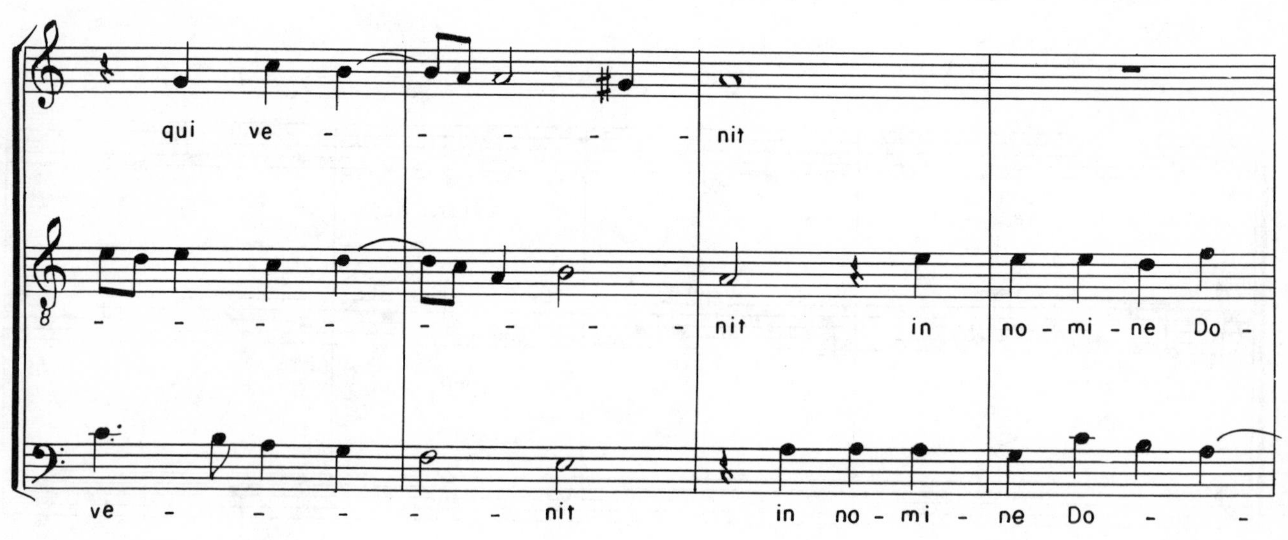
qui ve - - - - - - nit
- - - - - - - - - nit in no - mi - ne Do -
ve - - - - - - nit in no - mi - ne Do - -

in no - mi - ne Do - - - - - mi - ni,
- - - - - - - - - - - mi - ni,
- - - mi - ni, Do - - - - mi - ni, in

in no - mi - ne Do - - - - -
in no - mi - ne Do - - - - - - - - - - -
no - mi - ne Do - - - - - - - - - - mi -
- mi - ni,
in no - mi - ne Do -
- mi - ni,
in no - mi - ne Do - - - mi - ni,
- ni,
in no - mi - ne Do - - - - - mi - ni,
- - - - mi - ni, in no - mi - ne Do - - - mi - ni.
in no - mi - ne Do - - - - mi - ni.
in no - mi - ne Do - - mi - ni.

Missa ad imitationem moduli Puis que i'ay perdu: Benedictus

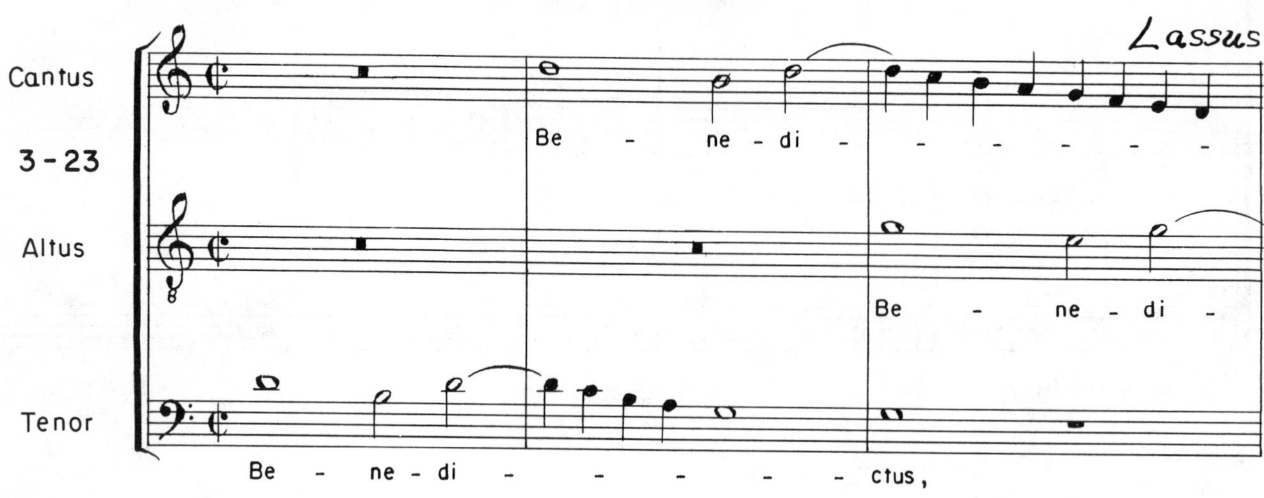

-ne Do - - - - mi - ni, in no - mi - ne
in no - mi - ne Do - mi - ni, in
Do - mi - ni, in no - mì - ne Do - mi-
Do - - mi - ni, in no - mi - ne, in no - mi -
no - mi - ne Do - - mi - ni, in no - mi - ne, in
- ni, in no - mi - ne Do - mi - ni, in no - mi -
- ne Do - - - - mi - ni, in no - mi - ne,
no - mi - ne Do - - - mi - ni, in no - mi - ne,
- ne Do - - - - mi - ni, in no - mi - ne
in no - mi - ne Do - - - mi - ni.
in no - mi - ne Do - - mi - ni,
Do - - - - - - mi - ni.

Missa Pro Defunctis: Benedictus

Lassus

Missa Mille regretz: Benedictus

in no - mi - ne Do - mi - ni,
qui ve - - - nit in no - mi - ne Do - mi - ni,
in no - mi -
in no - - - mi - ne Do - - mi - ni, in
in no - mi - ne Do - mi -
-ne Do - mi - ni, in no - - mi - ne Do -
no - - mi - ne Do - - - mi - - - ni, in
- - ni,
-mi - ni, in no - - - mi - ne Do - - - mi -
no - mi - ne Do - mi - ni, in no - mi - ne Do - mi - - ni.
in no - - mi - ne Do - mi - ni.
- - - ni, in no - mi - ne Do - mi - ni.

Missa ad Fugam : Agnus Dei

mi - se - re - - - - re no - - bis. A - gnus De -
- - - di, mi - se - re - - - - - - re no - -
mi - - se - - re - - - - re no - - -
- i, a - gnus De - - i, qui tol -
- bis, A - gnus De - - i, a - gnus De - - i,
- bis. A - - - gnus De - - - - - - -
- lis pec - ca - - - ta mun - di, mi - se -
qui tol - lis pec - - ca - - - ta mun - di,
- i, qui tol - lis pec - ca - ta mun - - - - - - di, mi -
- re - - - re no - - bis.
mi - se - re - re no - bis.
- se - re - re no - - - - bis.

Missa Vulnerasti cor meum: Agnus Dei

Morales

-ca - - ta mun - - - di, qui tol - lis pec - - ca -
-ca - ta mun - - - di, qui tol - lis pec - ca - ta mun - - -
pec - ca - ta mun - - - - - - di,

- ta mun - di, mi - se - re - re no - - - - - - -
- - - - - - - - - - di, mi -
mi - se - re - re no - - - - - - - - - - -

- - bis, mi - se - re - re no - - -
- se - re - re no - - - - - - - - - bis,
- bis, mi - se - re - re no - - - - - - - -

- - - bis, mi - se-re-re no - bis,
mi-se-re - re no - - - - bis, mi-se-re -
- bis, mi-se-re - re no - - - - - - - -

mi-se-re - re no - - bis, mi-se-re - re no -
-re no - - - - - bis,
- - - - bis, mi - se-re-re no - - bis, mi-se-re -

- - - bis, mi-se-re - re no - - - bis.
mi-se-re - re no - - - - - - - - - bis.
-re no - - - - - bis, mi - se-re-re no - - - bis.

Mass: De Feria: Kyrie. Palestrina.

son, Ky - ri - e e - - lei - - - - - - son.
- - - lei - - - - son, ... Ky-ri-e e - - - - - - - - - - lei - - - son.
- e e lei - - - - - - - - - - - - son.
Ky - - ri - e e - - lei - - - - - - - - son.

20
Chri - - ste .... e - lei - - - - - - - - - son
Chri - - - - ste e - - - - lei - son, Chri - - - - ste .... e - lei - - - - - son,
Chri - - - -
Chri - - - ste e - - - - lei - son, Chri - - ste.....

30
Chri - - - - ste ...... e - - - lei - - - - - - - - - - - son,
Chri - - - - - ste ...... e - lei - - - son, Chri - - ste ...... e - - - lei - - - - - son, Chri -
- - - - - ste e - lei - - - - - - - son, ... e - lei - - - son, Chri -
.... e - lei - - son, Chri - - ste e - - - - - -
Chri - - ste .... e - lei - - - - son, Chri -
- - - ste e - - - - - - - - - - lei - - - son, Chri - - - ste e - - - - - lei - son, Chri - - ste e - lei - -
- - - - - - - - - - ste e - - lei - - son, Chri - ste .... e -
- lei - - son, Chri - - ste e - - - - - - - - - - - - lei - - son,
40
- - ste .... e - lei - - - - - - - - - - - - - - son.
- son, Chri - - - ste e - - - - - - - - lei - - - - son.
- - lei - son, Chri - - ste .... e - lei - - - - - son.
Chri - ste e - lei - - - , - - - - - - son, e - - - - lei - - - son.

50
Ky- rie e- lei-
Ky- rie e- lei-
Ky- rie e- lei- son, Ky- ri- e e- lei-
Ky- rie e- lei- son, Ky- rie e- lei- son,
son, e- lei- son, Ky- rie
son, Ky- rie e- leison, Ky- rie e- lei-
son, Ky- rie e- lei-
Ky- rie e- lei- son, Kyrie e- lei-
60
e- lei- son, Ky- rie e- lei-
son, Ky rie e- lei- son, Ky- rie e- lei-
son, Ky- rie e- lei- son, Ky- rie e- lei-
son, Ky- rie e- lei- son,

70
---son, Ky-rie e-lei---son.
son, Ky-rie e-lei---son, Ky-rie e-lei---son, e-lie---son,
---son, Ky-rie e-lei---son, Ky-rie e-lei---son.
Ky---rie e-lei---son, Ky---rie e---lei---son, Ky--rie e---lei---son.

Mass: Dies Sanctificatus:

Kyrie. Palestrina.

20
Chri - - - ste e -
Chri - ste e - lei - - - son,
Chri - - ste e - - lei - - - - - - son, e -
Chri - - - ste e - - - lei - son, e -
- - lei - - - son, Chri - ste e - lei - - - - - son,
Chri - - - ste e - - lei - son, Chri - ste e -
- lei - son, Chri - - - ste e - - - lei - - -
- - lei - - - - son, Chri - - - ste e -
30
Chri - - ste e - lei - - - - - - son,
- lei - son, Chri - - - - ste e - lei - -
- - - son, Chri -
- - lei - son, Chri - - ste e - lei - - - - - - -
40
Chri - - ste e - - lei - son.
- - - - - - son, Chri - ste e - lei - - - son.
- - ste e - - - lei - son, Chri - ste e - lei - son.
- - son, Chri - - - - ste e - lei - - - - son.

Ky - rie e - lei - - - - - son, Ky - rie e - lei -
Ky - rie e - lei - - - - - - - - - - son, Ky -
Ky - rie e - lei - -
Ky - rie e - lei - -
50
- - - - - - son, Ky - rie e -
- rie e - lei - - - - son, e - lei - son, Ky - rie
- - - - - son, Ky - rie e - lei - son,
- - - - son, e - - - - - - - lei - son, Ky - - - -
- lei - - - - - son, Ky - rie e - - - lei - son, Ky - rie
e - lei - - - - - - - - - - son, Ky -
Ky - rie e - lei - - - - - son,
- rie, Ky - rie e - lei - - -
60
e - lei - son, Ky - rie e - lei - - - - - - - - son.
- rie e - lei - son, Ky - rie e - lei - - - - - - son.
Ky - rie e - lei - - - - - - - - son.
- son, Ky - rie e - lei - - - - - - - - son.

Mass: Gabriel Archangelus: Hosanna.

Palestrina.

sis, ho - san - na in ex- cel sis, ho-
ho - san - na in ex- cel - sis, ho - sanna in ex cel
in ex- cel - sis, ho - san - na in ex cel - sis,
ho - san - na in ex cel - sis, ho - sanna in
30
sanna in ex- cel - sis, in excelsis, ho - sanna in ex- cel
ho sanna in ex- celsis, ho - sanna in ex- cel - sis
ho - sanna in ex- cel - sis, ho - sanna in ex cel - sis,
ex- cel - sis, ho - sanna in ex- cel - sis, ho - sanna in
40
sis, ho - sanna in ex- cel sis, ho - sanna in ex- cel - sis.
ho - sanna in excel-sis hosanna in ex cel - sis.
ho - sanna in ex- cel - sis.
ex- cel- sis, ho-sanna in ex- cel - sis.

Mass: Sine Nomine: Sanctus.

Palestrina.

Cantus
San - - ctus, San - - - - - - - - -

Altus
4 - 4
San - - - ctus, San - - - - - - - - - ctus, San - - - -

Tenor

Bassus

10

20
Sa - ba-oth, Do- minus De- us Sa-
Do-mi-nus De-us Sa- ba- oth.
ba- oth, Sa- ba- oth, Dominus
minus De- us Sa- baoth, Do- minus De- us Sa-
30
baoth, Sa- ba- oth. Ple-ni sunt coe-li, et ter- ra
Ple-ni sunt coe-li, et ter- ra, ple-
De- us Sa- ba- oth. Ple- ni sunt coe - li
ba- oth. Ple-ni sunt coeli, et ter- ra, ple-ni sunt coeli et ter-
glo- ri- a tu- a Hosanna
ni sunt coe - li et ter- ra, Ho- sanna in ex- cel-
et ter- ra glo- ri-a tu-
ra glo - ri-a tu-

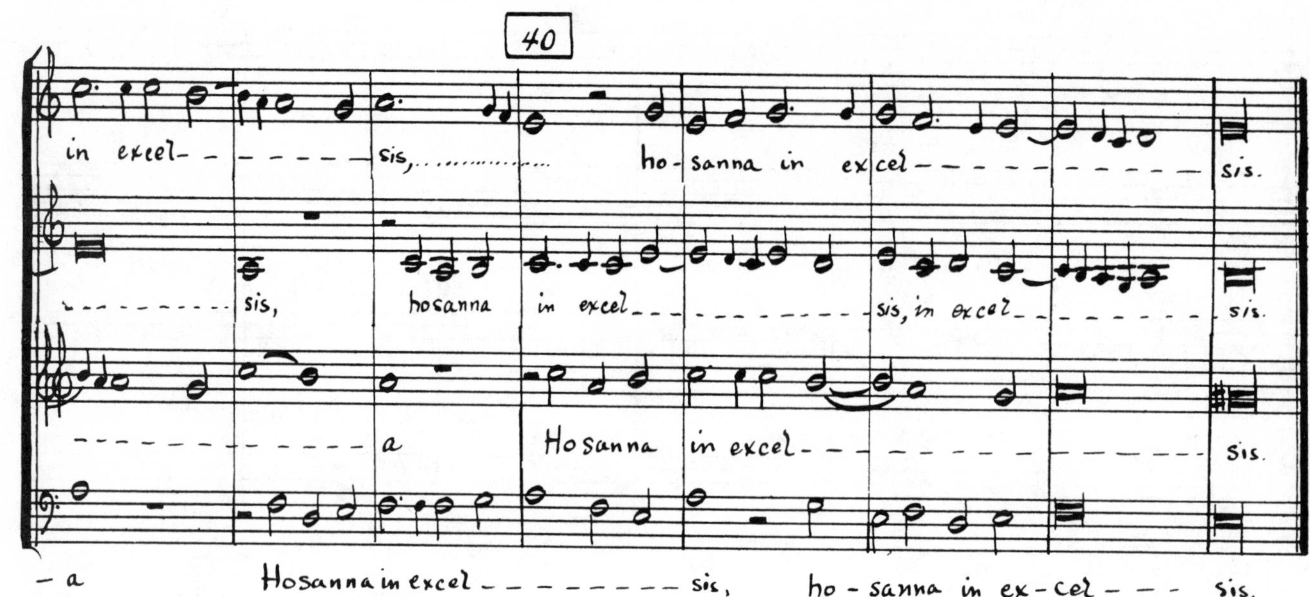
40
in excel- - - - - - - - sis, ... ho- sanna in ex cel- - - - - - - - - - - - - sis.
- - - - - - - - - sis, hosanna in excel- - - - - - - - - - - - sis, in excel- - - - - - - - - sis.
- - - - - - - - - - - - a Hosanna in excel- - - - - - - - - - - - - - - - - - sis.
- a Hosanna in excel - - - - - - - - - sis, ho - sanna in ex - cel - - - sis.

Motet: Dies Sanctificatus.

Palestrina.

ve-ni-te gen-tes et ad-o-
-tes gen-tes ve-ni-te gen-tes et
te gen-tes ve-ni-te gen-tes et
-ni-te ve-ni-te gen-tes
30
-ra-te Do-mi-num et ad-
ad-o-ra-te Do-mi-num et ad-o-ra-te Do-
ad-o-ra-te Do-mi-num et ad-o-ra-te Do-mi
et ad-o-ra-te et ad-o-ra-
40
-o-ra-te Do-mi-num, qui-a ho-di-e de-
-mi-num, qui-a ho-di-e-de-scen-dit
-num Do-mi-num, qui-a ho-di-e descen-
-te Do-mi-num, qui-a ho-di-e

-scen - dit lux ma - gna in ter - - ris de - scen - - dit
lux magna in ter - - ris de - scen -
dit lux ma - gna in ter - - ris descen - dit
de - - scen - dit de - -
50
descen - dit lux ma - gna in ter - ris; haec di -
-dit lux ma - gna in ter - - ris; haec di - - -
lux magna in ter - ris lux ma - gna in - ter - - ris; haec di -
-scen - - dit lux ma - gna in ter - ris; haec di - - es
- - es quam fe - cit Do - - - - mi nus
-es quam fecit Do - - - - mi nus quam fecit Do - mi - nus haec di - - es
es haec di - - - es
haec

60
haec di . . . es quam fecit Do . . . . mi-
...... quam fecit Dominus haec di . . . . . . es quam fecit Do . . . . mi-
quam fecit Do . . . . . mi-nus quam fe . . cit . . . . Do - mi-
di - - - es quam fe - - - cit Do . . . . mi-
70
-nus. Ex - ul - te - mus et lae - te - mur in e - - a et lae - te - mur
-nus. Ex - ul - te - mus et lae - te - mur in e - a ex - ul - te mus et lae - temur in
-nus. ex - ul - te - mus et lae - temur in e - a ex - - ul - te - mus et lae - te - mur
-nus. Ex - ul te - mus ex - ul - te - mus et lae - te - mur
80
in e - a ex - ul - te - mus et lae - te - mur in e - a.
e - - a ex - ul - te - mus et lae - te mur in e - a ex - ul te - mus et lae te - mur in e - a.
in e - a ex - ul - te - mus et lae - te - mur in e - - a ex - ul te - mus et lae te - mur in e - a.
in - e - a ex - ul - te - mus et lae - te - mur in e - a ex - ul - te - mus et lae - te - mur in e - a.

Hymn: In Festo Transfigurationis Domini.

Palestrina.

20
- - - nis glo - - - - - - ri - ae, glo - - - - - - - ri - ae.
- - - - - - - - - - - - - - - - ri - ae, si gnum per-en - - - - - - - - nis glo - - - - - - - ri - ae.
glo-ri - ae, signum per- en - - - nis, si-gnum per-en- - - nis glori-ae.
si - gnum per - en - - - - - - - - - - - nis glo-ri- ae, glo - - - - - ri - ae.
30
Hic il - - - - - - - - - - - le
Hic il - - - - - - - - - - le rex est gen - - - - - - - ti - um,
Hic il - - -
Hic il - - - - - - - - le rex est gen-ti-um, hic
rex est gen- - ti - um, po - pu-li - que rex Juda - i - - - - - -
po- pu-li - que rex Ju- da - i - ci, rex Ju-da-
- - - - - - - le rex est gen - - - ti - um, po- pu-li - que rex Ju-
il - le rex est gen - ti - um, po-pu-li - que rex Ju-da-i -

40
-ci, ... pro - missus A-brahae pa- tri, a- - -
- - - i - ci, ... promissus A - bra hae patri, pro- missus A- - - -
-da-i- ci, pro- - mis - sus A- brahae, promissus A- brahae pa- tri,
-ci, ... pro - mis - sus A - brahae pa- tri, pro-
50
- - - -brahae .... pa- tri e- jus - - - que in aevum
-bra-hae pa - - - - - - - - tri e- - - jus - que in aevum se-mi - ni, e-jus-que in ....
pro- mis-sus A - bra- hae pa - - - - - - - - - - - - - tri .... e - jus-
-missus A- bra- hae pa- tri .... e- jus - que in aevum se-mi-ni, e-
se-mi-ni, in ae - - - - vum se - - - - - - - - - mi - ni.
.... ae- vum se - mi - ni, in ae- vum se - - - - - - - - - - - - mi - ni.
- - - que in aevum se - - - - - - - - - - - - - - mi ni, se - - - - - - - - - - - mi - ni.
-jusque in ae- vum se- mi - ni, se- mi - ni.

60
Glo - - - - - - - - - - - - - - - - - - - ri - a
glo - - - - - - - - ri - a ti - - - - - - - - - - - bi Do - - - - - - - - - - - - - - - mi - ne,
glo - - - - - - - ri - a - - - - - - - - - - ti - bi - - - - - - - Do - mi - ne, - - - - - - - -
glo - - - - - - - - - - - - - - - -
ti - - - bi Do - mi - ne, glo - ri - a ti - - - - - - - bi Do - mi - ne,
glo - - - - - - - - - ri - - a ti - - - - - - - bi Do - - - - - - - - - mi - ne, qui
- - - - - glo - ri - a ti - - - - bi Do - - - - - - - - - - - - - - - - mi - ne, qui ap - pa - ru -
- - - - - - ri - a ti - - - - - - bi Do - - - - - - - - - - mi - - - ne,
70
qui ap - pa - ru - i - sti ho - di - e, - - - - - - - -
ap - pa - ru - i - sti ho - di - - e, ho - - - - - - - - - - - - - - - di - e,
- i - sti ho - di - e, ap - pa - ru - i - sti ho - di - e, cum patre et san -
qui ap - pa - - ru - i - sti ho - di - e, - - - - - - - - - cum patre et san -

80
cum patre et san - cto spi - - - - ri - tu.............
cum patre et san - - cto spi - - - - - - ri - tu............
- - cto spi ri - tu in sem - pi - ter - na sae - cu - la,.........
- - cto spi ri - tu, et sancto spi ri - tu in sem - pi - ter - na sae - - -
in sem - pi - - ter - na sae - cu - la,.................................... in
in sem - pi - ter - na sae - - - - - - cu - la, in sem pi - ter - - - - - -
...... sae - cu - la, in sempi - ter - na sae cu - la,
- - - - - - cu - la, in sem - -
sem - pi - ter - na sae - - - - - - - - - - - - cu - la.
- - - - - - - - - na, in sem - pi - ter - na sae - - - - - - - cu - - - la.
in sem - pi - ter - na sae - - - - - - - - - - - - - cu - la.
- pi - ter - na sae - cu - la.

Magnificat.
Palestrina.
Cantus
Altus
4-7
Tenor
Bassus
2. Et ex - - - - - sul - - - ta - vit,
2. Et ex - - - - - sul-ta - - vit, et
2. Et
2. Et
10
et ex - sul-ta - - vit spi - ri-tus me - us,
ex - - sul-ta - - - - vit spi - ri-tus me - us, spi -
ex - - - - sul - - ta - - vit spi - ri-tus me - us, spi -
ex - - - - - - sul-ta - - vit spi -
spi - ri-tus me - - - us in De - - o sa - lu -
- ri - tus me - us in De - - o, in De - o sa - lu-ta -
- ri - tus me - - us in De - - o, in De - - o
- ri-tus me - us in De - - - - - o
20
- ta - ri me - - o, sa - lu-ta-ri me - - - o, in De -
- ri me - - - o, sa - lu - ta - ri me - o, in De - -
sa - lu-ta - ri me - o, sa - lu - ta-ri me - o, in
sa - lu-ta - ri me - - - - - - o,

- - o, in De - - o sa - - lu - ta - ri me - o, sa - lu -
- - - - o sa - lu - ta - ri me - o, sa - lu - ta -
De - - - o, in De - - - o sa - lu - ta - ri me - o, sa -
in De - - - o sa - lu - ta - ri me - o,
30
- ta - ri me - - o, sa - lu - ta - ri me - - - - - - - o.
- - ri me - o, sa - lu - ta - ri me - o.
- lu - ta - ri me - - - - - o, sa - lu - ta - ri me - - o.
sa - lu - ta - ri me - o, sa - lu - ta - ri me - o.
40
4. Qui - a fe - - cit mi - hi ma - gna
4. Qui - a fe - cit mi - hi ma - - - - - - - -
4. Qui - a fe - - cit mi - hi
4. Qui - a fe - - cit mi - hi ma - - - gna qui
qui po - tens est, qui po - tens est,
- gna qui po - tens est,
ma gna qui po tens est, qui po - tens est,

50
po - tens est, qui po - tens
qui po - - - - - - - - - tens
qui po tens est:
qui po - tens est:
est: et san - ctum no - men e - - - - - - jus, et san - ctum no - men
est: et san - ctum no - men e - jus, no - men e - -
et san - ctum no - men e - - - - - - -
et san - ctum no - men e - - - - jus,
60
e - - - - - jus, et san - ctum no - men
- jus, et san - ctum no - men e - - jus, no - men
jus, et san - ctum no - men e - jus, no - - men
et san - ctum no - men e - jus, et san - ctum no - men
e - jus, et san - ctum no - men e - jus.
e - jus, et san - ctum no - men e - jus, no - men e - - jus.
e - jus, et san - ctum no - men e - - - - - - jus.
e - jus, et san - ctum no - - men e - - jus.

Altus I
Altus II
Tenor
Bassus
70
6. Fe - cit po-ten-ti-am, fe -
6. Fe - cit po-ten- ti-am, fe-
6. Fe - cit po - ten - ti-am,
6.Fe -
- cit po - ten-ti - am
- cit po - ten-ti-am
in bracchi - o
fe - cit po-ten-ti - am
in brac-chi - o, in
cit po - ten - ti-am in brac-chi - o su -
80
in brac-chi - o, in brac-chi - o su - o,
su - o, in brac-chi - o, in brac-chi-
brac-chi-o su - o, in brac-chi-
- o, in brac-chi - o su - o, in
in brac-chi - o su - o: dis-per - sit su-per -
- o su - o: dis - per - sit su-per - bos, dis-per -
- o su - o: dis - per - sit su - per - bos,
brac - chi - o su - o: dis - per - sit su - per - bos, dis -

Cantus
Altus
Tenor
Bass

8. E - - su - - - ri -
8. E - - su - - - ri - en - tes, e - su - -
8. E - - su - - - ri - en - - - tes, e - -

110
en - - - tes, e - su - - - ri - en - tes im - ple - vit bo -
- - - ri - en - tes, e - - su - ri - en - tes im - ple - vit
- su - - - ri - en - tes, e - su - ri - en - - - tes
8. E - - su - - - ri - en - - tes
- - nis, im - ple - vit bo - - - - nis, im - ple - vit
bo - - - - - - nis, im -
im - ple - vit bo - - - - nis, im - ple - vit
im - ple - - vit
120
bo - - nis: et di - vi - tes di - mi - sit in - a - nes,
- ple - vit bo - nis: et di - - vi - tes, et di - - vi - tes di -
bo - nis: et di - - vi - tes di - mi - sit in - a - - - - - -
bo - - nis: et di - vi - tes di - mi - sit in - a - - - -
et di - - vi - tes di - mi - sit in - a - nes, et di - vi - tes di -
- mi - sit in - a - - - - - - - - nes, et di - - vi - tes di -
- nes, di - mi - - sit in - a - - - - - - - nes,
- nes, et di - - vi - tes di -

130
-mi - sit in - a - - - - - - - - - - - - - - nes.
-mi - sit in - a - nes, di-mi - sit in - - - - a - nes.
et di - vi - tes di-mi - sit in-a - - - - - - nes.
-mi - sit in - a - - - - - - nes, in - - - - - a - - nes.
Cantus I
Cantus II
Altus
Tenor
10. Sic - ut lo-cu-tus est
10. Sic - ut
10. Sic - ut lo - cu-tus est
Sic - ut lo -
140
ad pa-tres no - - - - - stros, ad pa-tres
- lo - cu - tus est ad pa-tres
ad pa-tres no - - - - stros, ad
-cu - tus est
no - - - - - - - - stros, ad pa-tres no - stros: A - bra -
no - - - stros, ad pa - tres no - - - - - stros: A - bra -
pa - - - tres no - - stros: A - bra-ham
ad pa-tres no - stros, ad pa-tres no - stros: A -

150
-ham, ___ et se -
-ham, ___ et se - mi - ni e - jus ___
et se - mi - ni e - jus in sae - - cu - la, in
- bra - ham, et se - mi - ni e - jus in sae - - cu -
- mi - ni e - jus in sae - - cu - la, et se - mi - ni e - - -
___ in sae - cu - la, et se - mi - ni e - jus in sae -
sae - - - cu - la, ___ et se - mi - ni e - jus in
- la, in sae - cu - la, ___ et se - mi - ni e -
160
- jus in sae - - - - cu - la, et se - mi - ni e - jus,
- cu - la, in ___ sae - cu - la, et se - mi - ni e - jus in
sae - - cu - la, ___ et se - mi -
- jus, et se - mi - ni e -
170
et se - mi - ni e - jus in sae - - cu - la, in sae - cu - la.
sae - cu - la, et se - - mi - ni e - - jus in sae - cu - la.
- ni e - jus ___ in sae - - cu - la, ___ in sae - cu - la.
- jus in sae - - - - cu - la, in ___ sae - cu - la.

Cantus
12. Sic - - ut e - - - - - - - -
Altus
12. Sic - - ut e - - - - - - - - - -
Tenor I
12. Sic - - ut e - -
Tenor II
Bassus

- rat,
sic - ut
- - - - - - - rat, sic - ut e - raf
- - - - - - - - - - - rat, sic - - - - - - - -
12. Sic - - ut e - - - - - - - - - - rat, sic -
12. Sic - - - - - ut e - - - - -

180
e - - - - - rat in prin - ci - pi - o, in
in prin - ci - pi - o, in prin -
- ut e - - rat in prin - ci - pi - o,
- ut e - rat in prin - ci - pi - o, in
- rat in prin - ci - pi - o,

prin - ci - - pi - o et nunc et sem - - per, et
- ci - pi - o et nunc et sem - - - - per, et
prin - ci - pi - o et nunc et sem - - - - - -
in prin - ci - pi - o et nunc et sem - per,

190
nunc et sem - - - - - - - per et in sae - - - -
nunc et sem - - - - - per et in sae - cu - la,
et nunc et sem - - - - per et
- per, et nunc et sem - - per et in sae - cu - la,
et nunc et sem - - per

- cu - la sae - - - -
et in sae - - cu - la sae - - cu -
in sae - - - - cu - la, et in sae - - - - - cu - la
et in sae - - cu - la sae - cu -
et in sae - - - - cu - la

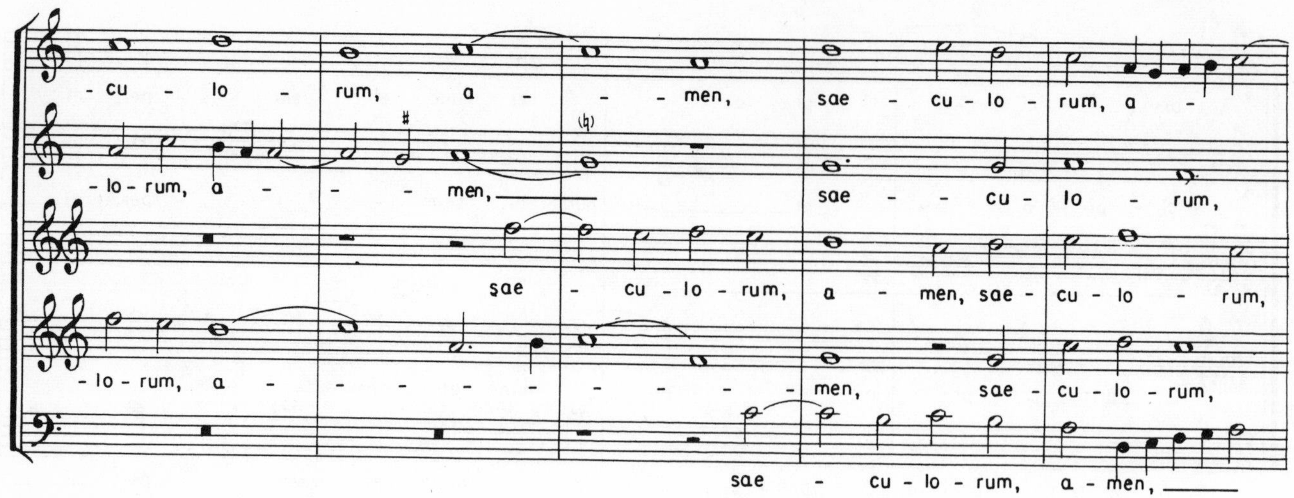
-cu - lo - rum, a - - men, sae - cu - lo - rum, a -
-lo - rum, a - - - men, sae - - cu - lo - rum,
sae - cu - lo - rum, a - men, sae - cu - lo - rum,
-lo - rum, a - - - - - men, sae - cu - lo - rum,
sae - cu - lo - rum, a - men,

200
- - men, sae - cu - lo - rum, a - men, sae - cu - lo -
a - men, sae - cu - lo - rum, a - - men, sae - cu - lo -
a - men, sae - cu - lo - rum, a - - - men, a - - men,
sae - cu - lo - rum, a - men, sae - cu -
a - - - - - - men, sae - cu - lo - rum,

rum, a - men, sae - cu - lo - rum, a - men.
- rum, a - men, sae - cu - lo - rum, a - - - men.
sae - cu - lo - - rum, a - - - men.
- lo - rum, a - - men.
a - men, sae - - - cu - lo - - - rum, a - men.

Mass: Sanctorum Meritis: Agnus Dei I and II. Palestrina.
I.
Cantus
Altus
4-8
Tenor
Bassus
A---gnus De-----i, A-gnus De--------i, A gnus........................
A----------gnus De-----------------------------------
A----------------gnus De-----i, A----gnus De--------
A------------gnus De-----
10
De-i, A-gnus De--
i, A--gnus De---i, A--gnus De-i, A-----------------gnus.............
---i, A-----------------gnus De---i,
--i, A-----------------gnus De--i, A-----------
20
------------------i, qui tollis pec-
De--------------i, qui tollis pec--ca-ta mun-di, pec------ca------ta mun-
A----gnus De-i,................................. qui
gnus......... De------i, qui tollis pec-ca-ta mun-di, pec------

-ca-ta mun - di, pec cata mun - di: mi - se-rere no- - - - bis, mi-se-
-di, qui tol- - lis pecca- ta mun- - - di:...... mi- se- rere no-
tollis pec- - cata mun- - di:........ mi - se- re - re,
ca-ta mun- - - - di: mi- - se- - rere no- - - - bis, mi- - - se- re - re
30
re- re no- - - - - - - - - - - bis, mi - se - re - - re no- - - - bis.
-bis, mi- - se- - - re- - - re no - bis,........ no- - - - - - - - - - - - bis.
mi- - se - rere no - bis, no- - - - - - - - - - - - bis.
no- bis, mi- -se- re- re no- - - - - - bis,...........
Cantus
Altus
II.
A- - gnus De- - - - - - - -
Tenor I
5-1
A- - - - gnus De- - - - - - - -
Tenor II
A- - gnus De- - - - - - i, A- - - - - gnus De- - - - - - - -
Bassus
A- - - - - - - - - gnus........ De- - i,

10
A-- gnus De--------i,........... qui tollis pecca--ta............... mundi,
i, A-- gnus De------i, qui tollis pec--ca-ta mun-di, qui
-i, A--gnus De----------------i,
----i, qui tol-lis pec-ca-ta mun-di,
A--gnus De------------i, qui

qui tol-lis pec--ca-ta mun-di,...............
tol-lis.......... pec-------------ca-ta mun-di, qui tollis
qui tollis pec-ca-ta mun-di,............ pec-ca------------ta
pec---ca-ta mun-di, A--------gnus De---i, qui
tollis pec--ca-ta mun-di,

20
qui tol lis pecca - - - ta mun - di, pec - - co - - - ta mun - di:
pec - - - ca - - ta mun - - - - - di: do - - - na no - - -
mun - di, qui tollis pec - - cata mun - - - di:
tollis pecca - - ta mundi, pecca - ta mun - - - - - di:
qui tollis pec - ca - ta mun - di, pec - ca - ta mun - di: do - - -

30
do - na no - - - - - bis pa - - - - - - - - - cem, do na no - - -
- - - bis pa - - - - - - cem, do - - na no - bis
do - na no - - - - bis pa - - - - cem do - na no - - bis
do - - - na no - - - - bis pa - - - - - - - cem, do - na
na no - - - - - - bis, do - na no - - - - - - bis. pa - - cem,

-bis pa - - - - - - - - - - - - - - - - cem, do - na no - bis pa - - - - - - - - -
pa - - - - - - - - - - - - - - - - - - cem, do - - - na no - - - - - bis pa - - - - - - - -
pa - - - - - - - - - - - - - cem, do - na no - bis .... pa - - - - cem, do - -
no - - - - - - - bis .... pa - cem, ...
do - - - na no - - - - - bis pa - - -

40
- - - - - - - - - - - - - - - - cem, do - na no - - - - - - - - bis pa - - - - - - cem.
- - - - - - - - - - - - - - - - - - - cem, do - - - na no - bis pa - - - - - - - - - - cem.
- - - - - na nobis, do - na no - - - - - - - bis pa - - - - - - - - cem.
do - - na no - bis pa - - - - - - - - - - - - - cem.
- - - - - - - - - - - - - - - - cem, do - na no - bis pa - - - - - - cem.

Mass: Petra Sancta: Kyrie.

Palestrina.

-ri-e e- - - le - ison, Kyrie e - le- - - - - -
Ky- - - ri-e e- - - le- ison, Ky-ri-e e-le-
- - - ison, Ky- - -ri-e e- - - le- ison, Ky-ri-e e-
e- le- - - ison, Ky-ri-e e-le- - - ison,
Ky-rie e- - le- ison, Ky- - ri-e e- - le- - -

20
- - - i-son, Ky - ri - e e- - le- - - ison.
- -ison Ky - ri-e e- - - le- - - ison.
- le - ison, Ky- ri-e e- - - le- i- son, e- - - le- ison.
Ky-ri-e e- - le- - - ison.
- ison, Ky- ri-e e-le- - - ison.

30
Chri - ste e-
Chri - ste e - le - - - - - - - - - - - - ison, Chri - ste e - - - - - - - - - - - - - le - ison,
Chri - - ste e - le - i - son, e - - - - - - - - - le - -
Chri - - ste e - le - i - son, Christe e - - - - - - - - le - ison, Chri-
Chri - ste e - le - i - - son, ... Chri -

- le - i - son ...... Chri - ste e - le - i - son, ...
Chri - ste e - le - i - - son, ... Chri ste e - le ...... ison,
- - - ison, Chri - ste e - le - i - son, ...
- ste e - le - - - - - - - - - - i - son, Chri - - - ste e - - le - - - - - - ison, Chri-
- ste e - le - - - - - - - ison, Chri - ste e -

40
Chri- ste e- le- i- - - son,
Chri- ste e- le- i- son, Chri-
Chri - - ste e- le- i- son,
- ste e- le- i- son, Chri- - ste e- le- i-
- le- i- son, Chri- - ste e- le- i-

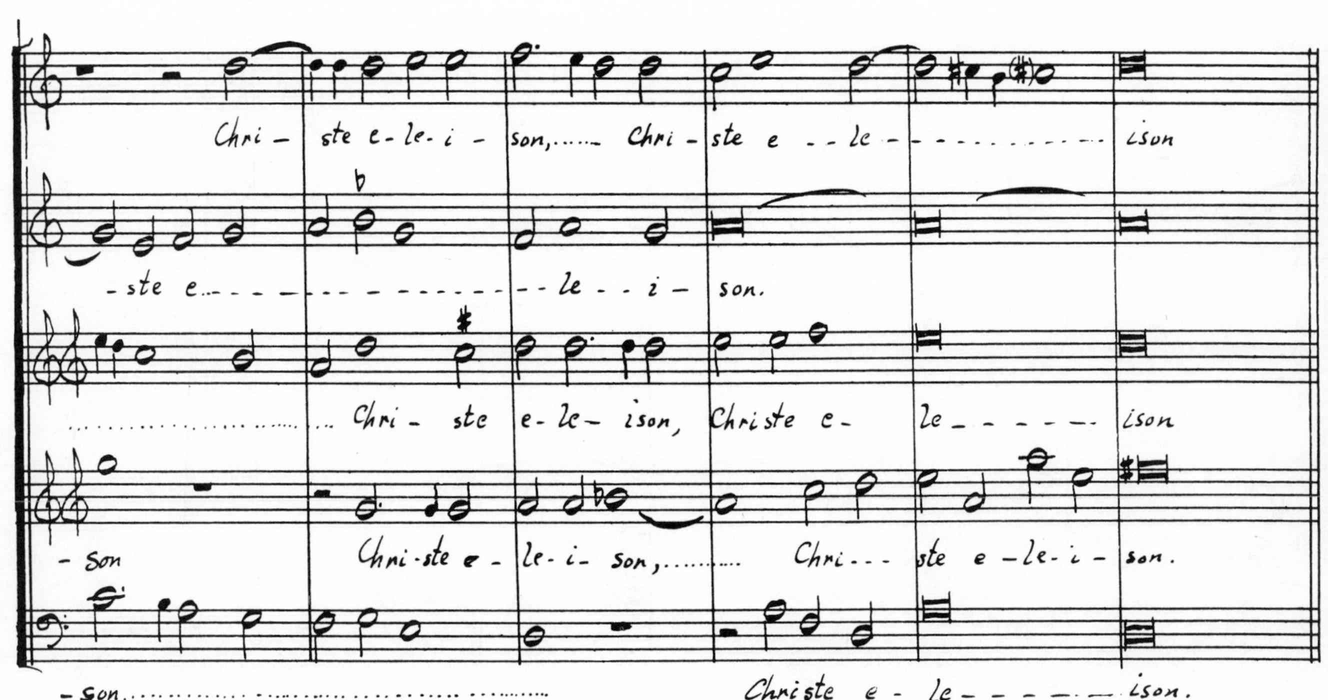
Chri- ste e- le- i- son, Chri- ste e- - le- ison
- ste e- le- - i- son.
Chri- ste e- le- ison, Christe e- le- ison
- son Chri- ste e- le- i- son, Chri- - - ste e- le- i- son.
- son, Christe e- le- ison.

50
Ky - ri - e e - le - i - son,
Ky - ri - e e - le -
Ky -
Ky - ri - e e - le - ison,

60
Ky - ri - e e - le -
Ky - ri - e e - le - i -
ison, Ky - ri - e e - le -
ri - e e - le - ison, Ky - rie e - le - ison,
Ky - ri e - le - ison,

-ison, Ky-ri-e e---le---ison,......
Ky-ri-e
-son, Ky-rie e-le....i-son, Ky.......ri-e e-le.......
-le-ison,.........
Ky-ri-e e---le-ison,.........
Ky.... ri-e e.........le.........i-son,.......
Ky-ri-e e--------le..........ison, Ky-ri-e

70
e---le.........i-son, Ky--rie e-le----ison.
.........i-son,...... Ky-ri-e e.......le.........i-son.
.........Ky-ri-e e--le.........ison.
Ky-ri-e e--le.........ison.
e--le--ison, Ky-ri---e e-le.........ison.

Mass: Vestiva i Colli: Kyrie

Palestrina.

20
ison,
Ky-rie e-le- - ison,
le-ison, Ky-rie
e- - - le-ison,
Ky-rie e-le
Ky-rie e-le- - - i-son,
Ky-rie e-le-i-son,
Ky-
i-son,
Ky-rie e-le- - - ison,
Ky-rie e-le
Ky-rie e-le- - - i-son,
Ky-rie e-le

Ky-rie e-le- - - i-son,
Ky-rie e-le- - - ison.
le- - ison, Ky-rie e-le- - ison,
Ky-rie e-le- - - i-son.
-rie e-le- - - i-son,
Kyrie e-le- - - i-son.
son,
Ky-rie e-le- - - i-son, Ky-rie e-le- - - ison.
ison,
Ky-rie e-le- - - ison.

30
Cantus
Altus
Tenor
Tenor
Christe e-le-ison, Christe e-le-ison,
40
50
60
Christe e-le-i-son.

Cantus
Kyrie ele
Altus
Kyrie ele i-son, Kyrie e-
Tenor
Kyrie e-le ison, Ky-
Tenor II
Kyrie e le- ison, Ky- rie e- le- ison,
Bassus
Kyrie e- le i-son, Ky- ri-e e-le

70
ison, Kyrie e-le
leison, Ky-rie e-le ison, Ky rie e- le- ison, Ky- ri-e e-
rie e-le i-son, Ky-rie e- le- ison,
Ky-rie e-le-i-son, Ky-rie e- le ison, Ky-
ison, Ky-rie e-le-ison, Ky-rie e-le- ison, Ky-ri

80
i_son, Ky_ _ri_e e_le_ _ _ i_son, Ky_rie e_
_ _ le_ _ _ i son, e_le_ _ ison, Ky_ri_e e_le_ _ _ i_
Ky_ri_e e_le_ _ _ i_son, Ky_ri_
rie e _le_ _ison, Ky_rie e_le_ _ _ ison, Ky_ri_e e_ _ _
_e e_le_ _ _ ison, Ky_rie e_le_ _ _ ison,

90
_le_ _ _ i_ son, Ky_ _rie e_le_ _ _ ison, Ky_ rie e_le_ _ _ ison.
son, Ky ri_e e_le_ _ ison, Ky_rie e_le_ _ _ i_ son.
_e e_ _ _ le_ _ _ ison. Ky_ rie e_ le_ _ _ ison.
_ _ _ le_ _ _ ison, Ky rie e_le_ _ _ i_ _son, Ky_ _ ri_e e_le_ _ ison.
Ky_ ri_e e_le_ _ _ i_ son, Ky_ _rie e_le_ _ ison.

Mass: Vestiva i Colli: Gloria. Palestrina.

20
te.......... Be_nedi_ci_mus te. Ad_ _o_ ra_ _ _ mus te. Glo_ri_ fi_ _ca_mus te........
te....... Be_ne_ di_ _ _ _ _ _ _ _ci_mus te.......... Ad_ _ _o_ ramus te. Glo_ri_fi_ _ _
_ne_di_ci_ mus te. Ad_ _ o_ramus te......... Glo_ri_fi_ ca_mus te.........
Laudamus te. Be_nedi_ci_ mus te.......... Ad_ _ _o_ _ra_ _ _ mus
_di_ci_mus te. Ad_ o_ ramus te. Glo_ri_fi_camus

.... Gra_ ti_as a_ gi_mus ti_ bi..........
_ca_ _ _ mus te. Gra_ tias a_ _ _ gi_ mus......... ti_ bi propter magnam
Gra_ti_as a_ gi_mus.............. ti_ _ _ _ _bi propter magnam...... glo_
te Glori_fi_ ca_ _ _ mus te. Gra_ ti_as a_ gi_ mus ti_ bi propter magnam glo_ri_am
te. Gra_ti_as a_ _ gimus ti_ _ _ _ _ _ _ _ _ _ _ _ _bi propter magnam glori_ om

30
propter magnum glo - - - ri.am tu - am. Do -
glo - ri - am tu_am
Domine De_us, Rex coe -
- ri_am tu_am Do mine De_us, Rex coele - - stis, Rex coe_le - -
tu - - - am, tu - - - am. Do_mine De_us, Rex coele - - -
tu - am. Domine De_us, Rex coe_le - - -

40
- mine, De_us, Rex coe le - - stis, De - us Pa - ter o - - mni - - -
- le - - - stis, De - - us Pa - - - ter omni - po - tens,
stis, De - us Pa - - - ter o - - mni - - - po - tens
- stis, Rex coe_le - - - stis, De - us Pa - - - ter o - - mni - -
stis, De - us Pa - - - ter o - - - mni - - -

50
po.tens...... Do_ mine Fi.li u_ nige.ni_ te,...... Je...... su
o_ mni.... po_tens. Domine Fi.li u.ni_ge.ni_te, Je.... su Chri...
Do_ mine Fi li u_ni_ge.. ni_ te, Je_ su Chri.. ste, Je_ su
_ po.tens...... Domine Fili u... ni.ge.ni_ te, Je_ su,...... Je_ su......
_ po.tens...... Je_ _ su Chri...

Chri...... ste. Fi_lius Pa......
...... ste. Do_mine De.us, A... gnus De_ i, Fi_ lius Pa......
Chri...... ste...... Do_mine De_ us, Agnus De_ i,
...... Chri... ste. Do_mine Deus, Agnus De...... i, Fi_ li_ us
...... ste. Domine De.us, Agnus De...... i,

60
tris, Filius Pa_ _ _ _ tris, Fi lius Pa_ _ _ tris Pa_ _ _ _ tris.
tris, Fi_li_us Pa_tris, Fi lius Pa_ _ _ _ tris.
Fi lius Pa_ _ _ tris...... Pa_ _ _ _ tris, Fi_lius, Pa_ _ _ tris.
Pa_ _ _ tris, Fi_li_us Pa_ _ _ tris, Fi_li_us Pa_ _ tris, Fi_li_us Pa_ _ _ tris, Pa_ _ tris.
Fi_lius Pa_ _ _ _ tris, Fi_ lius Pa_ _ _ _ tris.

70
Qui tol_lis pec_ ca_ ta mun_ _ _ di,
Qui tol_ _ _ lis pec_ca ta:...... mundi, pec_ca_ ta mun_ di,
Qui tollis pec_ _ca_ _ta mun_ _ _ di, mun_ _ _
Qui tollis pec_ _ ca_ ta mun
Qui tol_ _ _ lis pec_ca_ta..........

80
mi - sere - re ... no - - - - - - bis, mi - - se - re - - - - re no - bis ...
mi - sere - re no - bis, mi - se - re - re no - - - - - - - - - - - - bis.
- - - di, mi - sere - re no - bis, mi - sere - re no - bis. Qui
- - di, ... mi - sere - re no - - - - - - - - - - - bis, no - - - - bis. Qui tollis
mun - di, mi - se - re - re no - - - - - - - - - - - - bis. Qui tol - - - - -

Qui tol - - - lis, qui tol - lis pec ca - ta mun - di, su - - - sci - pe
Qui tol - - - - - - lis pec - ca - ta mun - di, su - - sci - pe de - pre -
tollis pecca - ta mun - di, pec - ca - - - ta mun - di, su - sci - pe de - pre -
peccata mun - di, qui tol - - - - - - - lis pecca - ta mun - di, su - - sci - pe de - pre -
lis pecca - ta mun - - - - di, su - sci - pe de - pre -

90
de_ pre_ca_ti_ o nem no_ stram.
_ca_ti_onem no_ stram, de_preca_ti_onem no_ _ _ stram. Qui sedes ad dex_
_ca_ti_ onem no_ _ stram, de_preca_ti_ onem no_ stram. Qui sedes ad dex_ _te_ram Pa_
_ca_ti_ onem no_stram, de_ preca_ ti_onem no_ _ strum, Qui se_des ad dex_teram Pa_
_ca_ti_onem no_ stram. Qui sedes ad dex_ _teram Pa_

100
Mi_ se_re_ re no_ _ _ _ _ _ bis. Quo_ ni_am tu so_lus san_
te_ram Pa_tris, mi_se_re_ re no_ _ _ _ _ _ bis. Quoni_am tu, quo_
_ _ _ tris,........ Quo_ ni_am tu so_ _ _ lus san_
_tris, mi se_re_ re no_ _ _ _ bis........ Quo_ ni_ am tu so_lus
_tris. Quoni_am tu............ solus san_

110
-ctus, tu so_lus Domi nus, tu solus Al_tis.si nus, Altis_si_mus, Je___
_niam tu solus san____ctus, tu solus Dominus, tu solus Al_ tis.si mus,
-ctus, san____ctus, tu solus Do mi_ nus,........... tu solus Al_
san____ctus, tu solus Do__mi nus,...... tu solus Al_tis si mus,........
__ ctus, tu solus Al__tissimus, Al_tissimus,

__su Chri_ste, Je su Chri____ ste..... Cum sancto Spiri_tu...............
Je_ su..... Chri.ste. Cum sancto Spi_______________ri_tu in gloria..De
_tissi mus, Je_su Christe. Cum sancto Spi_ri_tu,..........cum sancto Spiri_tu in gloria De_i
Je_____ su Chri_______ ste...... Cum san_cto Spi_ri_ tu........
Je_ su...... Chri____ste. Cum sancto Spiri_tu in gloria De_i

120
in glo-ria De-i Pa-- tris, De-i Patris. A------ men,
-i Patris. A---- men, De- i Patris A----- men, in gloria De-i
Pa------- tris. A--- men, in glo ria De-i Pa-- tris. A---
in gloria De-i Patris. A--- men in gloria De-i Patris. A--
Pa-tris. A-- men, ... in glo-ria De-i Pa--tris. A---

130
in gloria De-i Pa----- tris. A----- men, Dei Pa-tris. A---------- men.
Pa-tris A------------ men
-- men, in gloria De--- i Patris. A---- men, De--- i Pa-- tris. A--- men.
------ men, Dei Pa--tris. A- men, in gloria De-i Patris. A---------- men,
-men, in gloria De-i Pa---tris. A----------- men.

Motet: Alleluia Tulerunt.

Palestrina.

al — — le- lu — — — ja!
-ja ... al — — le-
al — — le - lu — — — — ja ... al — — — le —
— lu — — ja ... al — le- lu — — —
al — — le — lu ... ja al — le ... lu—

20
tu-lerunt Do — mi-num me — — — — —
lu — — — — ja! ... tu-lerunt Do — mi-num me — — — — — —
lu — — ja al — — le — lu — — — — ja! ... tu—
-ja al- — le-lu — — — — — — — ja! tu — lerunt Do — mi-
-ja ... al - le lu — — — — ja!

um tu- lerunt Do- mi-
um, tu- ler-unt Do- mi num me
-le-runt Do - mi num me - - - um, Do - - mi - num me - um,
-num, tu-lerunt Do- minum, tu-ler-unt Do- - mi num .... me
tu-lerunt Do- minum me - - - um, me - - - um

30
num .... me - - - um
-um, tu- lerunt Do- minum me.um Al - - - le - - lu - -
tu- lerunt Do- minum me - - - um Al - - - le - lu - - ja Al-
-um, tu- lerunt Do- minum me- - - - um Al - - - le - - lu-
Al - - le - lu - - - -

40
al - - le - lu - - - - - - - - - - - - - - - ja! et ne - - scio u - bi po - - - su -
- - - - - - - - - - - - - - - ja! . . . . et ne - scio u -
- - - - - le - lu - - - - - - - ja! et ne - sci - o u - bi po - - - su - e - runt e - - - - - -
ja! et ne - scio u - - bi po - - - su - e - runt e - - um
ja! et ne - sci - o u - bi po - - su - e - runt e - - - - - - - um . . . .

- e - - runt e - - - - - - - - - - - - - - - - um al - -
- bi po - su - e - runt e - - - - - - um u - bi po - su - e - runt . . . . e - - - -
- - - - - - - - - um et ne - scio u - bi po - - - su - e - runt e - - -
et ne sci - o u - - - - - - - - - - bi po - - suerunt e - - - - - - - - - -
et ne - sci - o u - bi po - - - - su - e - runt e - - - um

50
le-lu ja! si tu su-
um al-le-lu-ja! si tu su-stuli-sti
um al-le-lu ja al-le-lu-ja!
um al-le-lu ja al-le-lu ja si tu su-stuli-
al-le-lu-ja!

60
stuli-sti e um, di-cito mi-
e-um si tu su-stuli-sti e-um, di-cito
si tu su-stuli-sti e um, di-ci-
-sti e um si tu su-stu-li-sti e um,
si tu su-stu-li-sti e um,

hi di - cito mi - - - - hi, Al - - - - le - lu-
mi - - - - hi, al - - - le - lu - - - -
- to mi - - - - hi di - ci - to mi - - hi, al - - - le - lu - - - -
di - cito mi - - - - - - - - hi al - le - lu - ja
di - cito mi - - - - - - - - hi,

70
ja! et e - go e - - um tol - - lam tol - - - -
ja al - - le - lu - - ja! et e - go e - - - um tol - -
ja! et e - go e - - um tol - - - lam
al - - - - le - - lu - ja! et e - go e - - um tol - - -
al - - - - le - lu - - - - ja!

80
-lam et e-go e-um tol-lam.
-lam et e-go e-um tol-lam. Al-le-lu-
et e-go e-um tol-lam. Al-le-lu-
-lam et e-go e-um tol-lam. Al-le-lu-
et e-go e-um tol-lam. Al-

al-le-lu-ja al-le-lu-
-ja al-le-lu-ja
ja al-le-lu-ja al-le-lu-ja
ja al-le lu-ja al-le
-le-lu-ja al-le-lu-ja

90
ja al - le - lu - ja!
al - le - lu - ja
al - le - lu - ja!
al - le - lu - ja
al - le - lu - ja!
lu - ja
al - le - lu - ja!
al - le - lu - ja
al - le - lu - ja!

Hymn: In Dominicis Quadragesima.

Palestrina.

Hymn: In Dominicis Qudragesima.

Palestrina.

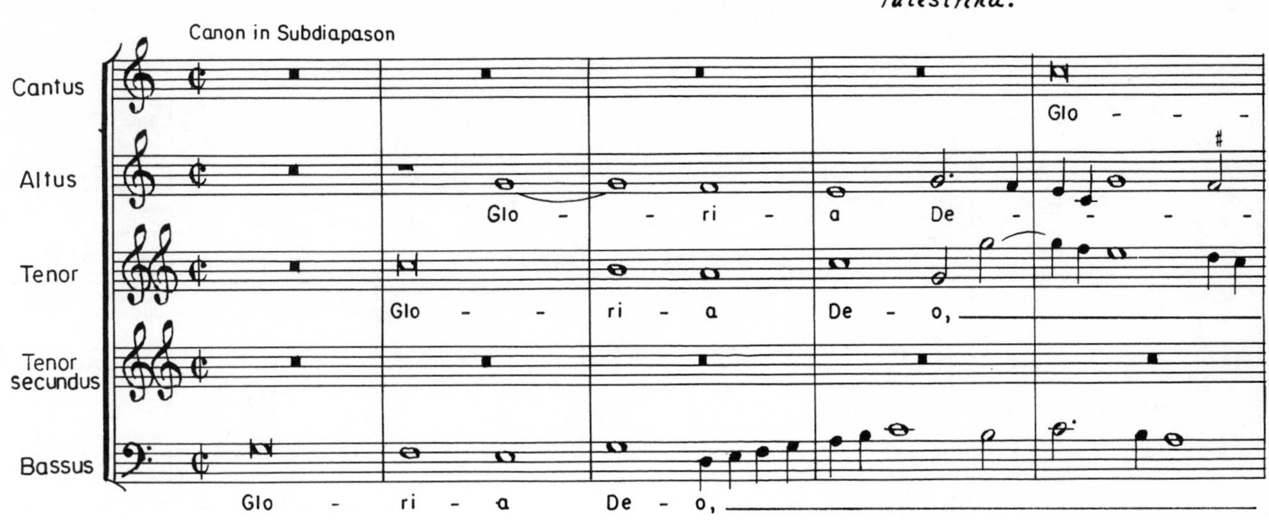

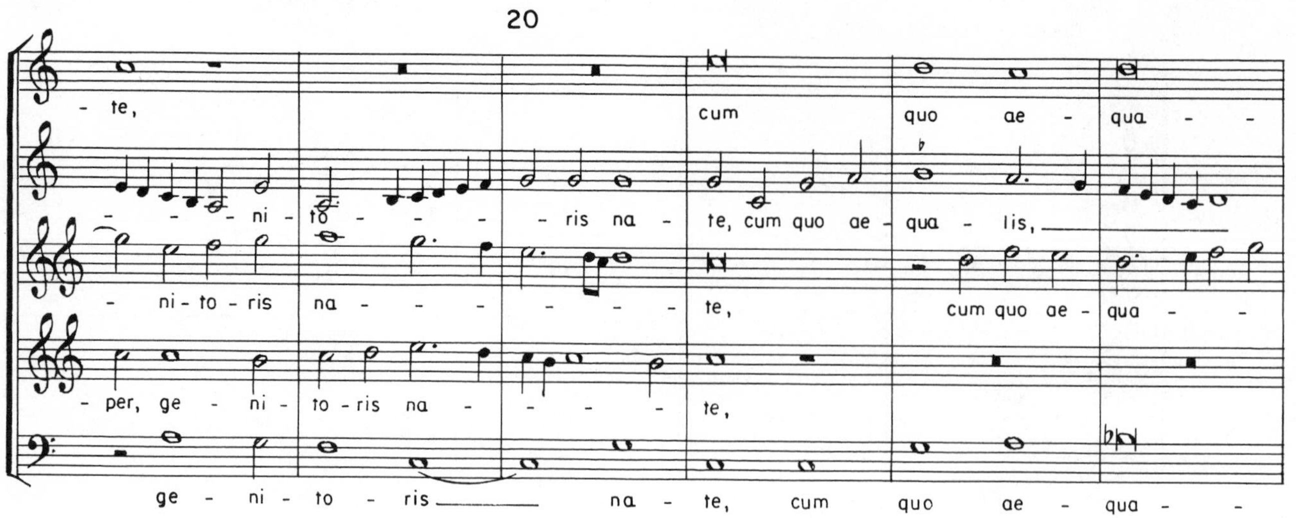
20
- te, cum quo ae - qua - -
- - - ni - to - - - - ris na - te, cum quo ae - qua - lis,
- ni - to - ris na - - - - - - te, cum quo ae - qua - -
- per, ge - ni - to - ris na - - - - te,
ge - ni - to - ris na - te, cum quo ae - qua - -

- lis spi - ri - tus per cun - cta sae - cu -
cum quo ae - qua - lis spi - ri - tus per cun - cta sae - cu -
- lis spi - ri - tus per cun - cta sae - cu - la
cum quo ae - qua - lis spi - ri - tus per cun - cta
- lis spi - ri - tus per cun - cta

30
- la re - - gnat, per cun - cta sae - cu - la re - - - gnat.
- la re - gnat, sae - cu - la re - gnat, sae - cu - la re - gnat.
re - gnat, sae - - - - - - - - cu - la re - - gnat.
sae - cu - la re - - - gnat.
sae - cu - la re - - - - gnat, sae - cu - la re - gnat.

Offertory: Laudate Dominum.
Palestrina.

Cantus
Lau - da - te Do - - - mi -
Altus
Lau - da - te Do - - - mi - num, lau - - - da -
5 - 7
Tenor
Quintus
Lau - - da -
Bassus

10
- num, lau - da - - te Do - mi - num, lau - da - te
- - te Do - - - - - - mi - num, lau -
Lau - - da - te Do - - - - - mi - num, lau - da -
- te Do - - - mi - num, lau - da - - - te Do - - -
Lau - - da - te Do - - -

Do - mi - num, qui - a be - ni - gnus est,
- da - te Do - - mi - num, qui - a be - ni - gnus, qui -
- te Do - mi - num, qui - a be - ni - - - gnus est,
- mi - num, qui - a be - ni - gnus est,
- - - mi - num, qui - a be - ni - - gnus est,

20
qui - a be - ni - - gnus est, qui - a
- a be - ni - - - gnus est, qui - a
qui - a be - ni - gnus est,
qui - a be - ni - - - - gnus est, qui - a be - ni -
qui - a be -

be - ni - gnus est: psal - li - te no - mi-ni e - - -
be - ni - - gnus est: psal - li - te no - mi-ni
qui - a be - ni- gnus est: psal - li - te no - mi - ni,
- - - - - - - gnus est: psal - li-
- ni - - - - gnus est: psal - li - te no - mi-ni e - - -

30
- - - - - - jus, psal - li-te no - mi-ni e - - -
e - - - - - jus, psal - li-te no - mi - ni e - jus, no -
psal - li-te no - mi-ni e - jus,
- te no - mi-ni e - - - jus, psal - li-te no - mi-ni, no - mi-ni
- - jus, psal - li-te no -

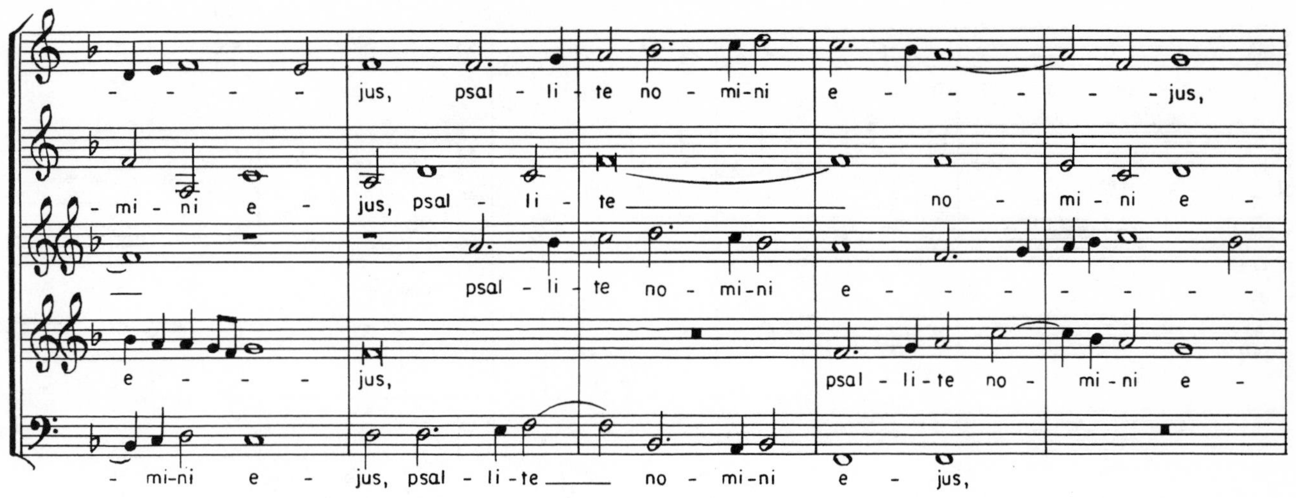
- - - - jus, psal - li - te no - mi-ni e - - - - - jus,
- mi - ni e - jus, psal - li - te no - mi - ni e -
psal - li - te no - mi-ni e - - - - - - -
e - - - jus, psal - li - te no - mi - ni e -
- mi-ni e - jus, psal - li - te no - mi-ni e - jus,

40
quo - ni - am, quo - ni - am su - a - - vis est, quo - ni -
- jus, quo - ni - am su - a - - vis est, quo - ni -
- jus, quo - - ni - am su - a - - vis est, quo - ni - am:
- jus, quo - ni - am, quo - ni - am
quo - - ni - am, quo - ni - am

- am su - a - vis est: o - mni-a quae -
- am su - a - - vis est: o - mni - a quae - cum - que vo - lu - it,
o - mni-a quae - cum-que vo - lu - it, fe -
su - a - - vis est: o - mni-a quae - cum-que vo - lu - it, fe -
su - a - - vis est:

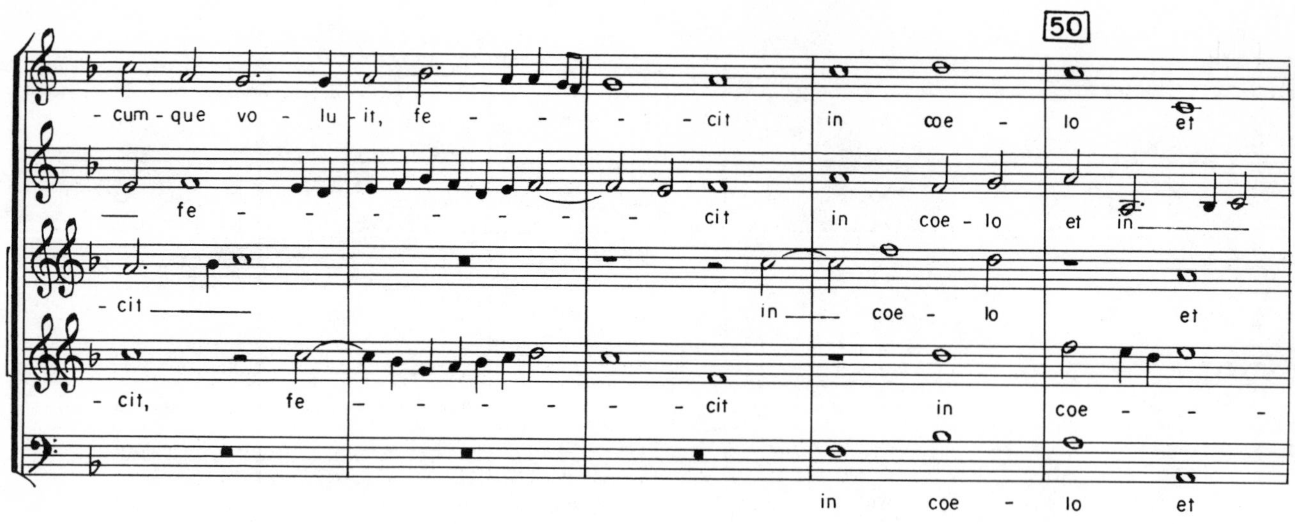
50
- cum - que vo - lu - it, fe - - - - cit in coe - lo et
fe - - - - - - - - - cit in coe - lo et in
- cit in coe - lo et
- cit, fe - - - - - - - cit in coe - - -
in coe - lo et

in ter - - - - - - ra, o - mni - a quae - cum - que vo - lu - it,
ter - - - - - - - - ra, o - mni-
in ter - ra, et in ter - ra, o - mni-a quae-cum-que, o - mni-
- lo et in ter - - ra, o - mni-a quae - cum-que vo -
in ter - - - - - - - ra, o - mni - a quae-cum-que vo - - lu -

60
o - mni-a quae - cum-que vo - lu - it, fe - - - - cit
- a quae-cum-que vo-lu-it, fe - - - - cit, fe - - -
- a quae-cum-que vo - - lu - it, fe - - - - cit
- lu - it, fe - cit, fe - - - -
- it, fe - - - -

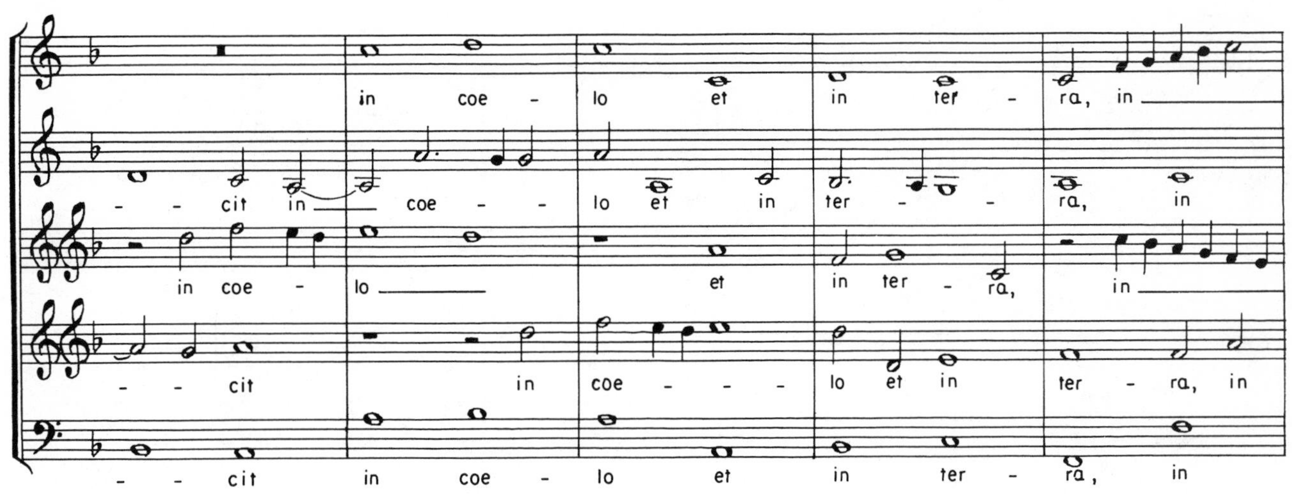

Offertory: Improperium. Palestrina.

cor me - - - - - - - - - um, im pro - pe -
um ex - pe - cta - vit cor me - - - - um, cor
um, cor me - - - - - um, im - pro - pe - ri - um, im -
Im - - - pro - pe - - ri - um ex -

ri - um ex - pe - cta - vit, ex - pe - cta - vit cor me -
me - um, im - pro - pe - ri - um ex - pe - cta - vit cor me - um
pro - pe - - ri - um ex - - - - pe - cta - vit cor
pe - cta - vit cor me - um, ex - pe - cta - - vit cor me -
Im - - - pro - pe - - ri - um ex - pe - cta - vit cor

- - - - um et
et mi - se - - - - - - ri - am,
me - um et mi - se - - ri - am, et mi -
um et mi - se - - - - - ri - am, et mi - se - -
me - um, et mi - se - - -

mi - se - - - - - - - ri - am: et su - sti -
et mi - se - - - - ri - am: et su - sti - - nu -
- se - ri - am: et su - sti - - nu - i
- ri - am, et mi - se - - ri - am: et su - sti - - nu -
- ri - am: et su - sti - - nu -

30
- nu - i qui si - mul me - cum con -
- i qui si - mul me - cum con - tri - sta - re - tur, con -
qui si - mul me - - cum con - tri - sta - re - -
- i qui si - mul me - - cum con - tri - sta - re - - -
i qui si - mul me - cum con - tri - sta - re - tur,

- tri - sta - re - tur, et non fu - - -
- tri - sta - re - tur, et non fu - it, et non fu -
- - - - tur, et non fu - - - it:
- - tur, et no fu - - - - - - - it:
et non fu - - - it:

40
- it: con - so - lan - tem me quae - si -
- it: con - - so - lan - tem me quae -
(♯)
con - so - lan - tem me quae - si - vi, con - so - lan - tem me quae - si -
con - so - lan - tem me quae - si - vi,
con - so - lan - tem me quae - si - vi,

- - vi, et non, et non in - ve - - - ni:
- si - vi, et non in - ve - ni, et non in -
- vi, et non, et non in - ve - - - -
et non in - - - ve - ni, et non in - ve -
et non in - ve - - - - ni, et non in - ve -

50
- ve - ni: et de - de - - - runt in e - stam me -
- ni: et de - de - runt in e - stam me - - am fel,
- - - - ni: et de - de - runt in e - stam me - am fel,
- - - - - ni: et de - de -

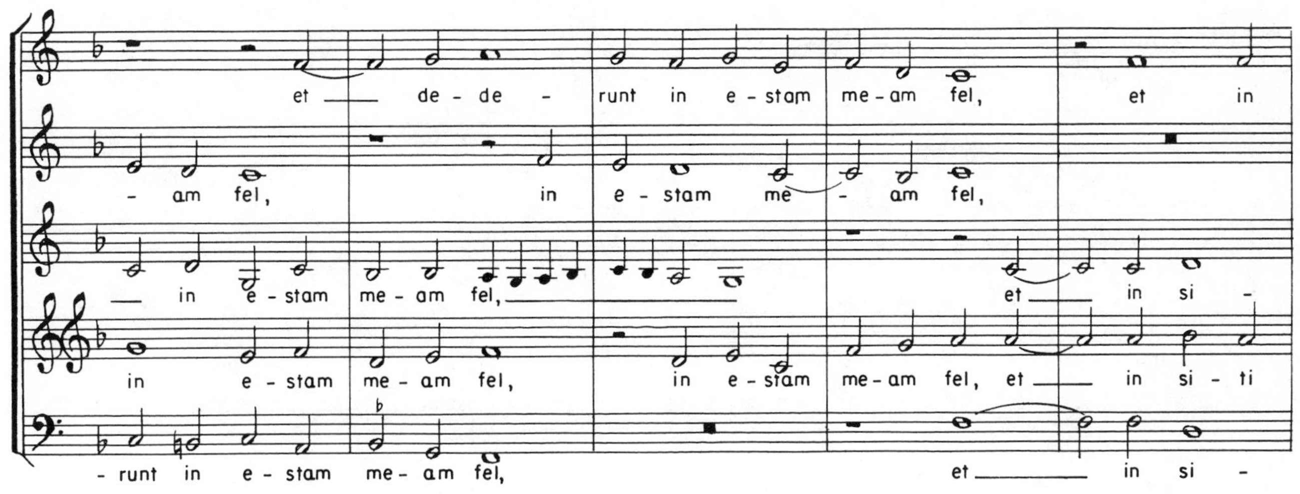
et — de-de - runt in e-stam me-am fel, et in
- am fel, in e-stam me - am fel,
— in e-stam me-am fel, — et — in si -
in e-stam me-am fel, in e-stam me-am fel, et — in si - ti
- runt in e-stam me-am fel, et — in si -

60
si - ti me - - - - - - a
et — in si - ti me - a po - ta - ve - runt,
- ti me - a, et — in si - ti me - a po - ta -
me - a, et in si - ti me - a po - ta - ve - runt —
- ti me - a po - ta - ve - runt

po - ta - ve - runt me — a - ce - to, — et —
po - ta - ve - runt me a - ce - - - to,
- ve - runt me a - ce - to, et — in si -
— me a - ce - - - to, — et in
me a - ce - to, et in

70
— in si - ti me - - - a po - ta - ve-runt me a -
et in si - ti me - a po - ta-ve-runt
- ti me - a po - ta-ve-runt me a-ce - to,
si - ti me - a po - ta-ve - runt, po - ta -
si - ti me - - - a po - ta-ve - runt me a -

- ce - to, po - ta - ve - runt me a - ce - to.
me a-ce - to, po-ta-ve-runt me a-ce - - - - - - to.
po - ta-ve - runt me a - ce - - - to.
- ve-runt me a - ce - to, po - ta-ve-runt me a-ce - to.
- ce - - - - to, po - ta - ve-runt me a - ce - to.

Offertory: Exaltabo Te.
Palestrina.

Cantus
Ex - al - ta-bo te, Do - - - - -
Altus
Ex - al - ta-bo te, Do - - - -
5-9
Tenor I
Ex -
Tenor II
Bassus

- - - mi - ne, ex - al - ta - bo
- - - mi - ne, ex - al - ta - bo te, Do - - mi - - ne,
- al - ta - bo te, Do - - - mi - ne, ex - al - ta - bo te, Do -
Ex - al - ta - bo te, Do - - - - - -
Ex - al - ta - bo te, Do - - - mi -

10
te, Do - - - - mi - ne, ex - - - al - ta - bo
ex - al - - ta - bo te, Do - - - - - - -
- - - - - - - - - mi - ne,
- mi - ne, ex - al - - ta - - - - - bo
- ne, ex - al - ta - bo

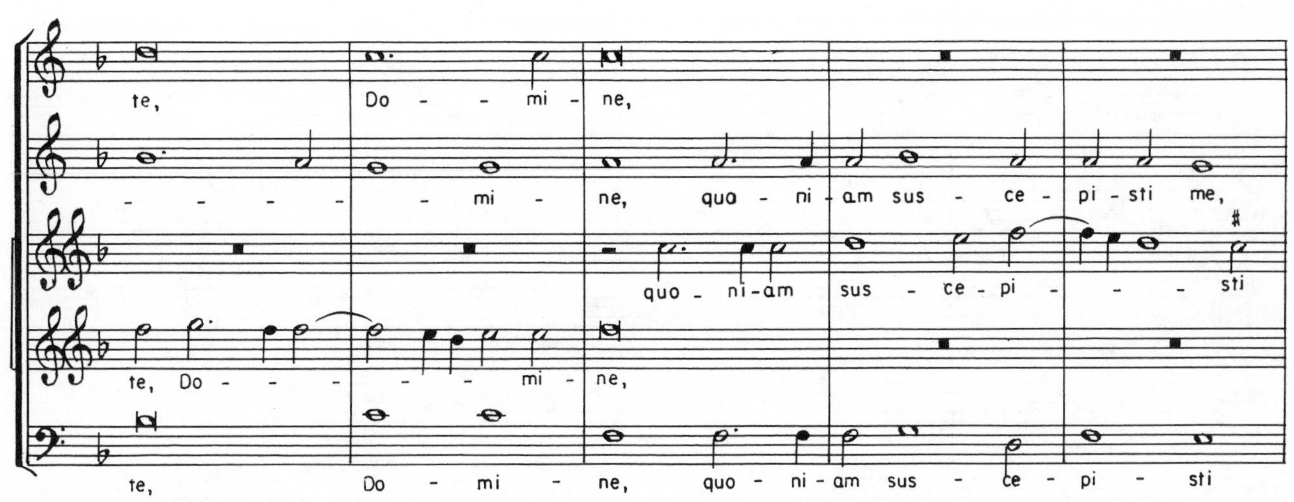
te, Do - - mi - ne,
- - - - - mi - ne, quo - ni - am sus - ce - pi - sti me,
quo - ni - am sus - ce - pi - - - sti
te, Do - - - - - mi - ne,
te, Do - mi - ne, quo - ni - am sus - ce - pi - sti

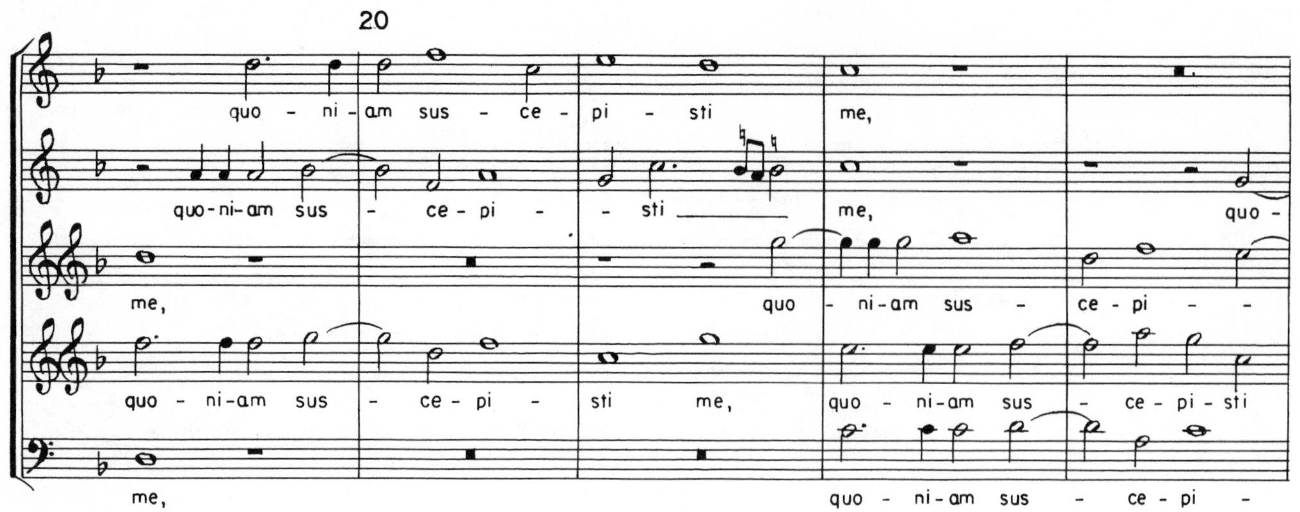
20
quo - ni - am sus - ce - pi - sti me,
quo-ni-am sus - ce - pi - - sti me, quo -
me, quo - ni-am sus - ce-pi - -
quo - ni-am sus - ce - pi - sti me, quo - ni-am sus - ce-pi-sti
me, quo - ni-am sus - ce - pi -

quo - ni - am sus - ce - pi - sti me, sus - ce - pi -
- ni-am sus - ce - pi - sti, sus - ce-pi - - - sti me, sus - -
- sti me, quo - ni-am sus-
me, quo - ni-am sus - - - ce - pi - sti me,
- sti me, quo - ni - am sus - ce - pi - sti me,

30
- - - - - - - - sti me,
- - - ce - pi - - sti me, nec
- ce - pi - sti me, nec de - le - cta - - - - -
nec de - le - cta - - - - - - -
nec de - le - cta - - - - - - -

nec de - le - cta - - - - - - - sti in -
de - le - cta - - - - - - - - - - sti
- - - - - - - - - - - - sti
- - sti, nec de - le - - - cta - - -
- - sti, in -

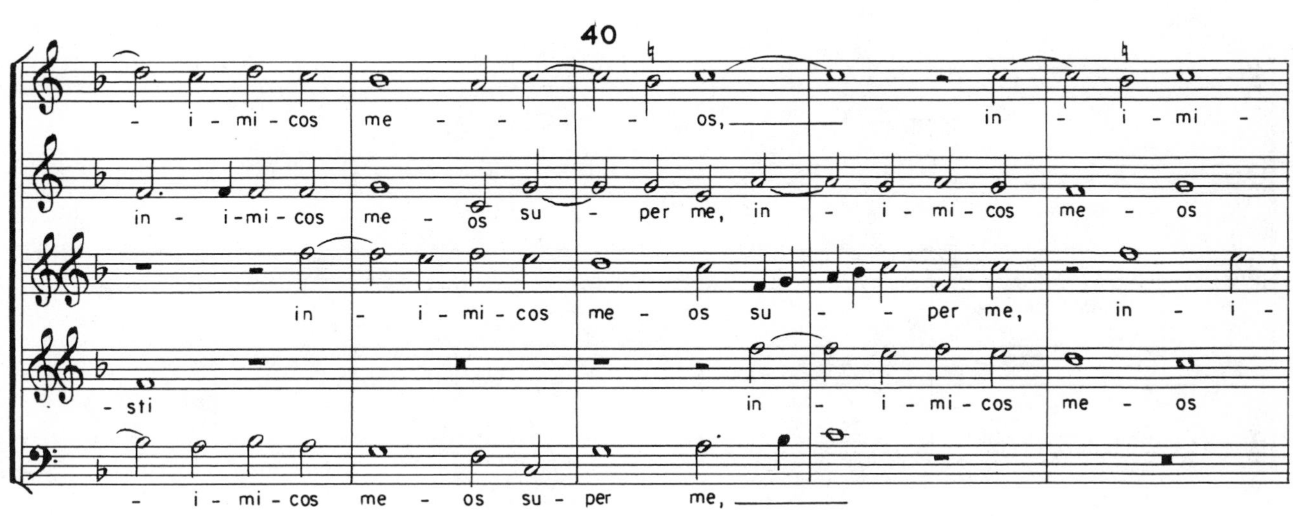

40
- i - mi - cos me - - - - os, in - i - mi -
in - i - mi - cos me - os su - per me, in - i - mi - cos me - os
in - i - mi - cos me - os su - - per me, in - i -
- sti in - i - mi - cos me - os
- i - mi - cos me - os su - per me,

- cos me - os su - per me: Do - mi - ne,
su - - - per me: Do - - mi - ne, cla - ma - vi ad
- mi - cos me - os su - per me: Do - mi - ne, cla ma - - -
su - per me: Do - mi - ne, cla - ma -
Do - - mi - ne, cla - ma -

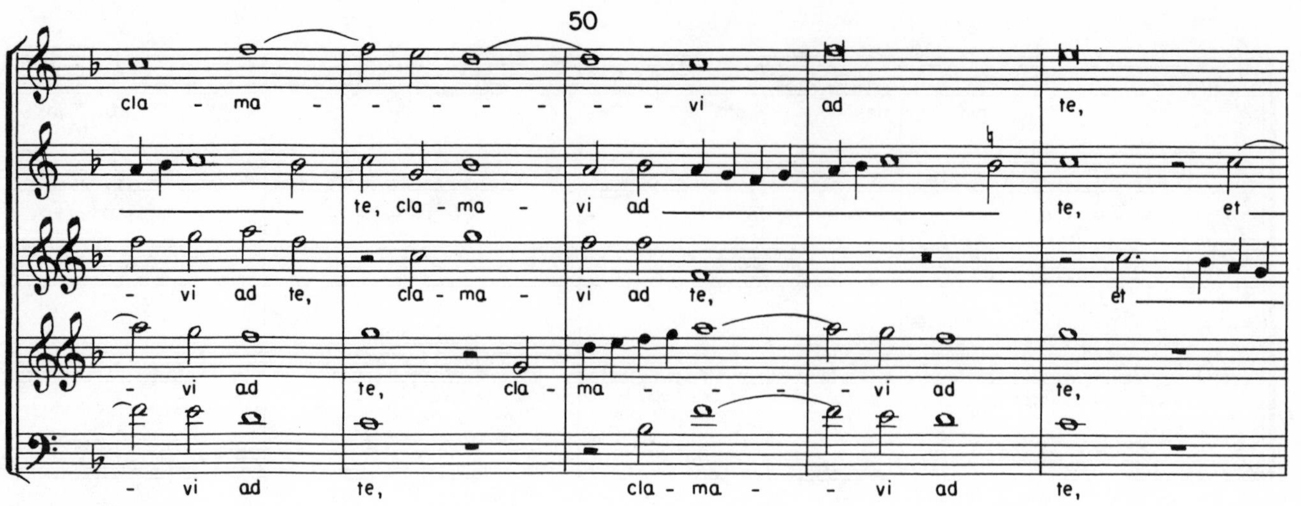
50
cla - ma - - - - - - - vi ad te,
te, cla - ma - vi ad te, et
- vi ad te, cla - ma - vi ad te, et
- vi ad te, cla - ma - - - - vi ad te,
- vi ad te, cla - ma - - vi ad te,

et sa - na - sti me, et sa - na - sti me,
sa - na - sti me, et sa - na - sti me,
sa - na - - - sti me, et
et sa - na - sti me, et sa - na - sti
et sa - na - sti me,

60
et sa - na - sti me.
et sa - na - - - sti me.
sa - na - sti me, et sa - na - sti me.
me, et sa - na - - - - - - - sti me.
et sa - na - - sti me.

Litaniae de Beata Virgine Maria.

Palestrina.

-us, mi - se - re.re no - bis. San - cta Ma.ri - a, o.ra.pro no - bis.
.us, mi.se.re.re no - bis. San.cta Ma.ri - a, — o - ra pro nobis
-us, mi - se - re.re no - - bis. San.cta Ma.ri - a, San.
mi - se - re.re no - bis, Sancta Ma.ri - a, o.ra pro no - - -
-us, Sancta Ma.ri - a, o.ra pro no.bis.

30
San.cta Virgo vir.gi.num, o.ra pro no - bis. Ma - ter Chri.sti, o.ra pro no - bis.
San.cta Virgo vir.gi.num, o.ra pro no - bis. o - ra pro no - - bis. Ma.
- - cta Virgo virgi.num, o.ra pro no - bis. Ma - ter Christi, o.ra pro no.bis. Ma.
.bis, o - ra pro no - bis. Ma ter Chri - sti. Ma ter ca.
San.cta Virgo virgi - num. Ma - ter Chri.sti. Ma.

40
O. ra pro no - - bis. Ma ter dulcis - - si - ma, o.ra pro
.ter ca.stis - si ma, o. ra pro no - - bis. Ma ter dulcis - si - ma, o - ra pro
.ter ca.stis. sima, o. ra pro no - - bis Ma ter dulcis - si - ma, o - ra pro
.stis - - si - ma, o. ra pro no - - bis.
.ter ca.stis - si - ma. Ma ter dul.cis - .si.ma, o.ra .... pro

no - bis. Ma - ter pi - is - si - ma, o - ra pro no - bis. O - ra pro no - -
no - bis. Ma - ter pi - is - si - ma, o - ra pro no - bis. O - ra pro no -
no - bis. Ma ter pi - is - si - ma, o - ra pro no - bis. Vir - go cle - men - tis - si - ma. Re -
Ma ter pi - is - si - ma, o - ra pro no - bis. Vir go clementis - si - ma, o - ra pro no -
no - bis. Vir - go cle - men - tis - si - ma.

50
- bis. Re - fu - gium pec - ca - to - rum. Con - so - la - trix af - fli - cto -
- bis. O - ra pro no - - bis. Con - so - la - trix af - fli - cto -
- fu - gi - um pec - - ca to - rum. Con - so - la - trix af - fli - cto -
- bis...... O - ra pro no - - bis. Con - so - la - trix af - fli - cto -
Re - fu - gi - um pec - ca - to - rum. Con - so - la - trix af - fli - cto -

60
- rum o - ra ...... pro no - - bis. Re - gi - na An - ge - lo -
- rum, o - ra pro no - bis, o - ra pro no - - bis. Re - gi - na An - ge - lo -
- rum, o - ra pro no - - bis. Re - gi - na An - ge - lo -
- rum, o - ra pro no - bis. Re - gi - na An - ge - lo -
- rum, o - ra pro no - bis. Re - gi - na An - ge - lo -

70
-rum, ora pro no-bis. Re-gi - - na Sanctorum o - mnium, o - ra
-rum, o ra pro no-bis. Re-gi - na Sanctorum omni-um, o ra pro no bis, o-
-rum, ora pro no-bis. Re-gi - - na Sanctorum omnium, ora pro no-bis, o-
-rum o ra pro no-bis. Re-gi-na Sanctorum o - - mnium, o ra pro no-bis,
-rum Re-gi-na San-cto-rum omni-um,

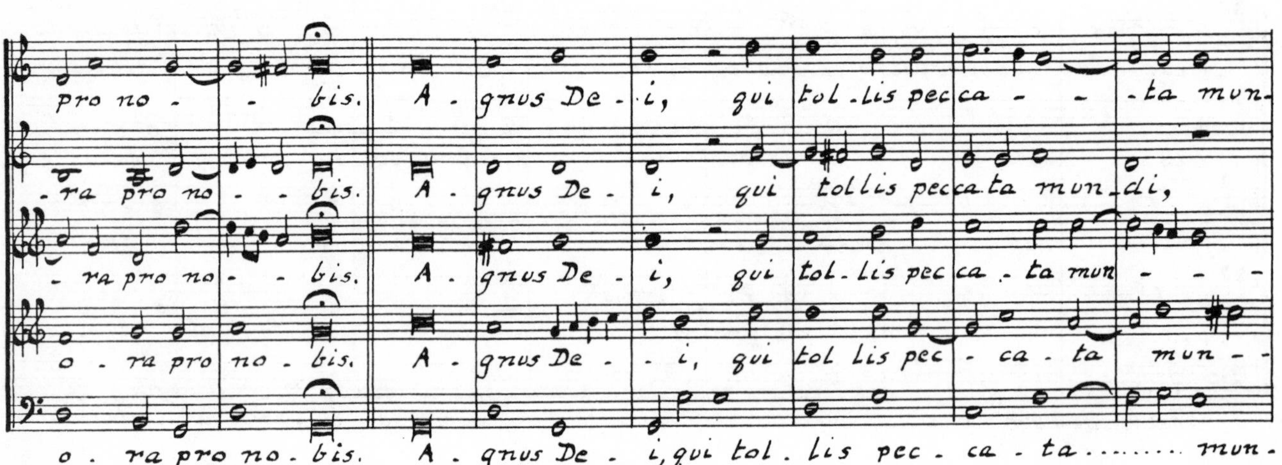
pro no - - bis. A-gnus De-i, qui tol-lis pec ca - - -ta mun-
-ra pro no - - bis. A-gnus De - i, qui tollis pecca-ta mun-di,
-ra pro no - - bis. A-gnus De-i, qui tol-lis pec ca-ta mun - - -
o - ra pro no-bis. A-gnus De - - i, qui tol lis pec - ca - ta mun - -
o - ra pro no-bis. A - gnus De - i, qui tol-lis pec-ca-ta....... mun-

80
-di, mise re-re nobis, mi-se-re - - re no - - - - - bis.
mise re - re no-bis, mi-se-re - - re nobis, mise-re-re no - - bis.
-di, mi-se-re-re no-bis, mi - se re - re no - bis.
-di, mi-se-re-re no - bis, mi-se-re-re no-bis, no - bis.
-di, mi-se-re-re no-bis, mi-se-re-re no - - bis, no - - - - bis.

Dominica in Palmis
24
CANTVS
Mproperium expectauit cor me um
Improperium expectauit expectauit cor me um & miseriam & sustinui qui simul mecum contristaretur
& non fuit consolantem me quæsi ui & non & non
inue ni & dederunt in escam meam fel & in siti me-
a potauerunt me aceto & in siti
me a potauerunt me aceto potauerunt me aceto.
Dominica in Palmis.
24
ALTVS
Mproperium expectauit cor meum cor me um Improperium Improperium ex pectauit cor meum & miseriam & miseriam & sustinui qui simul me cum contrista-
re tur & non fuit consolantem me quæsiui conso
lantem me quæsiui & non & non inue ni & dederunt in
escam meam fel in escam meam fel & in siti
mea & in siti mea potauerunt me aceto & in siti mea poto-
me aceto.

Dominica in Palmis
24
TENOR
Mproperium expectauit cor meum expectauit cor meum & mise riam & mise riam ij & sustinui qui simul mecum contristaretur & non fuit consolantem me quæsi ui & non inueni ij &
dederunt in escam meam fel in escam meam fel in escam meam fel & in
siti mea & in siti mea potauerunt me ace to & in siti me-
a potauerunt potauerunt me aceto potauerunt me aceto.
Dominica in Palmis.
24
QVINTVS
Mproperium expectauit cor meum cor meum Improperium expectauit cor meum & mise riam & mise riam & sustinui qui simul mecum contristaretur contristaretur & non fuit ij consolantem me quæsiui & non inueni
& non inueni & dederunt in escam me am fel in escā meam
fel & in siti mea potauerunt potauerunt me aceto & in siti mea
potauerunt me aceto potauerunt me ace to.

Dominica in Palmis
24
BASSVS
IMproperium expectauit cor meum & mise riam & ſuſtinui qui ſimul mecũ contriſta-
retur & non fuit conſolantem me quæſiui & non inue ni
& non inueni & dederunt in eſcam meam fel & in ſiti
mea potauerunt me aceto & in ſiti me a potauerunt me ace to potauerunt me aceto.

Mass: Ad Fugam: Kyrie. Palestrina.

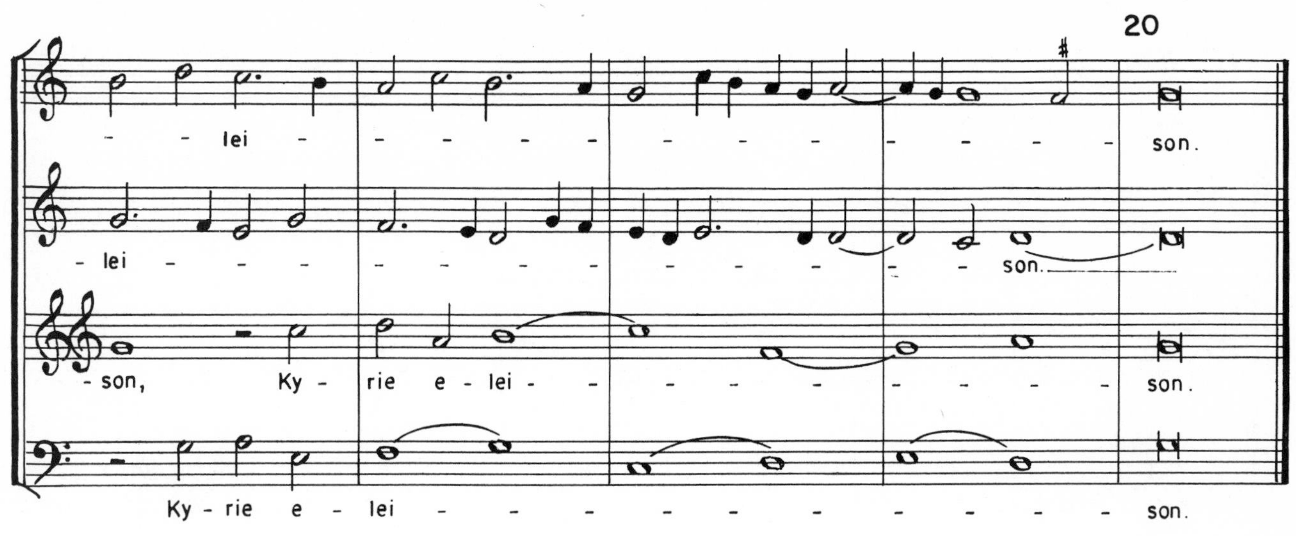

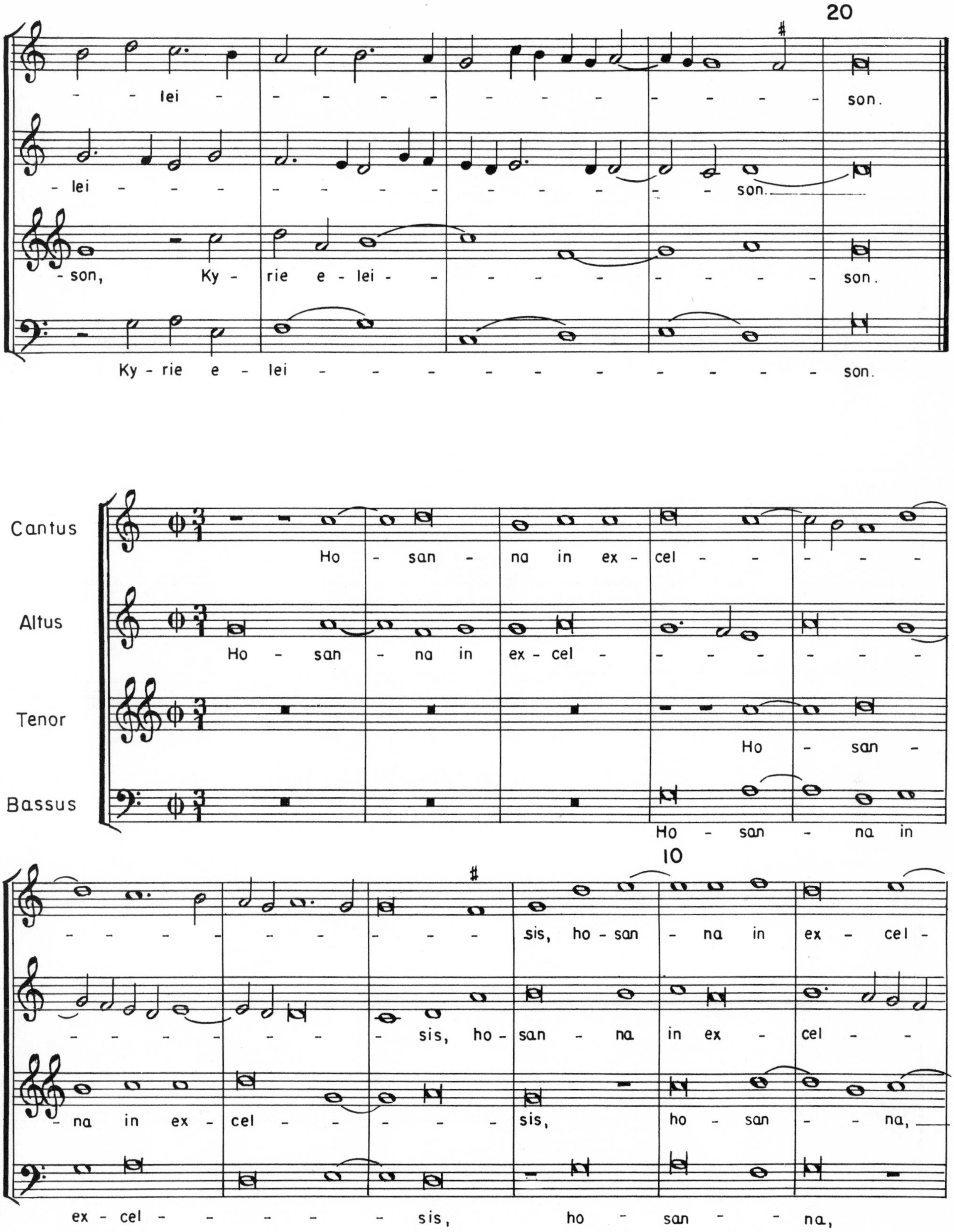
20
- - lei - - - - - - - - - - - - - son.
- lei - - - - - - - - - - - - - son.
- son, Ky - rie e - lei - - - - - - - - - son.
Ky - rie e - lei - - - - - - - - - - son.
Cantus
Altus
Tenor
Bassus
Ho - san - na in ex - cel - - - - -
Ho - san - na in ex - cel - - - - - - -
Ho - san -
Ho - san - na in
10
- - - - - - - - - - - sis, ho - san - na in ex - cel -
- - - - - - - - sis, ho - san - na in ex - cel - -
- na in ex - cel - - - - - sis, ho - san - - na,
ex - cel - - - - - - sis, ho - san - - na,

- - - - sis, ho - san - na in ex - cel -
- - - sis, ho - san - na in ex - cel - - sis,
ho - san - na in ex - cel - sis, ho -
ho - san - na in ex - cel - sis, ho - san -
20
- sis, in ex - - - - - - cel - sis, ho - san -
in ex - - - - - - cel - sis, ho - san - na in
- san - na in ex - cel - - - sis,
- na in ex - cel - - - - sis,
30
- na in ex - cel - sis, ho - san - na in ex - cel - sis.
ex - cel - sis, ho - san - na in ex - cel - sis.
ho - san - na in ex - cel - - sis.
ho - san - na in ex - cel - - - - sis.

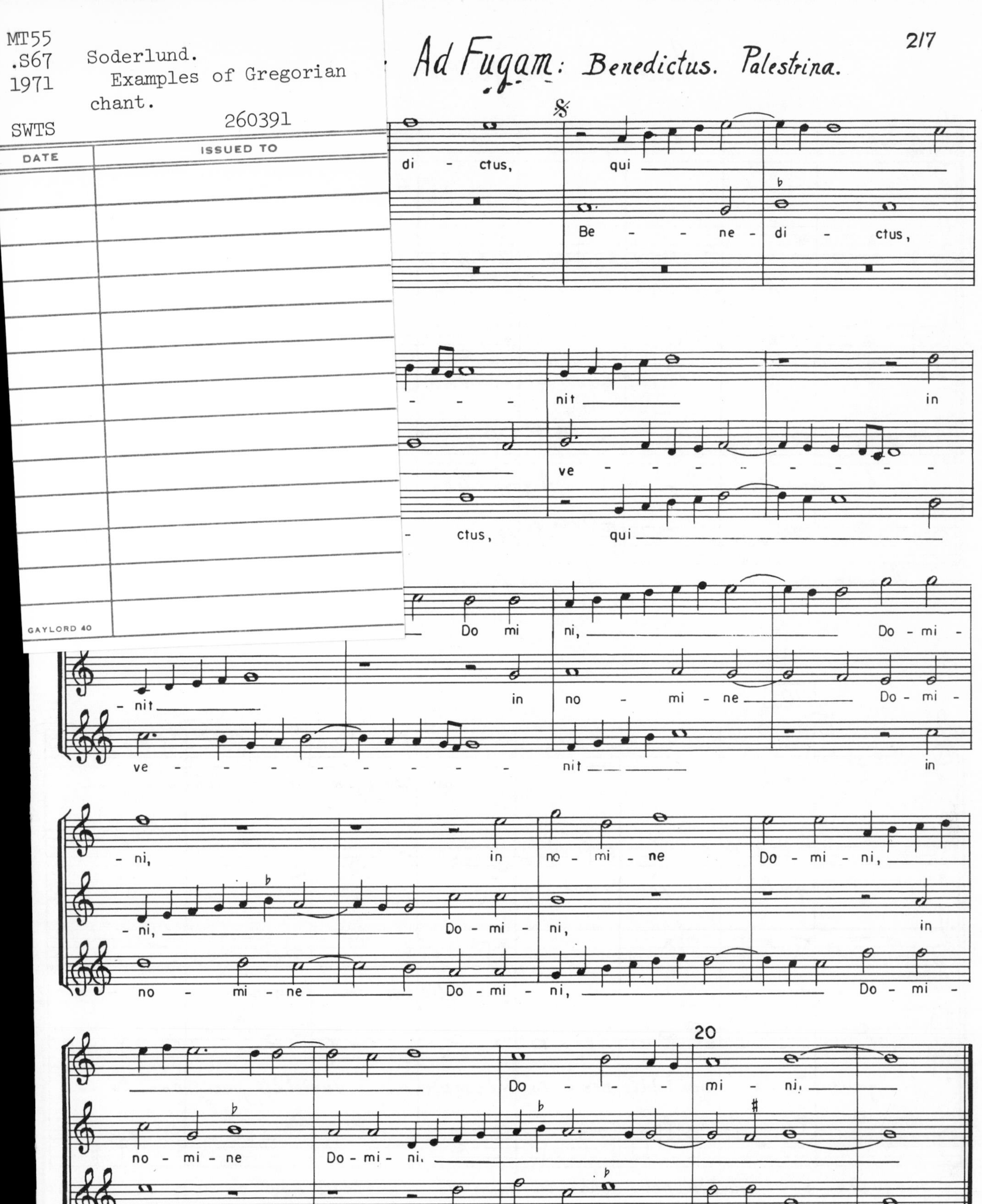
Ad Fugam: Benedictus. Palestrina.
di - ctus, qui
Be - - ne - di - ctus,
- - - nit in
ve - - - - - - - - - -
- ctus, qui
Do mi ni, Do - mi -
- nit in no - mi - ne Do - mi -
ve - - - - - - - - - - nit in
- ni, in no - mi - ne Do - mi - ni,
- ni, Do - mi - ni, in
no - mi - ne Do - mi - ni, Do - mi -
20
Do - - - mi - ni,
no - mi - ne Do - mi - ni,
- ni, in no - mi - ne Do - mi - ni.

Mass: Ad Fugam: Agnus Dei. Palestrina.

20
- - - - di: do-na no-bis pa - - - - - - - cem, do-na no-
do-na no-bis pa - - - - - - cem, do-na no-bis pa - - - - - - - - cem,
- - - - di: do-na no-bis pa - - - - - - cem, do-na no-bis
- - mun- - di: do-na no- bis pa- - - cem, do-na no- - - bis pa-cem, do-na nobis pa-cem, do-na
mun- - di: do-na no-bis pa- - - - cem, do-na no- - - - bis pa-cem, do-na no-bis pa-cem, do-na no-

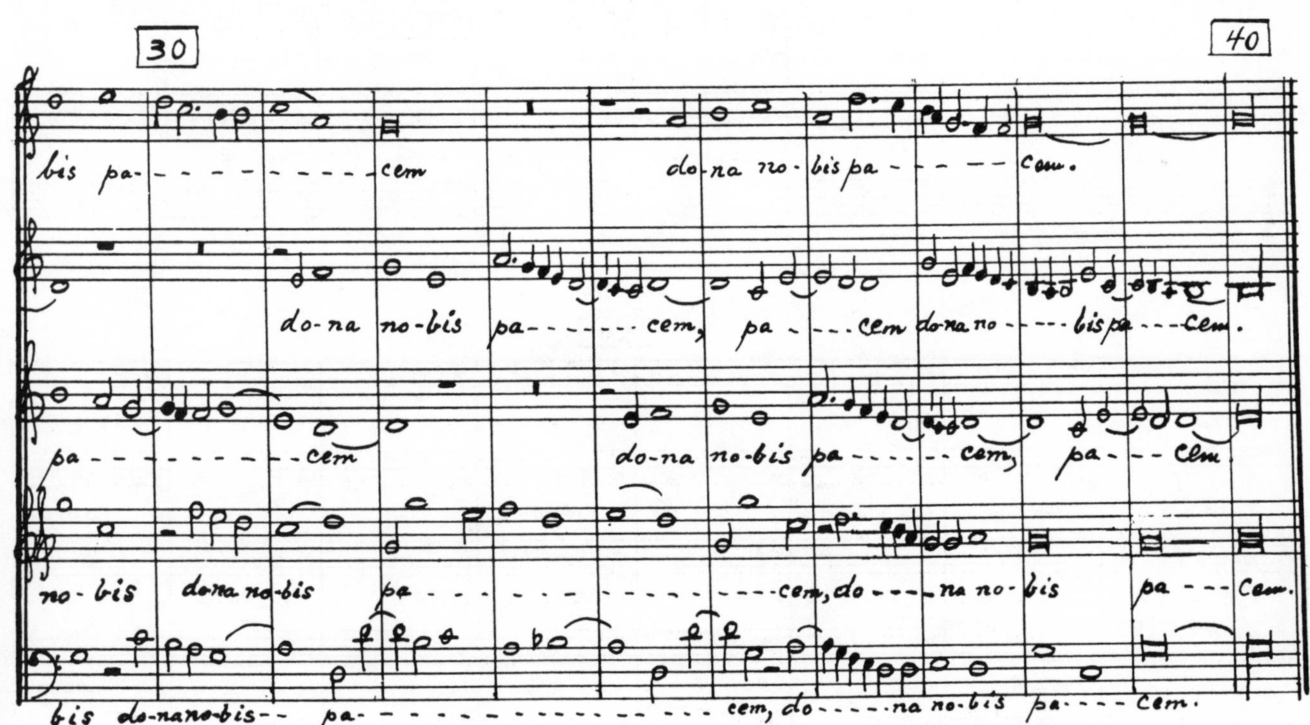
30
40
bis pa- - - - - - - - - - - - cem do-na no-bis pa - - - - - cem.
do-na no-bis pa- - - - - - - cem, pa - - - cem do-na no- - - - bis pa - - - cem.
pa - - - - - - - - - - cem do-na no-bis pa - - - - - - cem, pa - - - cem.
no-bis do-na no-bis pa - - - - - - - - - - - - - - - - cem, do - - - na no-bis pa - - - cem.
bis do-na no-bis- - pa - - - - - - - - - - - - - - - - - cem, do - - - - na no-bis pa - - - cem.

Mass: L'homme armé

Kyrie

Palestrina.

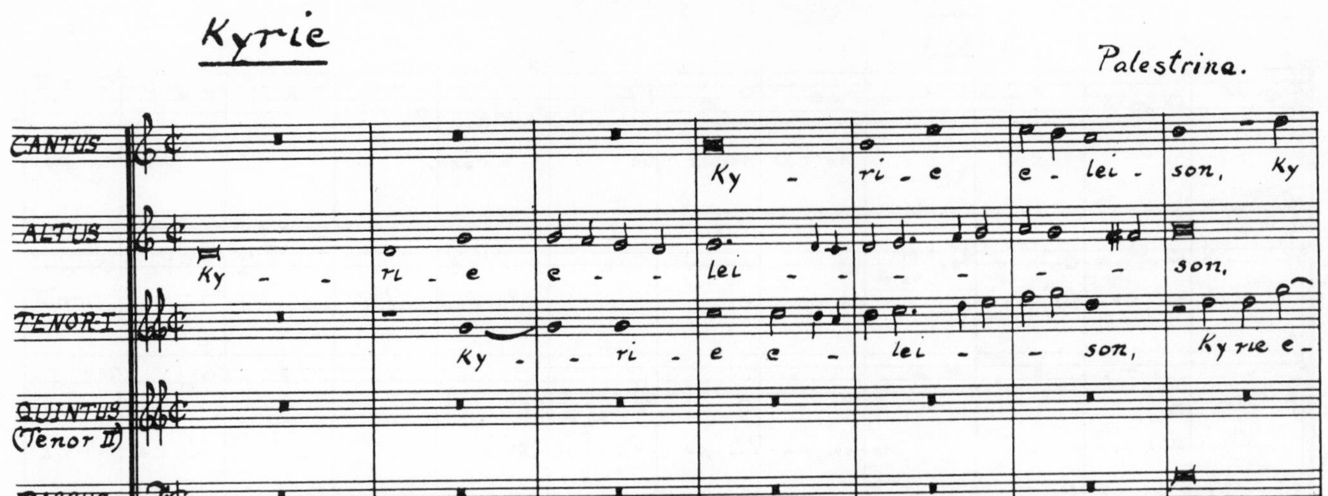

30
e_lei _ _ son......
Chri_ste
son. Chri_ste e _ lei
son. Chri_ste e _ lei

Chri_ste e _ lei _ son, Chri_ste e_
e_lei _ son, Christe e _ le _ son,
son, Christe e_lei _ son, Chri_
Chri _ ste,
son, Chri_ste e _ lei _ son,

40
lei _ son, Chri _ ste e _ lei _ son, Christe e_lei _ son, Chri
Christe e _ lei _ son, Christe e_lei _ son, Chri
_ste e _ lei _ son, Christe e_lei
Chri _ ste e_
Chri_ste e _ lei _ son, Chri_ste e_lei _ son, Christe e_

50
ste e - lei son.
ste e - lei son, Chri - ste e - lei son.
son, Christe e - lei son, Chri - ste e - lei son.
lei son.
lei son.

60
Ky - ri - e e - lei - son, Ky - ri - e e -
Ky - ri - e e - lei - son,
Ky - ri - e e - lei - son, Ky - rie e - lei -
Ky - ri -
Ky - ri - e e - lei -

lei - son, Ky - ri - e e - lei - son,
Ky - ri - e e - lei - son, Ky - ri - e e - lei - son,
son, Ky - rie - e - lei - son, Ky - ri - e
e e - lei - son, Ky - ri - e e - lei son, Ky - ri - e e - lei - son,
son Ky - rie e - lei - son, Ky - ri - e

Gloria in excelsis Deo.

CANTUS: Et in ter - ra pax ho - - mi - ni - bus, ho -

ALTUS: Et in ter - ra pax ho - mi - -

TENOR I: Et in ter - ra pax...................... ho - - mi - ni - bus....... ho -

QUINTUS (Tenor) II

BASSUS: Et in ter - ra

10
-mi - - - ni bus bo - nae vo. lun. ta - tis. Lau
-ni. bus...... bo nae.... volun - ta - tis.......... Laudamus
-mi - ni - bus bo - nae vo lun. ta - tis, bo - - nae volunta - tis.
Lau - - - da -
pax ho - mi - ni - bus bo - nae vo lunta - tis, bo - nae volun. ta. tis.

20
-damus te.......... Be - ne - di - ci mus te.......... Ad - o - ra -
te...... Be - ne - di. ci mus... te, be - ne di ci. mus te. Ad - o - ra - mus
Laudamus te.......... Be - ne - di - ci - mus te. Ad - o - ra - mus..
- - - mus - te Ad - - - - o - ra - - - -
Laudamus te. .... Ad - o - ra - -

30
-mus te......... Glo - ri - fi - ca - mus....... te, glo - ri - fi - ca mus te. Gra -
te.......... Glo - ri - fi camus te, glo - ri - fi. ca - mus te.
.... te. Glorifi. ca - - - - - mus........ te.
-mus te. Glo - ri - fi - ca - mus te.
-mus te. Glo. ri. fi. ca - - mus te.

- ti - as a - gi mus ti - - bi, a - gi mus ti - bi pro pter magnam glo - -
Gra - ti - as a - gimus ti - - - bi propter magnam . . . .
Gra - ti - as a - - gi - mus ti - bi propter magnam glo -
Gra - ti - as a - - gi mus ma - - gnam glo - ri
Gra - ti - as a gimus ti - - - bi propter mag - nam

40
- - - ri - am tu am tu - - - am. De - us
glo - ri - am tu - am . . . . De -
- - ri - am tu - - - - - am Do - mi ne De us, Rex coele - - - stis
- am tu - - am
glo - ri - am tu - am Do - mi - ne De us Rex coele - - - - - - stis,

50
Pater omni - po - tens, ... Domi - ne Fi - - li u -
- us Pa - ter omni - po - tens . . . . Domi - ne Fi - li u -
De - us Pa - ter o - mnipotens. Domi - ne Fi - - li u - - ni - ge - ni
Do - mi - ne De - -
Do - mi - ne Fi - li u - - ni - ge - ni -

80

Qui tol - lis peccata mun-di, pec - ca - - ta..... mun - di mi-

Qui tol - lis peccata mun-di, ...

Qui tol - lis peccata mun - - -

Qui tol - lis pec-

- se - re - - - - re no - - bis, mi - se - re - re no - bis. Qui tol -
mi - se re - re no - bis, misere - - re no - - bis. Qui tol - -
- di mi - se - re - - re no - - bis, mi - se - re - re no - -
Qui tol - lis pec - ca - -
- ca - ta mun - di, mi - se re - re no - bis.

90
- lis pecca - ta mun - di, pec - ca - ta ...... mundi, qui tol - lis pec - ca - - ta mun -
- - lis qui tol - lis pecca - - ta mun - di, pec - ca - ta mun - di: ......
- bis. Qui tollis pec - - ca ta mun - - di, qui tol - lis peccata mun -
- - ta mun - - - di: de - - - pre -
Qui tol - lis pecca - ta mun - - - - - -

100
- di: su - sci - pe .... de - preca - ti - o - nem no - stram, de - preca ti -
su - sci - pe, su - sci - pe depreca - ti o - nem nostram, de - - pre ca ti o nem
- di: su - sci - pe .... depreca - ti - onem nostram, depreca - ti - onem
- ca - - - - ti - o - - - - nem no - - - -
- di su - sci - pe depreca - ti - o - nem

110
.o.nem no . stram. Qui se - des ad de.xteram Pa -
...... no.stram. Qui se . des ad de - xteram Pa
no - stram. Qui se . des ad dexteram Pa - - tris,
..stram.
no - stram. Qui se.des ad de . xte ram...... Pa tris,

120
. . tris, mi. se re re no bis. Quo - ni.am tu so. lus san - - ctus,........
.tris, mi . se re re no - bis Quo.ni.am .... tu
mi. se . re re no - - - bis. Quo - ni . am tu. so. lus, tu
Tu so - -
mi . se . re re no - - - bis. Quo ni.am tu so. lus san - ctus,

...... tu so - lus Al . tis . si . mus, Je - su Chri - -
so . lus Do - mi nus, tu so lus Al tis si mus, Je - su Chri - -
so . lus Do - mi nus, tu so. lus Al tis . si . mus, Je - su Chri ste,.
- - - - lus Je - - - - - -
tu so. lus Al. tis . si. mus, Je - su Chri - -

130
-ste, Je - su Chri - ste. Cum sancto Spi-ri tu, cum sancto Spi - - ri-tu
-ste, Je - su Chri - ste. Cum sancto Spi-ri tu, cum sancto Spi - - ri-tu
...... Je - su Chri - ste. Cum sancto Spi-ri-tu, cum sancto Spi-ri-tu in glo -
-su Chri - - - ste. De - -
-ste, Je - su Chri - ste. Cum sancto Spiri tu......... in

140
in glo-ria De - i Pa - - - tris............ A - men.
.... in glo-ri-a De - i .... Pa - tris. A - - - - men.
-ri-a De - - - - i Pa - - - tris A - - - men.
-i Pa - - tris. A - men.
glo - ri-a De - i Pa - tris............................... A - men A - men.

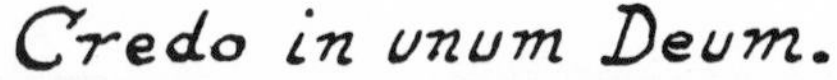
Credo in unum Deum.

CANTUS
ALTUS
TENOR I
QUINTUS (Tenor II)
BASSUS
Pa-trem o-mni-po -
Pa-trem o-mni-po-ten - - - tem, ...
Pa-trem o-mni-po-ten - - -
Pa trem o-mni po-ten - - - - - tem, omni po-ten-tem,

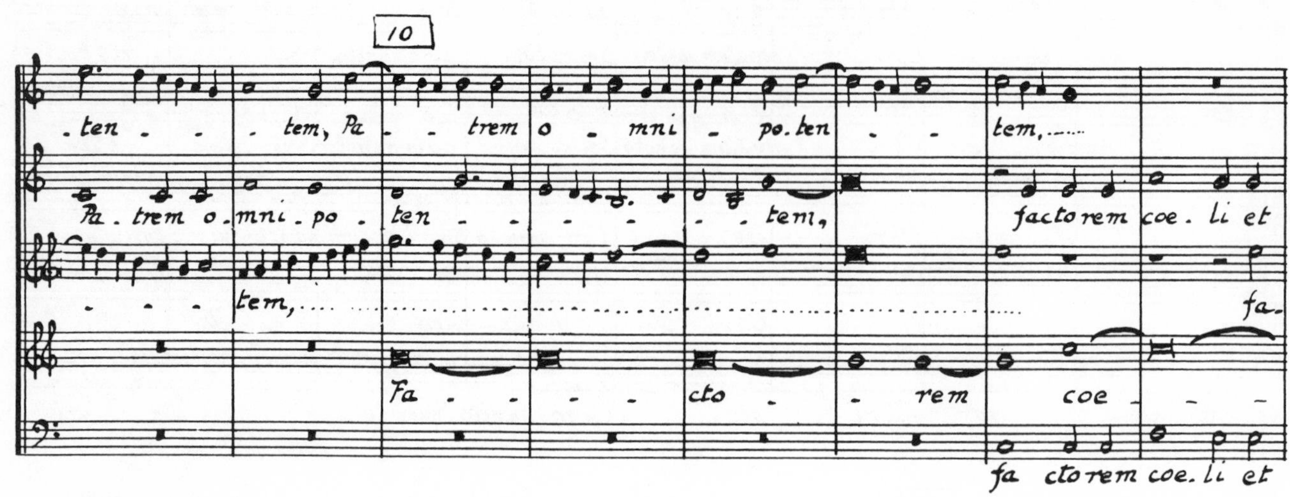
10
-ten - - - - tem, Pa - - trem o - mni - po-ten - - tem,......
Pa-trem o-mni-po - ten - - - - - - - - tem, factorem coe-li et
- - - tem,...... fa-
Fa - - - - cto - - rem coe - - -
fa ctorem coe-li et

20
factorem coe-li...... et ter - - - rae vi-si-bi-lium
-ter - - - - - - rae, vi - si bi-li-um....... o - mni-um
-ctorem coe-li et ter - - rae, vi - si - bi - li um omnium et
- - - - li et ter - - - - - rae
ter - rae,...... vi - si-bi li um o - mni

30
omni um et in-vi - si - bi-li - um. Et in u - num Do - - - mi-
et in vi - - - si - bi - li um........... Et in u - num Domi-
in-vi - si-bi - - - - - li - um Et in unum Do - - mi-num
Fi - - - - -
-um....... et in-vi - si - bi - li-um. Et in u-num Do - mi-num,

. num de . sum Chri - stum. . . . . . . Fi . li um De . i u - ni ge - - ni .
. num de - sum Chri . stum Fi . li um De i u . ni ge - - - - ni .
. . . . . . de . sum Chri . stum. . . . . .
. . li . - - - um. Et ex
de - sum Chri . stum.

40
. tum. Et ex Patre na . tum an . te o . mni . a sae - - - cu. la.
. tum. Et ex Patre na . tum an . te o . mnia sae . cu. la. . . . . . .
Et ex Pa. tre na . . - tum an . te o . mnia sae - cu . la. . . . . .
Pa - - - tre na - - - - - - tum.
Et ex Patre na . tum an . te o . mni a sae - - - cu. la.

50
Deum de De . o, lu men de lu mi . ne, De . um ve . rum de De. o
De . um de De . o lu men de lu mi . ne, De . um ve . rum. . . . .
De - um de De - o, ... lu men de lu mi . ne, . . . De . um
Lu - - - - - - men de
De - um de De - o lu . men de lumi ne De - um. . . . .

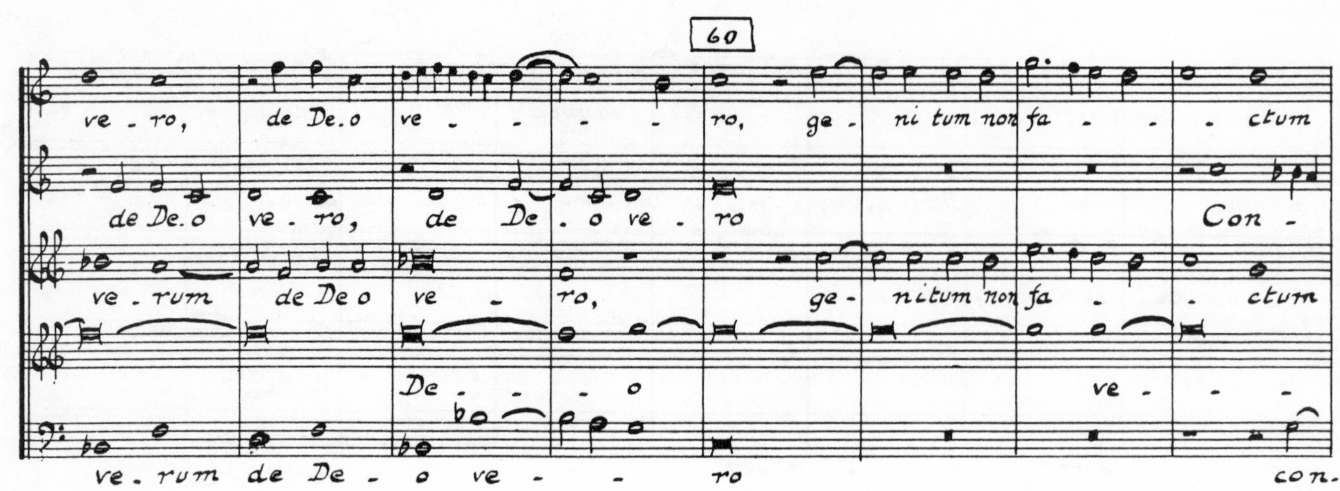
60
ve - ro, de De - o ve - - - - - ro, ge - ni tum non fa - - - ctum
de De - o ve - ro, de De - o ve - ro Con -
ve - rum de De o ve - ro, ge - ni tum non fa - - ctum
De - - - o ve - - -
ve - rum de De - o ve - - ro con -

70
con - substantialem Pa - tri: per quem o - mnia fa - cta sunt.
- - substanti alem Pa - tri: per quem omnia .... facta sunt. Qui pro - pter nos, ...
per quem o mni a fa - - cta sunt Qui propter nos
- - - - - - ro. Et
- sub stanti - a - lem Pa - tri. Qui propter nos ho -

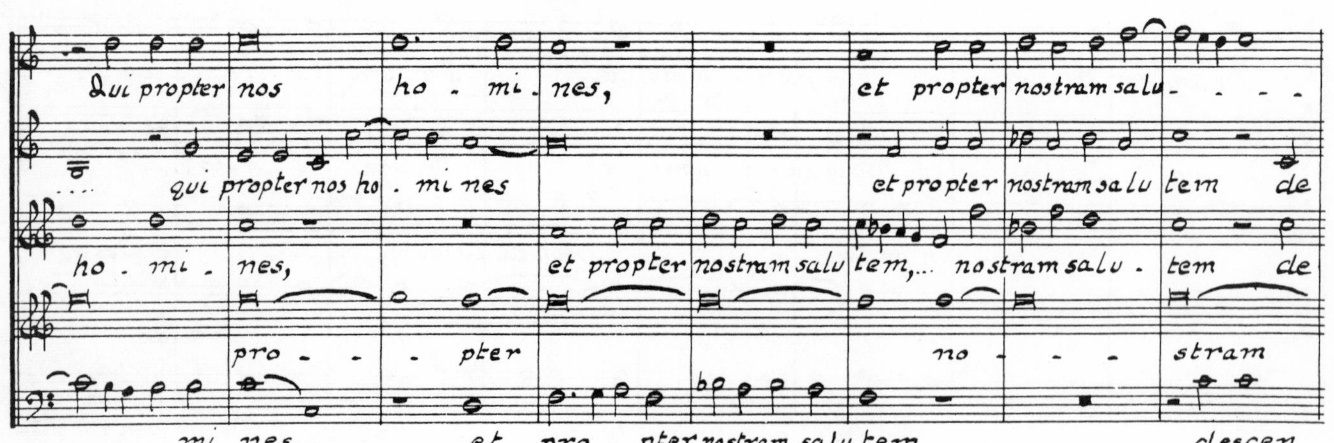
Qui propter nos ho - mi - nes, et propter nostram salu - - - -
... qui propter nos ho - mi nes et propter nostram salu tem de
ho - mi - nes, et propter nostram salu tem, ... nostram salu - tem de
pro - - pter no - - - stram
- - mi - nes, ... et pro - pter nostram salu tem descen -

80
.tem ...... descendit de .... coe. lis. Et in.
.scen - dit de coe - - - - - - - - - - lis. Et in.
.scen.dit de .... coe.lis de .... coe . . lis Et in_
sa - . lu - tem Et
. dit de .... coe lis descendit de .... coe - lis Et in.

90
.car.na. tus est de Spi.ri tu san.cto ex
.car.na tus est de Spiri - tu san.cto ex
.car.natus .... est de Spi - ri.tu san.cto ex
ho - - - mo fa - - - ctus
.car.na.tus est de Spi.ri.tu san.cto ex

100
Ma.ri.a Virgi.ne: .... Et ho.mo fa. . ctus est.
Ma. ri. a Vir. gi. ne: Et ho.mo fa.ctus .... est.
Ma - ria Vir- - gi. ne: Et ho. - mo fa.ctus est.
.... est. ....
Ma - ri.a Vir.gi ne: Et ho. - mo fa.ctus est.

CANTUS
ALTUS
TENOR
BASSUS
Cru.ci.fi.xus e.ti.am pro no.- - - - - - -
Cru - ci - fi - xus e - ti am pro no - - - -

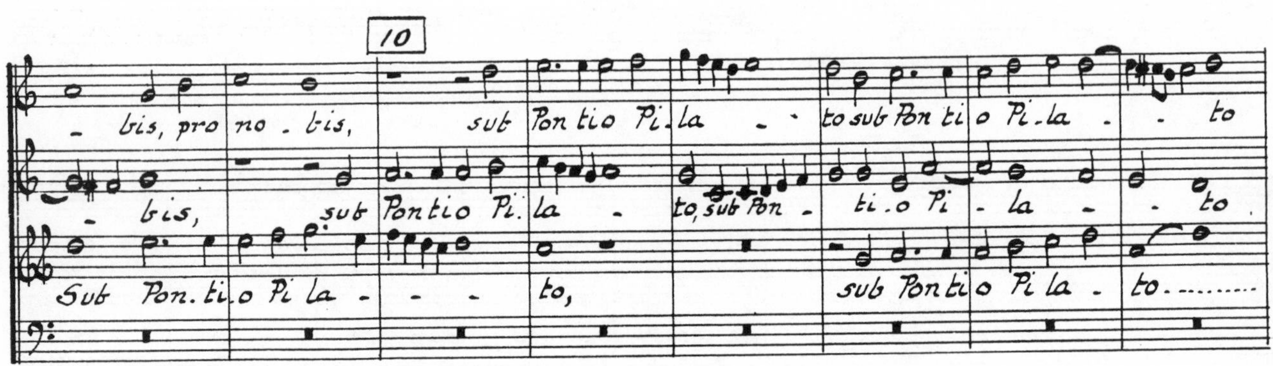
10
- bis, pro no - bis, sub Pon tio Pi - la - - to sub Pon ti o Pi - la - - to
- bis, sub Pon tio Pi - la - to, sub Pon - ti - o Pi - la - - to
Sub Pon. ti o Pi la - - - - to, sub Pon ti o Pi la - to........

20
pas - sus, et se pul - tus est.
pas - sus, et ...... se - pul - tus est.
pas - sus, et se pul - tus est. Et re sur - re - xit ter - ti a di - -
Pas - sus, et se - pul tus est. Et re sur re xit ter ti a di - -

30
se cun dum Scri - ptu - - ras, se cun dum Scri - ptu-
- e se cun dum Scri ptu - - - - ras, se cun dum Scri ptu - - - - - -
- e se cun dum Scri - ptu ras, se - - cun - dum Scri ptu -

Et a - scendit in coe - - lum. Et i - terum venturus
- ras Et a - scendit in coe - - lum. Et i - ter um venturus
- - ras. Se - det ad dexte ram......... Patris Et
- - ras. Se - det ad dexteram Pa - tris Et

40
est cum glo - ri a ju di ca re vi - vos et mor -
est cum glo - ri a ju di ca re. vi - vos........ et
i - terum ven - turus est cum glo - ri - a ju - di - ca - re vi - - - vos
i - terum ven turus est cum glo - ri - a ju - di ca - re vi - - vos et.......

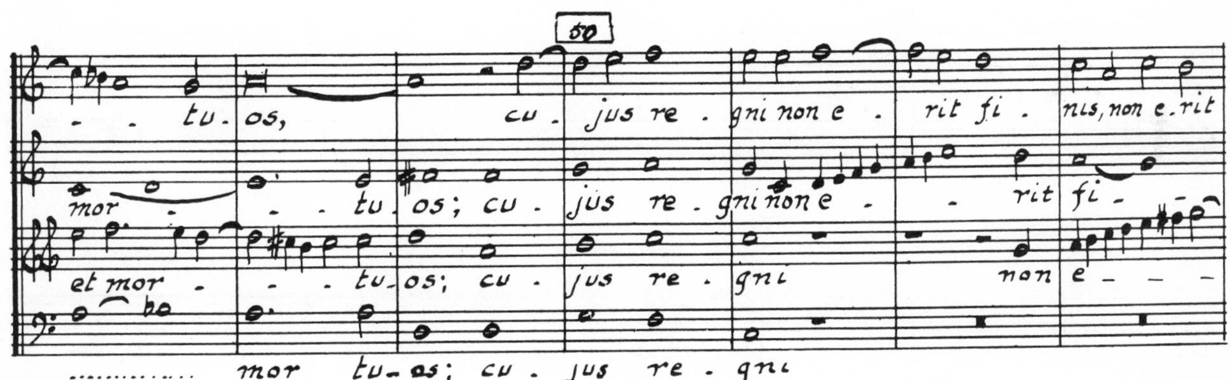
50
- - tu - os, cu - jus re - gni non e - rit fi - nis, non e - rit
mor - - - tu - os; cu - jus re - gni non e - - rit fi - -
et mor - - - tu - os; cu - jus re - gni non e - - -
.... mor tu - os; cu - jus re - gni

60
fi - nis non e - - rit fi - nis non e - rit fi - - nis.
- nis non e - rit, non e - rit fi - nis non e - rit fi - - - nis.
- rit fi - nis, non e - - rit fi - nis, non e - rit......... fi - - nis.
non e - - rit fi - nis, non e - rit fi - - nis.

CANTUS
Et in Spi ritum san ctum, Do - mi. num, et vi.
ALTUS
Et in Spi ritum san. ctum, Do . . . . mi. num et vi.
TENOR I
Et in Spi ri tum san - ctum, Do - mi. num, et vi
QUINTUS (TENOR II)
Et in Spi - - - ri - - tum
BASSUS
Et in Spi. ritum san. ctum, Do - mi. num, et vi.

10
. vi. fi. can - tem, qui ex Pa - tre Fi. li. o. que pro. ce - - - - -
. vi - . fi. can - tem, qui ex Pa - tre Fi. li. o. que pro - ce - - -
:vi - fi . can . tem. Qui
san - - - - ctum.
. vi - fi. can - tem. Qui

20
. dit. Si. mul ad. o. ra - tur, et con glo ri. fi. ca -
. dit. Si. mul ad. o. ra - tur, et con glo-ri. fi. ca -
cum Pa - tre et Fi. li. o si. mul. ad. o. ra - tur et con glo ri. fi. ca -
Pro - - - - - - phe - - -
cum Pa - tre et Fi. li. o si. mul ad. o. ra - tur,

30
.tur, qui lo. cu. tus est per Pro. phe . . . . . tas.
.tur, qui lo. cu. . tus est per Pro-phe . tas. Et u. . nam
.tur, qui lo- cu . tus est per Pro_phe . tas Et u . nam
-tas Et u . nam Ec . . cle. . -
qui lo. cu . tus est per Pro.phe . tas. Et u . nam

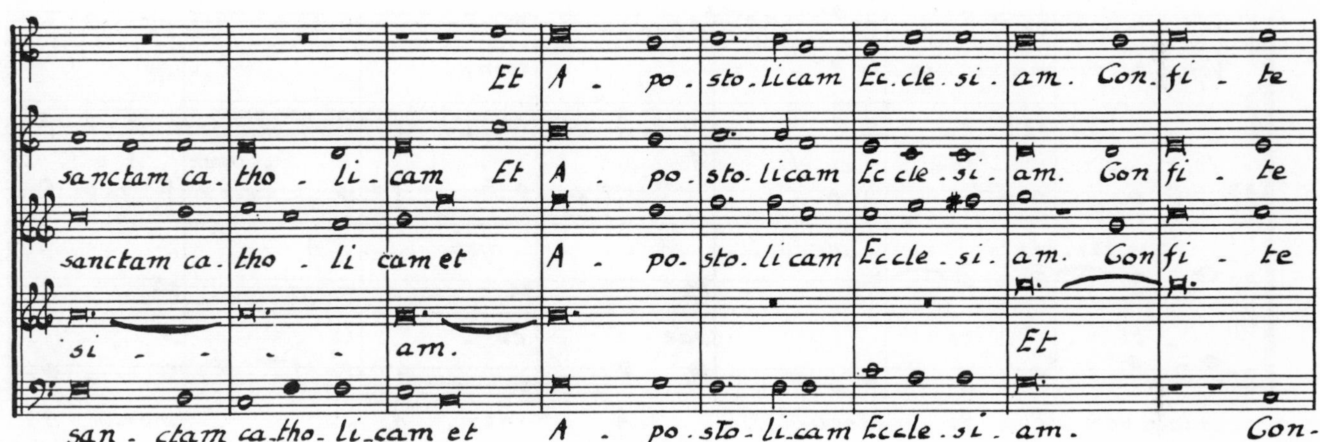
Et A . po. sto. licam Ec. cle. si. am. Con. fi . te
sanctam ca. tho . li . cam Et A . po. sto. licam Ec. cle. si. am. Con fi . te
sanctam ca. tho . li camet A . po. sto. li cam Eccle. si. am. Con fi . te
si . . . . am. Et
san . ctam ca.tho. li. cam et A . po. sto. li. cam Eccle. si. am. Con-

40
.or u . num baptí . sma in re. mis. si. o . nem pecca to . . . rum.
.or u_num bapti . . sma in re. mis. si. o . nem pec . ca . to . rum.
.or u. num ba . pti . sma in re. mis. si. onem pec. ca. to . rum.
ex . . spe . cto re . . . sur . re . . : cti . .
.fi . te. or in re. mis. si. o . nem pec. ca . to . rum.

50
Et ex - spe - - - cto re - sur recti - o - nem mor - tu - o - - rum. Et vitam
Et ex - spe - - - cto re sur recti - o - nem. Et vitam ven -
Et ex - spe - - - cto re surre cti - o - nem mor - - tu - o - rum.
- o - nem mor - tu - o - rum - Et vi - tam ven - -
Et ex - spe - - - cto re surrectio - nem Et

60
Ven - tu - ri sae - cu - li. A - - - - - men, A - - - -
- tu - ri .... sae - cu - li. A - - - - - - - men, A - - -
Et vi tam ventu - ri saecu - li. A - - - men, ... A - - - - - -
- - tu - - ri sae - - cu - - li. A - - -
vitam ven - tu - ri saeculi, ... A - men, A - - - men, A -

- men, A - - - men, A - - - - - - - - - men.
- - men, A - men, ... A - - - men.
- men, A - - - - - - men A - - - - men, A - - - men.
- - - - - - men
- - - - - - - - - - men, A - - - - - men.

Sanctus

CANTUS
San - ctus, San - ctus San - ctus, San - - -
ALTUS
San - - - - ctus, San - - - - - - ctus, San. ctus
TENOR I
San - - - - - — ctus, San - - .ctus,
QUINTUS (TENOR II)
San - -
BASSUS
San - - - -

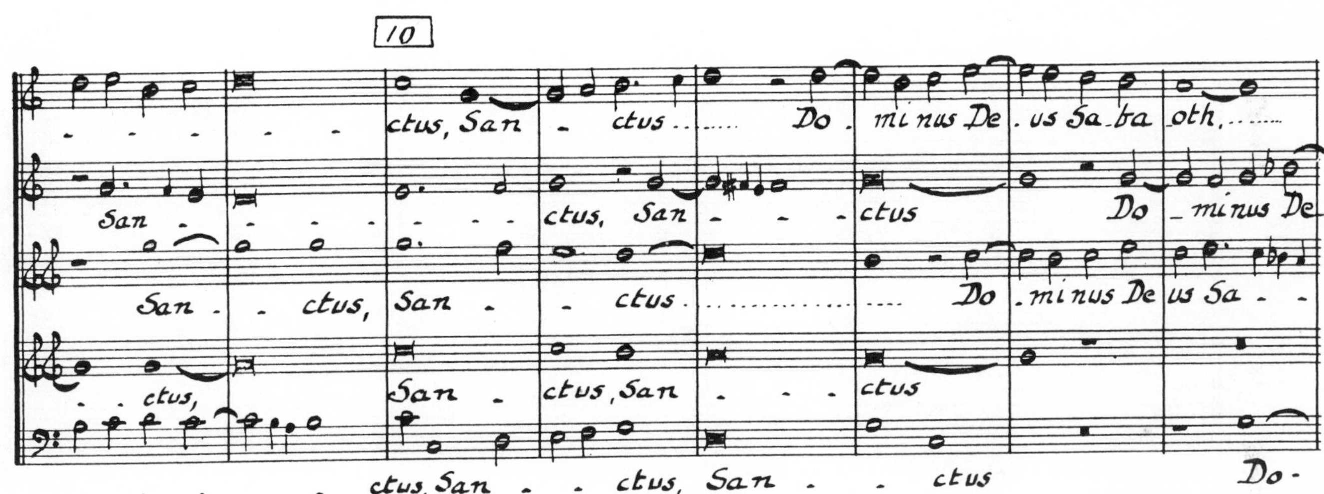
10
- - - - - - ctus, San - ctus...... Do. mi nus De . us Sa ba oth,.......
San - - - - - - - - ctus, San - - - ctus Do - mi nus De
San - - ctus, San - - ctus .... Do - mi nus De us Sa - -
. . ctus, San - ctus, San - - - ctus
- - - - - - - ctus, San - - ctus, San - - ctus Do-

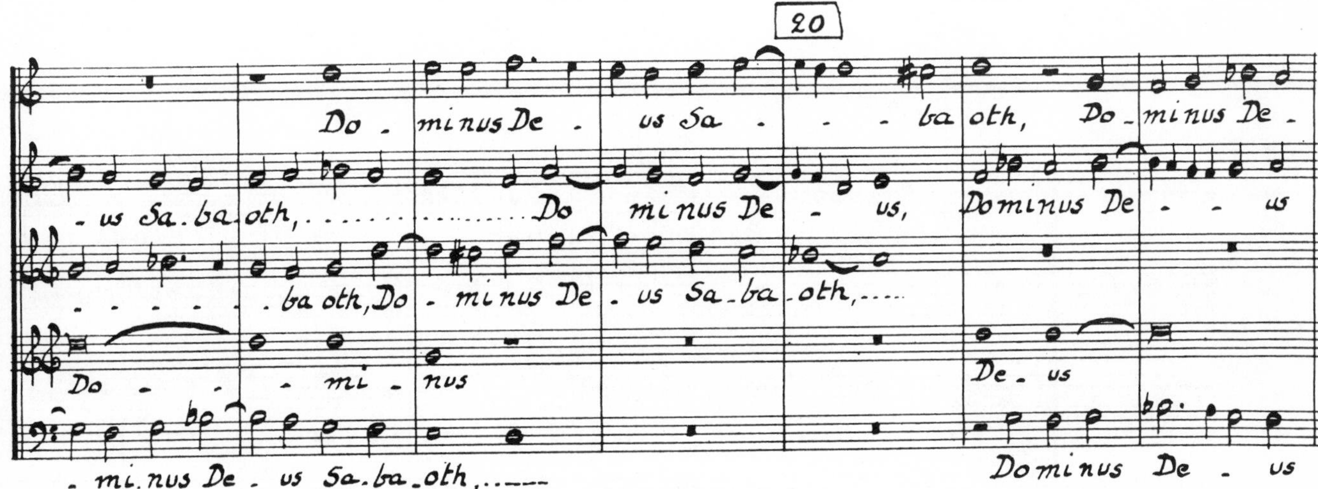
20
Do - mi nus De - us Sa - - - ba oth, Do - mi nus De -
- us Sa. ba. oth, ... Do mi nus De - us, Do mi nus De - - us
- - - - - - . ba oth, Do - mi nus De - us Sa - ba - oth,.....
Do - - mi - nus De - us
- mi. nus De - us Sa. ba. oth,...... Do mi nus De - us

. us, Do . mi nus De . . . . us Sa . ba . . . . oth, Do mi nus Deus
Sa . ba . oth, Do . minus De . us .... Sa . ba oth,
Do . mi nus De us .... Sa . ba . . . . oth, Do . mi .
Sa . . . ba . oth, ... De . . . us
Sa . ba . oth, De . . . . us Sa . ba . oth Do . minus Deus

30
Saba oth, Do . minus De us Sa . ba . oth, Do . mi nus De . us Saba . oth.
Do . mi . nus De . us Sa . . . ba oth.
. nus De us Sa . ba . oth. Do . mi nus De us Sa . ba . oth.
Sa . . ba . oth. ....
Sa . ba . oth, ... Do . mi . nus De . us Sa ba . oth.

40
CANTUS I
Ple . ni sunt coe . li et .... ter . . . . ra, et
CANTUS II
Ple . ni sunt coe . li et .... ter.
TENOR I
Ple . ni sunt coe . li et. .... ter . ra, et ..... ter . . .
QUINTUS (TENOR II)

50
ter - ra ple ni sunt coeli et ter -
ra ple - ni sunt coe - li et ter - - - - ra
ra, ple - ni sunt coe - li et ter - - ra glo-
Ple - ni sunt coe - li
ra glo ri a tu - - - - - a glo - ri a
glo ri a tu - - a, glo ri a tu - - - a, glo ri a
ri a tu - - - - a, glo - ri a tu - - - - a,
et ter - ra
60
tu - a, glo - ri - a tu - - - - - - - a glo-
tu - - - a, glo - ri - a tu - a, glo - ria
glo - ri - a tu - - a, tu - - a, glo-
glo - ri - a tu - a,
70
ri a tu - - a, glo ri - a tu - - - - - a.
tu - - a, glo ria tu - - - a, glo ria tu - - - - a.
ri a tu - - a, glo ri a tu - a, glo ri a tu - - - - a.
glo - ri - a tu - - a.

Hosanna

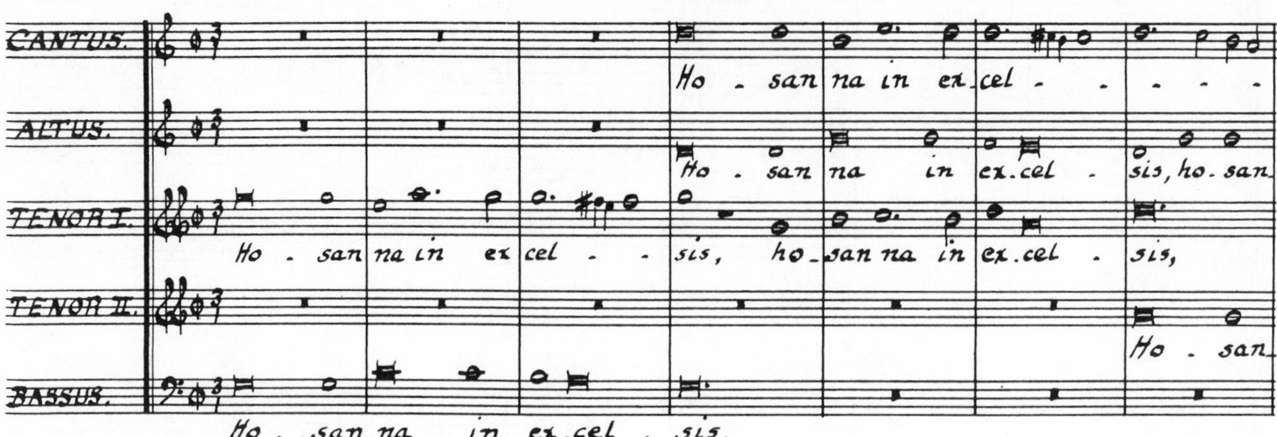

CANTUS.
ALTUS.
TENOR I.
TENOR II.
BASSUS.
Ho - san na in ex.cel - - - - -
Ho - san na in ex.cel - sis, ho.san
Ho - san na in ex cel - - sis, ho-san na in ex.cel - sis,
Ho - san
Ho - san-na in ex.cel - sis,

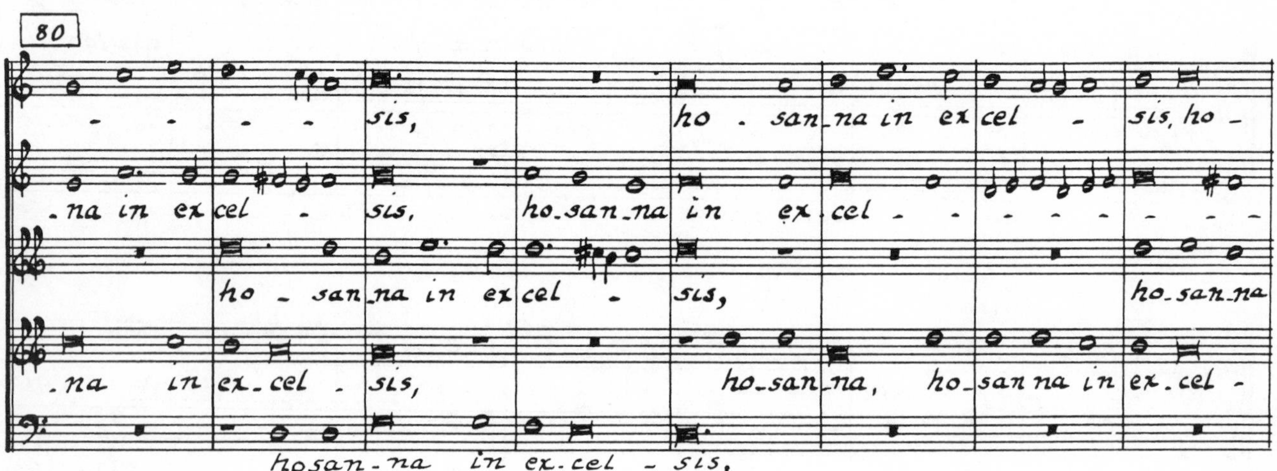

80
- - - - - sis, ho - san-na in ex cel - sis, ho -
-na in ex cel - sis, ho-san-na in ex cel - - - - - - - -
ho - san-na in ex cel - sis, ho-san-na
-na in ex-cel - sis, ho-san-na, ho-san na in ex.cel -
hosan-na in ex.cel - sis,

90
.san - - na in ex - cel-sis, in ex-cel - - - - - sis, ho - san
- sis in ex.cel - - sis, ho - san - na
in ex.cel - - - - - - - sis, ho - san-
- sis, ho - san-na in ex - cel-sis,
ho.san.na, ho.sanna in ex.cel - sis, ho - san-na in

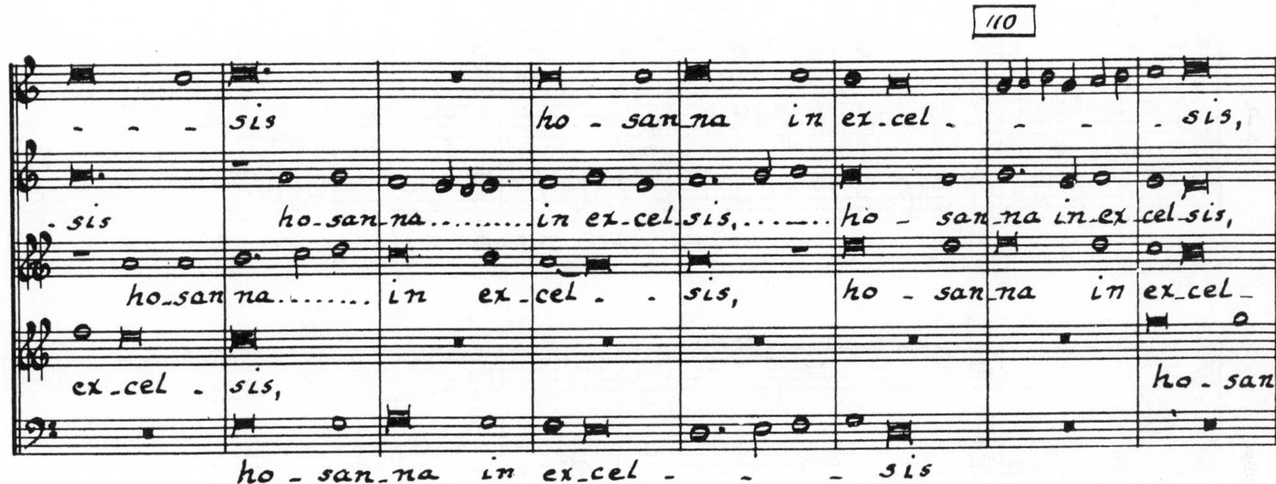

ho - san - na in ex-cel-sis, ... ho-san-na in ex - cel - sis.
-sis, ho - - - san - na in ex-cel-sis, in ex-cel - - - sis.
-sis, ... ho - san-na in ex-cel - sis, in ex - cel - - sis.
-na in ex-cel - sis, ho - san-na in ex-cel - - sis.
ho-san-na in ex-cel - sis, in ex-cel - - sis.

Benedictus

CANTUS.
ALTUS.
TENOR I.
BASSUS
Be - ne - di - ctus qui
Be - ne - di - ctus qui ve - - - - - nit
Be - ne - di - ctus qui ve - - - -

10
Be - - - ne - di - - - -
ve - - - - - - nit Be - ne - di - ctus qui ve - -
qui ve - - - - - nit be - ne - di - - ctus qui
- - - - - - - nit, be - ne - di - ctus qui ve - - - -

20
- ctus qui ve - - - - - - - -
- - - nit, qui ve - - - - - - - - -
ve - nit, be - ne - di ctus qui ve - nit, qui ve - - - - - -
- - - nit, be - ne - di - ctus qui.......

- nit in
- - nit.................. in nomi - ne.................. Domi - ni,
- - - nit in nomi ne........Do - mi ni in nomi
ve - nit in nomi - ne................Do - - - - - mi-

Agnus Dei I

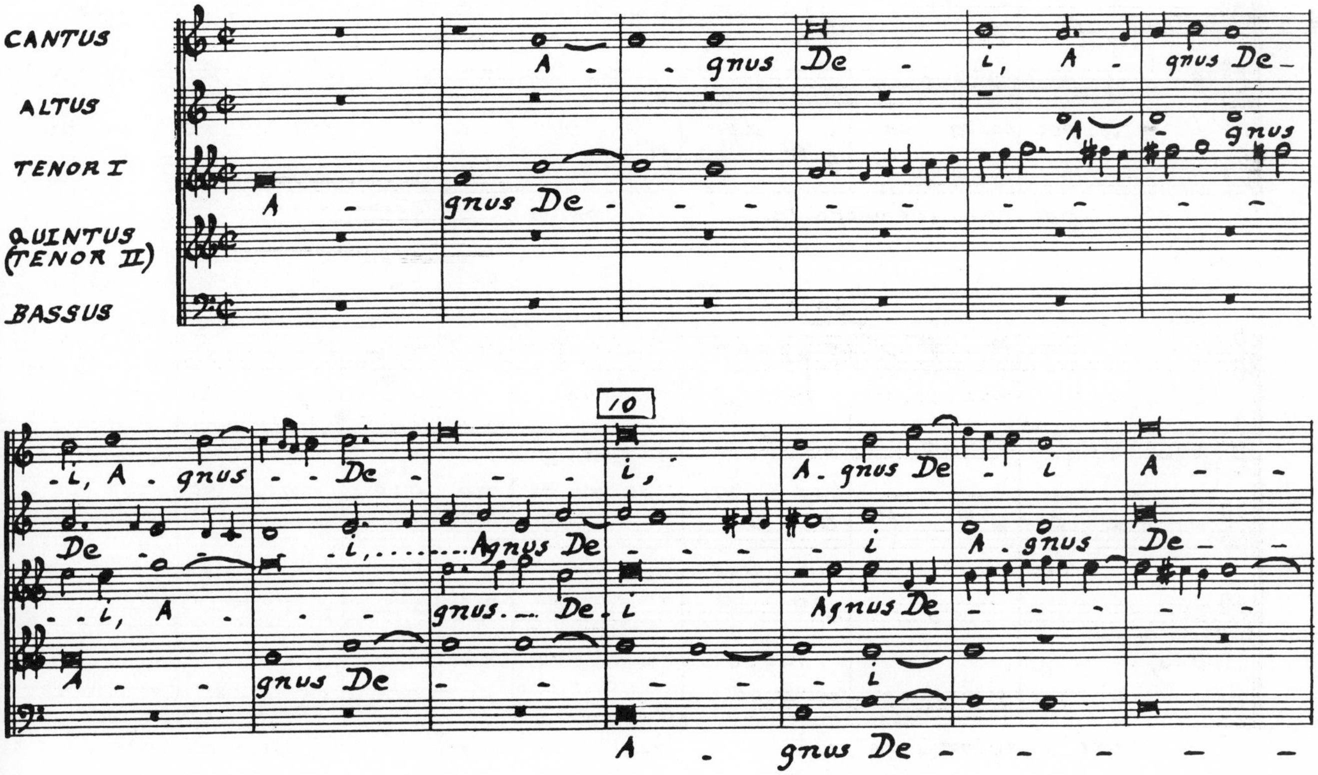

CANTUS

ALTUS

TENOR I

QUINTUS (TENOR II)

BASSUS

A - - gnus De - i, A - gnus De -

A - gnus

A - gnus De - - - - - - - - - -

10

- i, A - gnus - - De - - - i, A - gnus De - i A - -

De - - - i, ... Agnus De - - - - - i A - gnus De - -

- - i, A - - - gnus. - De - i Agnus De - - - -

A - - gnus De - - - - - - i

A - gnus De - - - - - -

20
-gnus De - - - i, qui tol - lis pecca - ta mun - di, pec-ca-ta mun-
-i, ... qui tol-lis pec-ca-ta mun - - - -
- - i, qui tol - lis pec-ca-ta mun - - - - di, ...
qui tol - lis qui tol-
-i, qui tol-lis pec-ca-ta-mun - di,

-di, qui tol - lis pecca-ta mun - - - di: mi - se-re - re no -
- di, qui tol - lis pec - ca-ta mun - di: mi - se re - re no -
qui tol - lis pec - ca - ta mun-di:
- lis pec ca-ta mun - di: mi-se-re - re no -
qui tol-lis pecca-ta .... mun - - di:

30
- - bis, mi-se-re - re .... no - - - bis
- - - - - bis mi - se-re-re no-bis mi - se - re-re no -
mi se-re - re no - bis mi - se - re - re
- bis, mi-se - re - re no - bis
mi - se-re - re no - bis mi-se-re - re

40
mi - se re - re no - bis, mi - se - re re no - - - - -
- - bis, mi - se - re - - re no - - bis, mi - se - re - re no -
no - bis, mi - - se - re - re no - bis,
mi - se - re - re no - -
no - bis mi - se - re re no - bis,

- bis mi - se - re - re no - - bis, mi - se - re - re no - - bis.
- bis mi - se - re - re no - bis. mi - se - re - re no - - - - bis.
mi - se - re re no - - - bis, mi - se - re - re no - - - bis.
mi - - se - re - - re no - - bis.
mi - se - re - re no - bis mi - se - re - re no - - - - bis.

Agnus Dei. II.

CANTUS I
A - gnus De - - - - - - i,
CANTUS II
A - gnus De - - - - - - - - - - i,
ALTUS
A - gnus De - -
TENOR I
A - gnus De - i, A - gnus..... De - -
QUINTUS TENOR II
A - - - - gnus De -
BASSUS
A - gnus

10
A - gnus De - - - - - - - i, A - gnus De - -
A - gnus De - i, A - gnus De - - - - - - -
i, A - gnus De - - i, A - gnus
i, A - gnus De - i, A - gnus De - - - -
i, qui
De - - i, A - gnus De - - - - i, A - -

20
i qui tol lis pec ca ta mun - di, qui tol - lis pecca ta mun -
i qui tol lis pec ca ta mun - di, qui tol -
De - i qui tol lis pec ca ta mun - di, qui tol
i qui tol - lis peccata mun -
tol - lis pec -
- gnus De - i, qui tollis peccata mun - di, qui tol -

30
- di, pecca - ta mun - di, do - na no
- lis pecca - ta mun - di pecca - ta mun - di, pec - ca ta mun - di do
- lis peccata mun di, pec ca - ta mun -
di, pecca - ta mun - di:
ca - ta mun -
- lis pecca - ta mun - di:

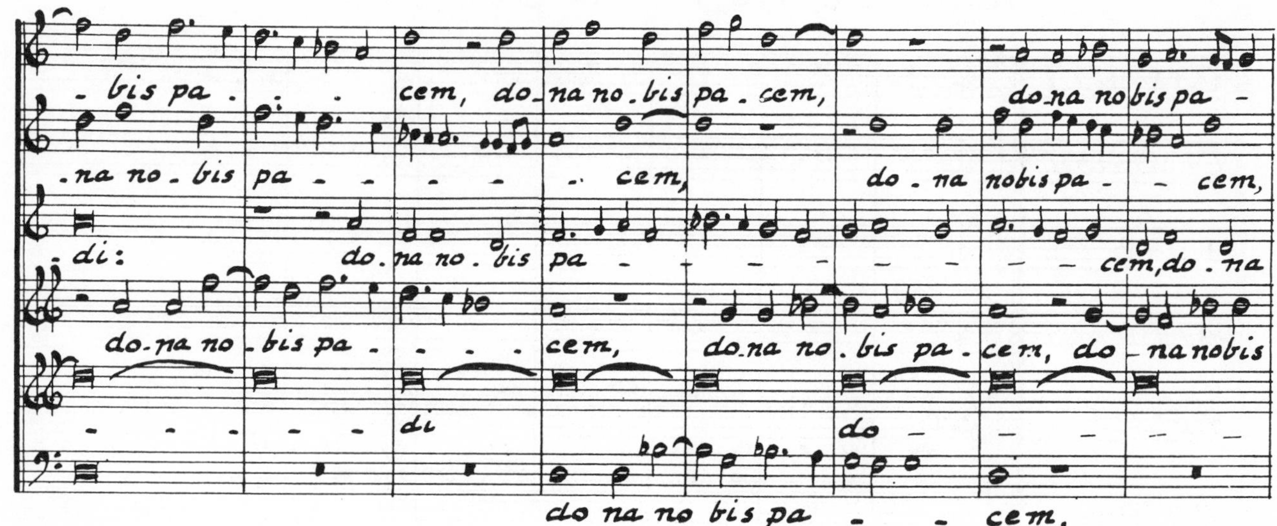
- bis pa - - cem, do - na no - bis pa - cem, do - na no bis pa -
- na no - bis pa - - - - - - cem, do - na nobis pa - - cem,
- di: do - na no - bis pa - - - - - - - - - cem, do - na
do - na no - bis pa - - - - cem, do - na no - bis pa - cem, do - na nobis
- - - - - - di do - - - - - -
do na no bis pa - - cem,

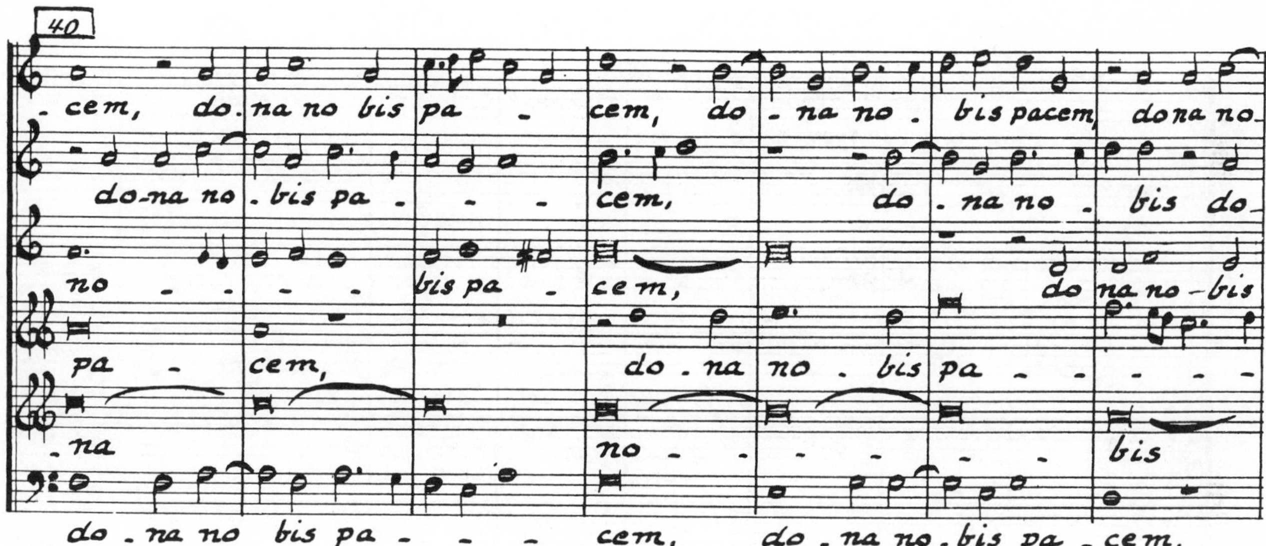
40
- cem, do - na no bis pa - cem, do - na no - bis pacem, do na no -
do - na no - bis pa - - - cem, do - na no - bis do -
no - - - - bis pa - cem, do na - no - bis
pa - cem, do - na no - bis pa - - - -
- na no - - - - - - bis
do - na no bis pa - - - cem, do - na no - bis pa - cem,

50
- bis pa - - - cem, do - na no - bis pa - - - cem.
- na no - bis pa - cem, do - na no - bis pa - cem.
pa - cem, do na no - bis pa - - cem.
- cem, do - na no - bis pacem, do - na nobis pa - cem.
pa - - - - - cem.
do - na no - bis pa - - - - - - cem.

Mass: Ut Re Mi Fa Sol La: Kyrie

30
Chri - - ste e - - - - lei son, Chri - ste...... e - lei - -
Chri - - - ste e - - - - - lei - - - - -
Chri - ste e - lei - - son, e - - - lei - son, e - lei - - son,
Chri - ste e - - lei - - - - - - - - - - - - - -
Chri - ste e - - lei - son, Chri - ste e - - lei - -
Chri - ste e - lei - - - - - - - - - - son, Christe e - lei

40.
- - - - son, ... Chri - ste e - lei - - - -
- - - - - - son, Chri - - -
Christe e - lei - son, Chri - ste e - - - - - lei - - - - -
- - son, Christe e - lei - - - son, Chri - ste e - lei - -
- - - - - - - son, Chri - ste e - lei - - - - son, Chri - ste e -
- - - son, Chri - ste e - lei - - son,

50.
- son, e - leison, Chri - - - ste e - - lei son, Chri -
- ste e - - - - lei - - - - - - -
- son, Chri - ste e - - - lei - - son, Chri - ste e - lei - - - -
- - - - son, Christe e - lei - - - - - -
- lei - - son, Christe e - - lei - - - - son, Chri -
Chri - ste e - lei - son, Christe elei - son, Chri - ste e - lei - - son,

- - ste e - - lei - - son. Ky - - ri - - e e -
- son. Ky -
- son, e - - - - - - lei - son. Ky - ri - e e - lei - - son,
son. Ky - ri - e e - lei -
- ste e - lei son. Ky - ri - e
Chri - ste e - lei - son. Ky - ri - e e - lei - son,
60
- - lei - - - - - son, e - - - - lei - son, e -
- ri - e e - - lei - - son, Ky - ri -
Ky - rie e - lei - - - son, Ky - ri - e e - lei - son, Ky - rie e - lei -
son, Kyri - e e - lei - son,
e - lei - son, Ky - rie e - lei - - son, Ky - -
Kyrie e - lei - son, Ky - ri - e e - lei -
70
- - lei - son, Ky - rie e - - lei - son, Kyrie e - lei - - son, Ky -
- e e - lei - son, Ky - ri - e e - lei - son, Ky - ri -
- - son, Ky - - rie e - lei - son, Ky - ri - e......... e - lei - - son
Ky - ri - e e - lei - - son, Ky - ri - e e - lei - - son, Kyrie e - lei - -
- rie e - lei - - - - - - son, Ky - rie eleison, Ky - ri - e e - lei
- son, Ky - rie e - lei - son, Ky - rie eleison, Kyrie eleison Ky - rie

Gloria in excelsis Deo

CANTUS I: Et in ter-ra pax homini bus bo-nae volun ta- tis. Lau- da- mus

CANTUS II: Et in ter-ra pax homini bus bo-nae volun ta- tis.

ALTUS I: Homini- bus bo-nae voluntatis Lau- da- mus

ALTUS II: Et in ter- ra pax homini- bus bonae volun- ta- tis. Lau- da- mus

TENOR: Et in ter- ra pax homini bus bo-nae volun ta tis. bo

BASSUS: Et in ter-ra pax hominibus bonae volun ta- tis. Lau- da- mus

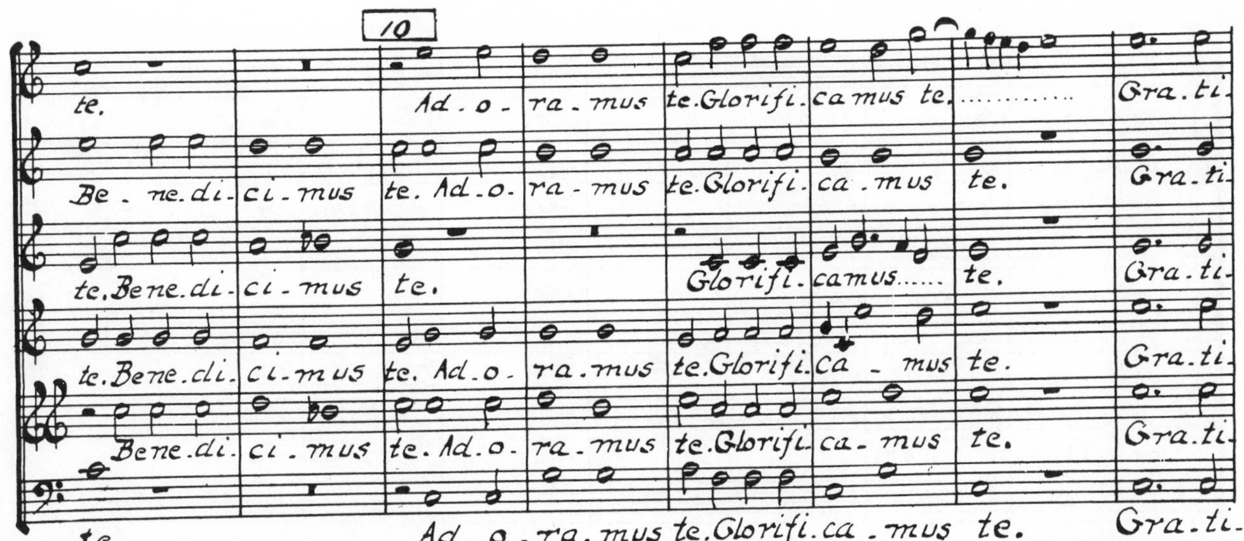

20
-as a-gimus ti-bi pro-pter ma-gnam glo-riam tu-am. Do-
-as a-gimus ti-bi pro-pter ma-gnam glo-riam tu-am. Do-
-as a-gimus tibi..........pro-pter ma-gnam glo-riam tu-am. Do-
-as a-gimus ti-bi pro-pter ma-gnam glo-riam tu-am. Do-
-as a-gimus........tibi pro-pter ma gnam......glo-riam tu-am.
-as a-gimus ti-bi pro-pter ma-gnam glo-riam tu-am. Do-

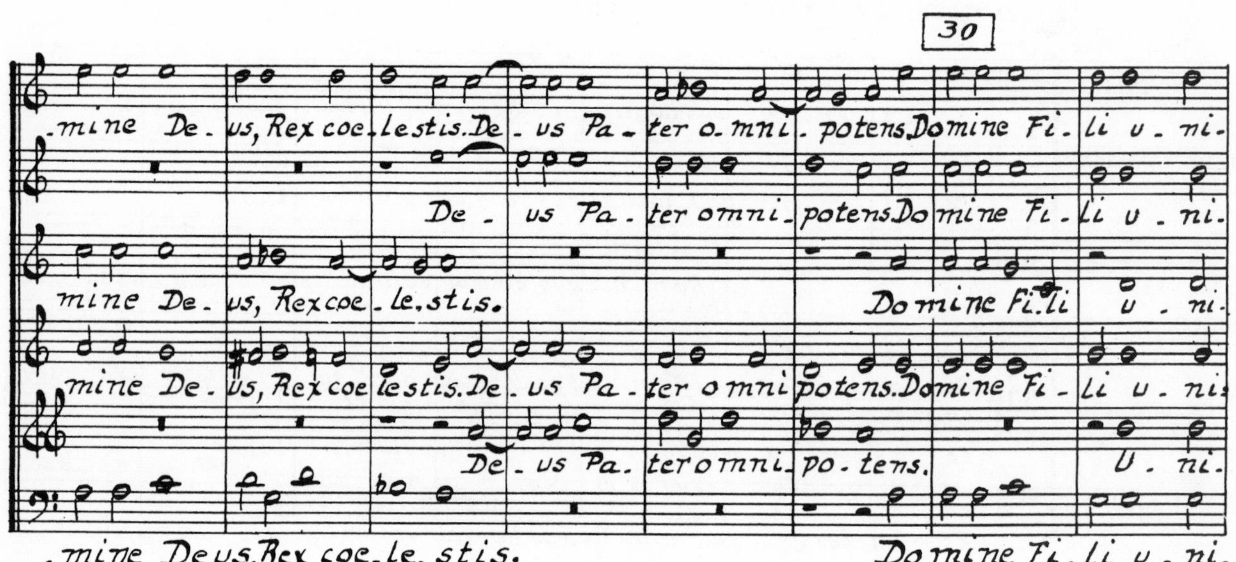
30
-mine De-us, Rex coe-lestis. De-us Pa-ter o-mni-potens. Domine Fi-li u-ni-
De-us Pa-ter omni-potens Domine Fi-li u-ni-
mine De-us, Rex coe-le-stis. Domine Fi-li u-ni-
mine De-us, Rex coe-lestis. De-us Pa-ter omni potens. Domine Fi-li u-ni-
De-us Pa-ter omni-po-tens. U-ni-
-mine Deus, Rex coe-le-stis. Domine Fi-li u-ni-

-geni-te Je-su Chri-ste. Domine De-us, Agnus
-geni-te Je-su Chri-ste. Domine De-us,
-geni-te Je-su Chri-ste. A-gnus
-geni-te Jesu Chri-ste. Domine De-us, Agnus De-
-genite Je-su Chri-ste. Domine De-us,
-ge-ni-te Je-su Chri-ste. A-gnus

40
De - i, Fi - lius....... Pa-tris, Filius Pa - - tris.
Fili-us....... Pa - tris, Fi - li - us....... Pa - tris.
De - i, Filius Pa tris, Filius Pa-tris, Fili-us......... Pa - tris.
i, Filius Pa-tris, Filius Pa - - - - tris.
Filius Pa - - - tris, Fi - lius......... Pa - - - tris.
De - i, Fi - lius Pa-tris, Fili-us Pa - tris.

50
Qui tollis pec-cata mun-di, mi-se-re-re no - bis, mi-
Qui tollis pec-cata mun-di, mi-se-re-re no - bis,
Qui tollis pec-ca - ta mun-di, mi-se-re - re no - bis,
Qui tol - lis peccata mun - di, mi-se-re-re no - bis,
Qui tol lis pec-cata.......mun - di, mi-se-rere no - bis,
Qui tollis pec-ca-ta mun-di, mi-se-re-re no - bis,

60
- - se-re-re no - bis. Qui tol-lis pec-cata mun - di,
mi-se-re-re no - bis. Qui tol-lis peccata mun - di,
mi-se-re - re no - bis. Qui tol-lis peccata mun - di,
mi-se-rere......... no-bis.
mi - se-re-re no - bis. Qui tol-lis pec-ca ta mun - di,
mi-se-re - re no - bis.

70
su - sci - pe de - pre . ca - ti - onem no - - - - - stram.
su - sci - pe de - pre - ca - ti - o - nem no - - stram.
su - sci - pe de - pre ca - - - ti . o - nem no - - - - stram. Qui
su - sci - pe deprecatio - - - nem no - - - - stram.
su - sci - pe de - pre - ca ti - onem no - - - - - stram.
su - sci - pe de - preca - ti - o - nem no - - - stram.

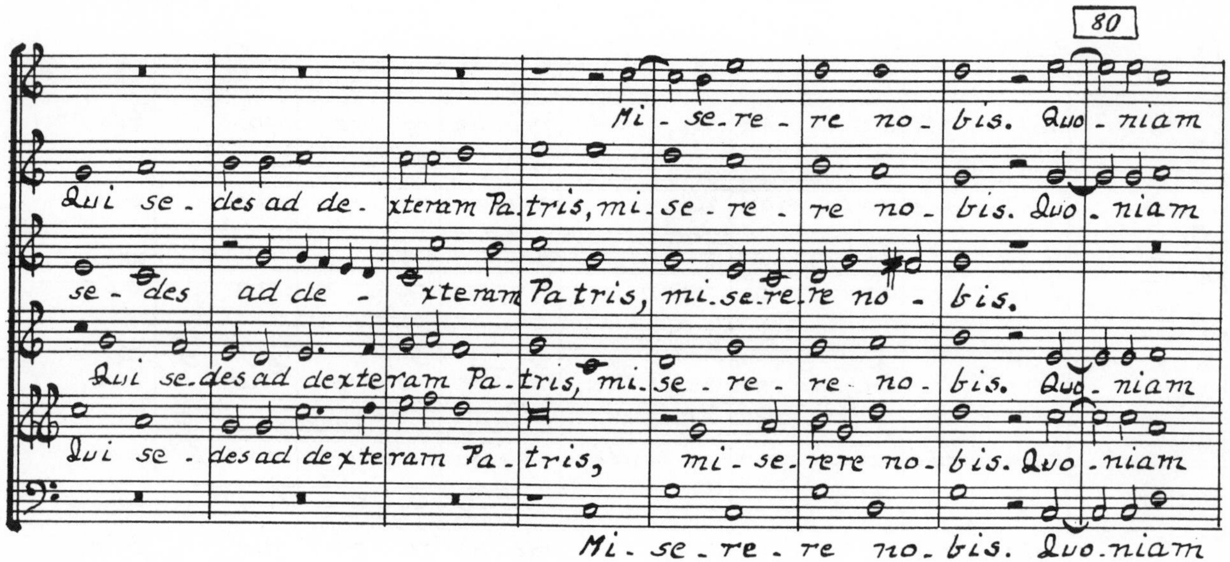
80
Mi - se - re - re no - bis. Quo - niam
Qui se - des ad de - xteram Pa - tris, mi - se - re - re no - bis. Quo - niam
se - des ad de - xteram Patris, mi . se . re . re no - bis.
Qui se - des ad dexteram Pa - tris, mi - se - re - re no - bis. Quo - niam
Qui se - des ad dexteram Pa - tris, mi - se - rere no - bis. Quo - niam
Mi - se - re - re no - bis. Quo - niam

tu solus sanctus, tu solus Al - tis - si - mus
tu so - lus sanctus, tu so . lus Do - mi - nus, tu so lus Al - tis - si - mus
Tu so - lus Do - minus, tu solus Al - tis - si - mus Je -
tu solus sanctus, tu so lus Do - minus, tu solus Al - tis - si - mus
tu so - lus sanctus, tu so lus Do mi nus, tu so . lus Al tissimus
tu solus sanctus, tu solus Altissi - mus

90
Je - su Chri - ste, Cum san - cto Spiri - tu
Je - su Chri - ste. In Glo. ri.
- - su Chri - - ste, Cum san - cto Spi - ri - tu in glo. ri.
Je. su - - Chri - - ste ...... Cum san. cto Spi. ri - tu in glo. ri.
Je. su Chri - - - ste, Cum Santo Spiri - tu in glo. ri.
Je - su Chri - ste Cum Sancto Spiritu ......

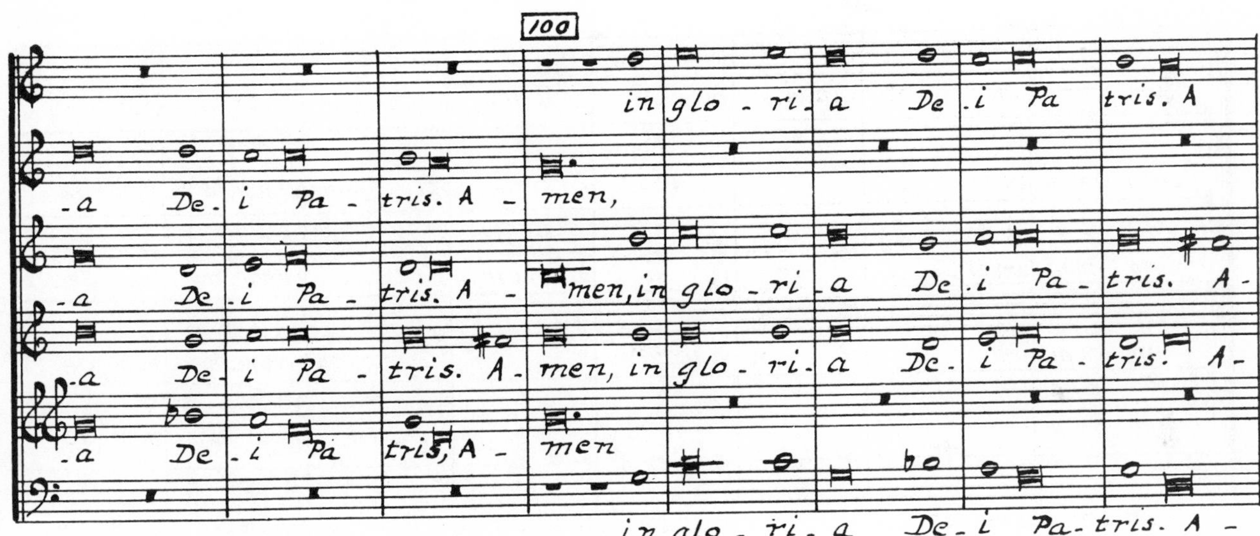
100
in glo - ri. a De. i Pa tris. A
. a De. i Pa - tris. A - men,
. a De. i Pa - tris. A - men, in glo - ri. a De. i Pa. tris. A -
. a De. i Pa - tris. A - men, in glo - ri. a De. i Pa - tris. A -
. a De. i Pa tris, A - men
in glo - ri. a De. i Pa. tris. A -

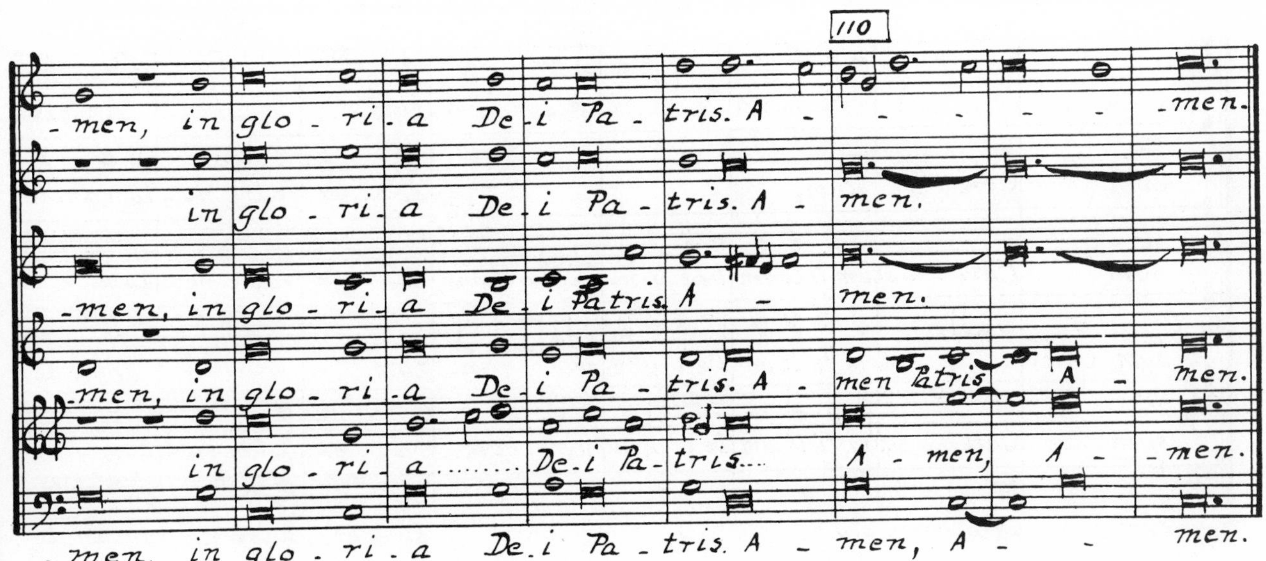
110
. men, in glo - ri. a De. i Pa - tris. A - - - - - - men.
in glo - ri. a De. i Pa - tris. A - men.
. men, in glo - ri. a De. i Patris. A - men.
. men, in glo - ri. a De. i Pa - tris. A - men Patris A - men.
in glo - ri. a .... De. i Pa - tris.... A - men, A - men.
. men, in glo - ri. a De. i Pa - tris. A - men, A - - men.

Credo in unum Deum.

30
o - mnia .... saecu - la. De - um de De - o, lumen de lumi - ne, De - - um ve - rum de
o - mnia sae - cu la. Lu - men de lumi ne, De - um ve - rum de
De um de De - o, lu men de lumi ne, De - um verum de
o - mnia sae - cu la. De um de De - o, lumen de lu mi ne, De - um verum de
De - um de De o, lumen de lumine De - um .... - ve - rum
o - mnia sae - cu la. Lumen de lumi ne, De - um ve - rum de

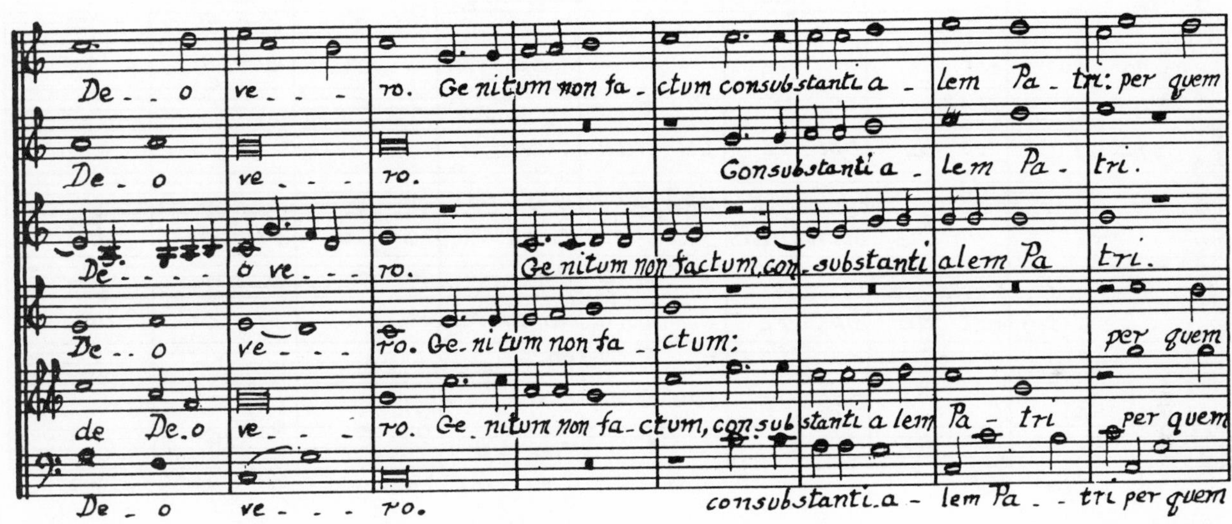
De - - o ve - - - ro. Ge nitum non fa - ctum consubstanti a - lem Pa - tri: per quem
De - o ve - - - ro. Consubstanti a - lem Pa - tri.
De - - - - o ve - - - ro. Ge nitum non factum con - substanti alem Pa tri.
De - - o ve - - - ro. Ge nitum non fa - ctum: per quem
de De - o ve - - - ro. Ge - nitum non fa - ctum, consubstanti a lem Pa - tri per quem
De - o ve - - - ro. consubstanti - a - lem Pa - - tri per quem

40
omni - a facta sunt. Qui propter nos, homi - nes, de -
Qui propter nos, ho mi - nes, et propter nostram salu - tem
Qui propter nos, homi - nes, et propter no-stram sa lu - tem de -
omnia fa - cta sunt. Et propter nostram salu - - tem de -
omnia facta sunt. Qui propter nos, homi nes, et propter nostram salu - tem de
omni a facta sunt. Qui propter nos, et propter no-stram salu - tem

50
-scen-dit de coe-lis, de-scendit de coe- - - - lis. Et in-car-
de-scen-dit de coe- - lis. Et in-car-
-scen-dit de coe-lis, de-scen-dit de coe- - - lis.
-scen dit de coe- - - lis, descendit de coe- - - - - - - - lis. Et in-carna-
-scen dit de coe- lis, de scen- - - dit de coe- - lis.
de-scen-dit de coe- - lis. Et in-car

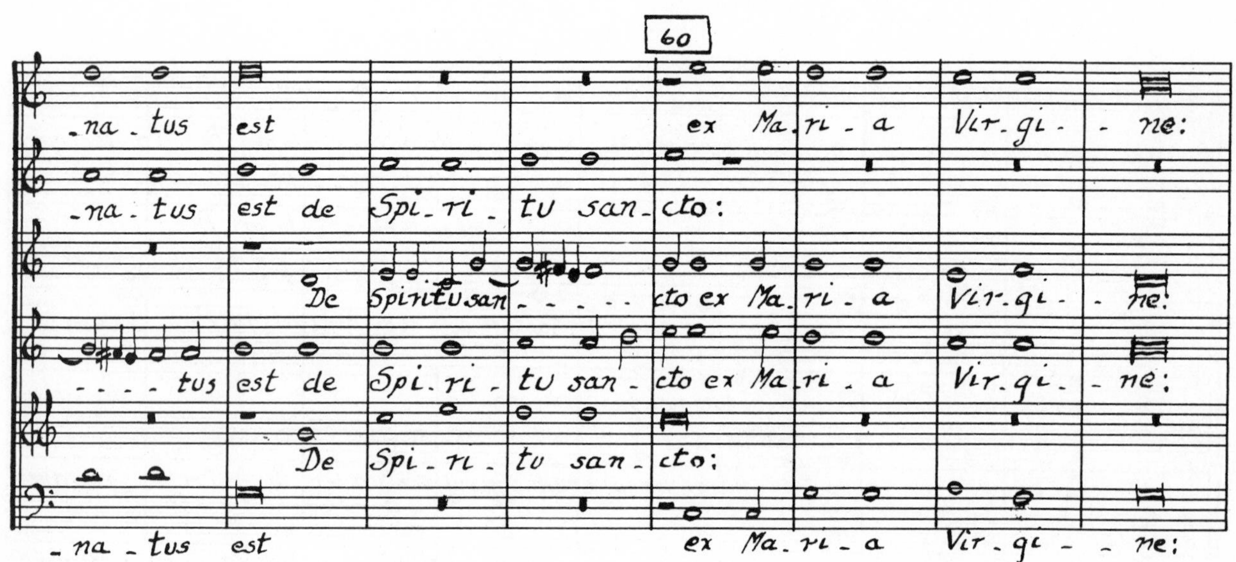
60
-na-tus est ex Ma-ri-a Vir-gi- -ne:
-na-tus est de Spi-ri-tu san-cto:
De Spiritu san- - - - cto ex Ma-ri-a Vir-gi- -ne:
- - - tus est de Spi-ri-tu san-cto ex Ma-ri-a Vir-gi- -ne:
De Spi-ri-tu san-cto:
-na-tus est ex Ma-ri-a Vir-gi- -ne:

70
Et ho- - mo fa- - ctus est.
Et ho- - mo fa- - ctus est.
Et ho- - mo fa-ctus est fa- - ctus est.
Et ho- - - mo fa- ctus est et homo fa- - ctus est.
Et ho-mo fa-ctus est fa- - - ctus est
Et ho- - mo fa- - - - - - - ctus est.

CANTUS I
CANTUS II
ALTUS I
ALTUS II
Cruci - fi - xus
Cru-ci - fixus ...... e - ti - am pro no - bis,
Cru-ci fi-xus e-
Cru-ci fi-xus e - tiam pro no - - - - - - - bis, e - ti-
10
...... e - ti - am pro no - bis, sub ponti-o Pi - la - to pas-
sub ponti-o Pi - la - - - - - - - to pas-
- ti-am pro no - - - - - - bis, sub ponti-o Pi - la - - - - to
-am pro no - - - - - - - bis, sub Ponti-o Pi - la - - - - - - - to pas-
20
- - sus, et .... se - pultus est, et se - pul - tus est. Et resur-rexit ter-
- - - sus, et se - pul - - - tus .... est. Et resurrexit terti-a
pas - sus, et se-pultus est, pas - sus et se-pul-tus est. Et resur-rexit ter-
- - - sus, ... pas-sus, et se - pul - tus est.
30
-ti-a di - e, se-cundum Scri - ptu-ras. Et ascen-dit in coe - - - - - -
di - - - e, Et ascen-dit in coe - - - - - - -
ti-a di - e, se-cundum Scri - ptu-ras ....
Se-cundum Scri - - - - ptu - - - ras. Et ascendit in

lum, se-det ad dexte-ram, Pa - tris ad dexte-ram..... Pa-tris. Et i-te-rum, et
lum, se-det ad dexte-ram...... Pa-tris. Et i-te-rum
se-det ad dexteram Pa - - - - - - - tris. Et iterum ven-turus est,
coe- - - lum, se-det ad dexteram Pa - - - - - - tris....... Et iterum ven-
40
i-te-rum ven-turus est cum glo-ri-a ju-di-ca-re vi- -vos et mor-
ven-tu-rus est cum glo-ri-a ju-di-ca-re vi-vos et.........
et i-te-rum venturus est cum gloria ju-di-ca-re vi- -vos et mor-tu-os, vi-vos
turus est cum glo-ri-a ju-di-ca-re cum gloria ju-di-ca-re vi-vos et mor- -
50
- - - - tu-os: cu- -jus regni non e- - - -rit fi- - -nis fi- - -
mor-tu-os:.............. cu- -jus regni non e-rit fi- - - - - - - - -nis,
et mortu- - - - - - - os cu-jus
- - - - tu-os:............... cu-jus regni non e- - -rit fi- - -
60
- - - -nis, cujus re-gni non... e-rit fi-nis, non e-rit fi- - - - - -nis.
cu-jus re-gni non e- - -rit fi nis.
regni non e-rit, cujus regni non e-rit, non e- - -rit, non e-rit fi- - - - - - nis
- - - - - - - nis, cu-jus regni non e-rit fi- - - - - nis.

CANTUS I
Et in Spiri-tum san-ctum, Domi-num, qui ex
CANTUS II
Et in Spiri-tum san-ctum, Domi-num, et vi-vi-fi-can-tem, qui ex
ALTUS I
Et vi-vi-fi-can-tem qui ex
ALTUS II
Et in Spi-ri-tum san-ctum, Do-mi-num, et vi-vi-fi-can-tem qui ex
TENOR
Et in Spiritum san-ctum, Domi-num, qui ex
BASSUS
Et vi-vi-fi-can-tem, qui ex

10
Patre Fi-li-o-que pro-cedit. Qui cum Pa-tre et Fi-li-o, et conglo-
Patre Fi-li-o-que pro-ce-dit.
Patre Fi-li-o-que pro-ce-dit. Si-mul ado-ra-tur, et conglo-
Pa-tre Fi-li-o-que pro-ce-dit. Qui cum Pa-tre et Fi-li-o si-mul ad-o-ra-tur, et conglo-
Patre Fi-li-o-que pro-ce-dit. Qui cum Pa-tre et Fi-li-o si-mul ad-o-ra-tur et conglo-
Patre Fi-li-o-que pro-ce-dit. Si-mul ado-ra-tur:

20
ri-fi-ca-tur: qui lo-cutus est per Prophe-tas Et
Et unam sanctam ca-tholi-cam
-rifica-tur: qui lo-cutus est per Pro-phe-tas. Et unam sanctam ca-tho-li-cam
ri-fi-ca-tur: qui lo-cutus est per Pro-phe-tas. Et unam sanctam ca-tholicam et
ri-fi-ca-tur, qui lo-cutus est per Pro-phe-tas. Et unam sanctam ca-tholi-cam et
qui locutus est per Pro-phe-tas.

30
Apos-to-li-cam Eccle-si-am. In remissi-o-nem pec-ca-to - - - -
Confi-te-or unum ba-pti-sma.
Confi-te-or unum ba-pti-sma in remissi-onem pec-ca to - - - -
Apos-to-li-cam Eccle-si-am. Confi-te-or unum ba-pti-sma in remissi-o-nem pec-ca-to - - - -
Apos-to-li-cam Eccle-si-am. Confi-te-or unum ba-pti-sma in remissi-o-nem pec-ca
Apos-to-li-cam Eccle-si-am. Unum ba-pti-sma

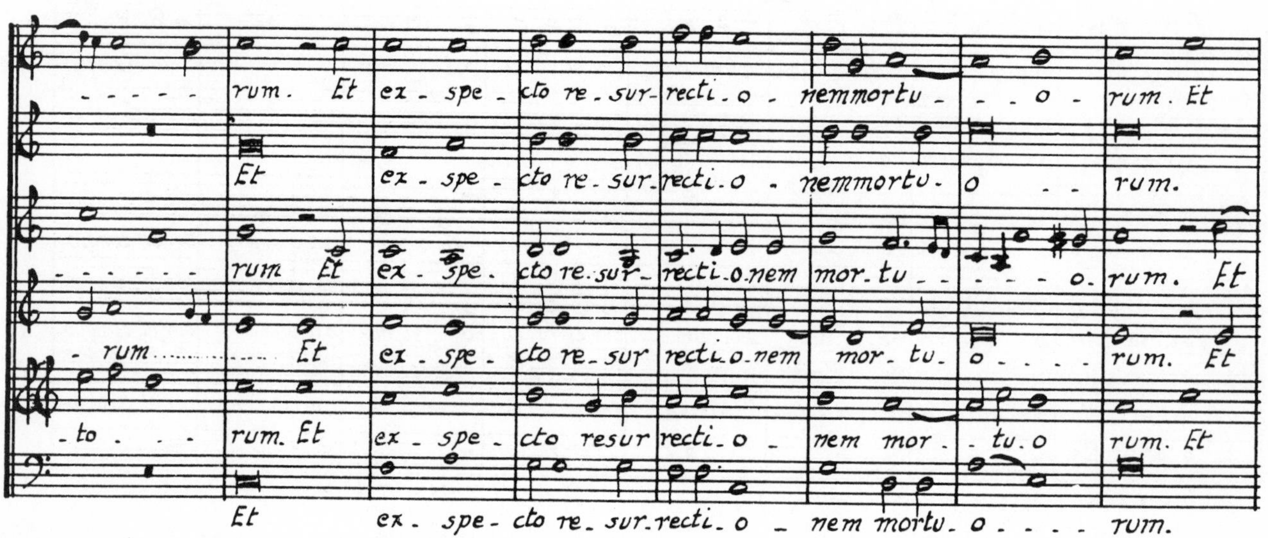
- - - - - rum. Et ex-spe-cto re-sur-recti-o-nem mortu - - o - rum. Et
Et ex-spe-cto re-sur-recti-o-nem mortu-o - - rum.
- - - - - - rum Et ex-spe-cto re-sur-recti-o-nem mor-tu - - - - o. rum. Et
- rum ...... Et ex-spe-cto re-sur recti-o-nem mor-tu-o - - - rum. Et
- to - - rum. Et ex-spe-cto resur recti-o - nem mor - tu-o rum. Et
Et ex-spe-cto re-sur-recti-o - nem mortu-o - - - - rum.

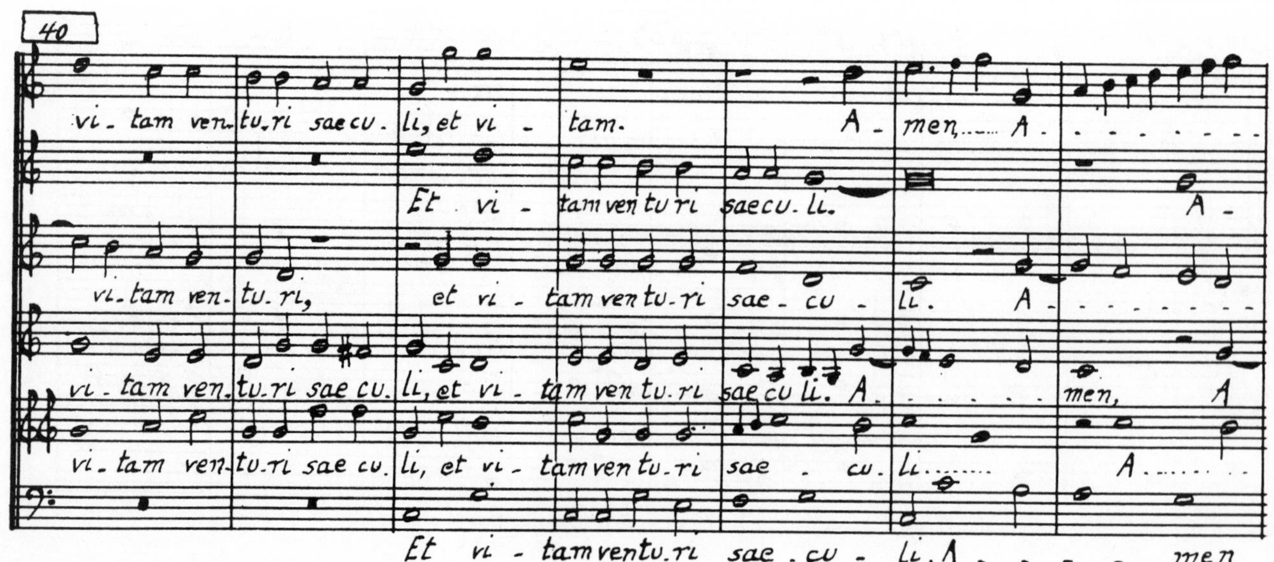
40
vi-tam ven-tu-ri saecu-li, et vi-tam. A-men ..... A - - - - - - -
Et vi-tam ventu-ri saecu-li. A -
vi-tam ven-tu-ri, et vi-tam ventu-ri sae-cu-li. A - - - - - -
vi-tam ven-tu-ri sae cu-li, et vi-tam ven tu-ri sae cu li. A - - - - - men, A
vi-tam ven-tu-ri sae cu-li, et vi-tam ventu-ri sae - cu-li .... A ....
Et vi-tam ventu-ri sae-cu-li. A - - - - men

50
men, A - - men, A - - men.
men.
men, A - - men.
men, A - - men.
men, A - men, A - - men.
A - - men. A - - men.

Sanctus
CANTUS I
San - - ctus, San - - ctus,
CANTUS II
San - ctus, San - ctus,
ALTUS I
San - ctus, San -
ALTUS II
San - ctus, San - ctus
TENOR
San - ctus, San -
BASSUS
San - ctus, San -

10
San - ctus, San - ctus.
San - ctus, San - ctus
ctus, San - ctus, San - ctus, San -
San - ctus San - ctus Do
ctus, San - ctus, San - ctus Do-
ctus, San - ctus

20
Do - minus De - us Sa - - - - - - - ba - oth, Do - minus De
Do - minus De - us Sa - ba - oth,
ctus Do - minus De - us Sa - - - ba oth, ... Do -
minus De - us Sa - - - ba - oth, Do - mi - nus De - us
minus De - us Sa - - - ba - oth, Do - mi - nus
Do - minus De - us Sa - - - ba - oth,

us Sa - - - - ba - oth, ... Sa - ba - oth, Do - minus De -
Do - minus De - us Sa - ba - oth, Do - mi - nus De -
mi - nus De - us, Do - minus De - us Sa - - ba - oth, Do -
Sa - - ba - - - oth, Do - minus Deus Sa - - ba - oth, Dominus De - - -
De - us Do - - - - mi - nus ...... De - us Sa - ba - oth, ... Do - mi - nus
Do - minus De - us Sa - - - ba - oth, Do - minus De -

30
us Sa - - - - - - - - - - - - - - - - - -
us Sa - ba - oth, Do - mi - nus De - us Sa - ba - oth,
minus De - - us Sa - baoth, ... Do - mi - nus De - - us Sa - - - -
- - - us, Do minus De - us Sa - - - ba - oth, Do - minus De - us Sa - -
De - us Sa - ba - oth .... Do - minus De - - - us Sa - - ba - oth
- us, Do - minus De - - - - us Sa - - - - -

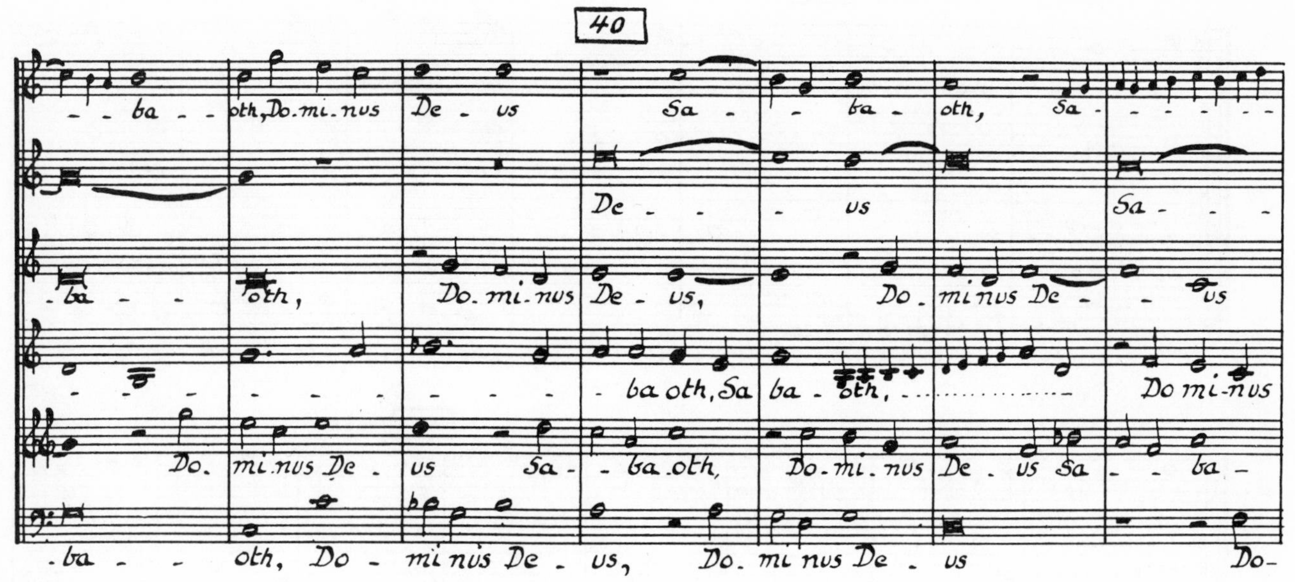
40
ba - - oth, Do.mi.nus De - us Sa - - ba - oth, Sa -
De - - - us Sa -
ba - - oth, Do.mi.nus De - us, Do.mi nus De - - us
ba oth, Sa ba - oth, Do mi.nus
Do. mi.nus De - us Sa - ba.oth, Do.mi.nus De - us Sa - - ba -
ba - - oth, Do - mi nus De - us, Do. mi nus De - us Do-

50
ba - oth.
ba - - - - oth.
Sa - baoth, Do.mi.nus De - us Sa - - ba - - oth.
De - us sa - - ba oth, Do.mi.nus De us sa - - ba - - oth.
oth Do.minus De - - us Sa ba oth.
minus De - - - us Sa - - ba - - oth.

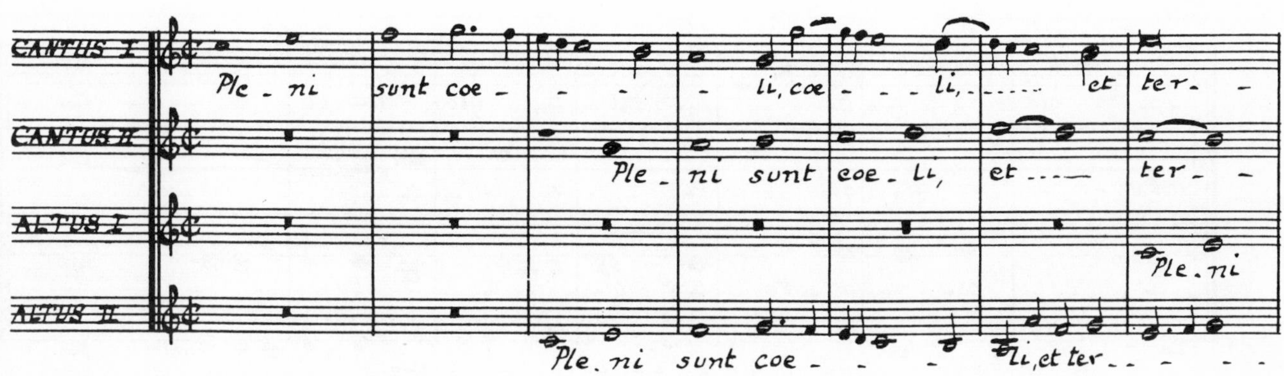
CANTUS I
Ple - ni sunt coe - - li, coe - - li, et ter -
CANTUS II
Ple - ni sunt coe - li, et ter -
ALTUS I
Ple.ni
ALTUS II
Ple.ni sunt coe - - li, et ter - -

60
-ra, ple-ni sunt coe-li, ple-ni sunt coe - li et ter-
- - ra, ple - ni sunt coe - li et ter-
sunt coe - - li, ple - ni sunt coeli et ter-ra, ple-ni sunt coe-li
-ra, ple - - ni sunt coe - li, ple-ni sunt coe-li et ter-
70
-ra glo-ri-a tu-a glo - - ria tu - a, glo-ri a tu-
- - ra glo-ri-a
et ter- - - ra glo-ri-a tu-a,
- - ra glo-ri-a tu-a,
80
- - a, glo-ri a tu-a, gloria tu-a glo-ri-
tu - - a, glo-ri-a
glo - ria tu - - a, glo-ri a - tu - -
glo-ri-a tu-a, glo-ri-a tu-a glo-
-a, glo - ri-a tu-a, glo-ri-a tu - a.
tu - a, glo - ri - a tu-a.
-a, glo-ri-a tu-a, glo-ri-a tu - a.
-ri-a tu - a, glo-ri-a tu - a.

Hosanna
90
CANTUS I
CANTUS II
ALTUS I
ALTUS II
TENOR
BASSUS
Ho - - - san - -
Ho - - san - - na - - in - - ex - - cel - - —
Ho - - - san - - na in - ex cel - - - - - - - - -
Ho - - san - na in excel - - - - - - - -
Ho - - san - na in ex - cel - - - - - sis, ho
Ho - san - na in ex - - -

100
- na in ex - - - cel - - - - - - - -
- sis in ex - - cel - - sis, ho - - -
- - - - - - - - - sis, in ex - cel - - -
- sis, ho - - - san - na in ex - cel - sis,
- - san - na .... in excel - - - - - sis, ho - san - -
- cel - - - - - - - - - - - - - - sis,

- - - - - - - - - - - - - sis, ho - - san - na
- san - - na in ex - - cel - - sis, in
- sis, hosanna inexcelsis, in ex - cel - sis -
ho - - san - - - - - na .... in ex - -
- na in ex - cel - - sis, ho - - san - na in ....
ho - san - na in ex - cel - sis ho - san -

in ex - cel - - sis, ho - san - na in ex - cel - - sis,
ex - - cel - - sis, ho - - -
in excelsis, ho - san - na in ex - cel - sis, ho - -
- cel - - - sis, ho - san - na in ex - cel - -
ex - - cel - sis, in - ex - cel - sis, ho - san - na
- na in ex - - cel - sis, ho - san - - - - - na.

120

ho - san - na in ex - cel - - - - sis, ho - san - - -
- san - - - na in ex - - cel - - sis,
- - san - na in ex - - cel - sis, ho - san - na
- - - - - sis, in ex - cel - sis, ho - san - na
in excel - - - - sis, ho - san - na in ex - -
ho - san - na in ex - - - cel - - - - -

- - - - - - - - na in - ex - - - cel - sis.
in ex - cel - sis.
in ex - - - cel - - - - sis, in ex - cel - sis.
in ex - cel - - - - sis in ex - - cel - sis.
- cel - - - - sis.
- - - sis.

Benedictus
CANTUS II
ALTUS I
TENOR
BASSUS
Be - ne - di - ctus qui ve - - - - - - - - nit
Be - ne - di - ctus qui ve - - nit, qui ve - - - - - - - - nit, be
Be - ne - di - ctus qui ve -
Be -

10
be - ne - di - ctus qui ve - - - - - -
- ne di - ctus qui ve - - - - - - - - nit, qui ve - - - - -
- - - - - - - - - nit, be - ne - di ctus qui ve - nit,
- ne - di - ctus qui ve - nit, be - ne - di - ctus qui ve - - -

20
- nit be - ne - di - ctus qui ve - - - -
- - nit be - ne - di - ctus qui ve - - - - nit, be - ne - di
be - ne di - ctus be - ne - di - ctus qui ve - nit, qui
- - - - - - nit, be - ne - di - ctus qui ve - nit qui ve -

- - - - nit in no - mi - ne Do - - - - -
- ctus qui ve - nit in no - - mi - ne Do - - - - - - - - - -
ve - nit in no - - mi - ne Do - mi - ni, in
- nit in no - - mi ne Do - mi - ni in no - - mi - ne Do - mi -

30

- - mi - ni, in no-
in no - mi - ne ...... Do - - -
no - - - mi-ne, in no - - mi-ne Do - - - mi-
ni, in no - - - - mi-ne .... Do - mi - ni....

40

- mi - ne Do - - - - mi - ni,
- mi - ni, in no - - mine Domini, ... in no mi ne Do-
- ni, in no - - mi - ne Do - - - - - - mi - ni, in
in no - mi - ne Do - - - mi - ni, in no - mine ..... Do

in no - mi - ne Do - - - - mi - ni.
- mi - ni, in nomine Do - - - - - mi - ni.
no - mi - ne Do - mi - ni in nomine Do - - mi - ni.
- mi - ni, in no - mine Do - - - mi - ni.

Hosanna ut supra

Agnus Dei I

10
- i, A - gnus De - - - - i,
- - - - - - - - i, A - -
A - - - gnus De - - - - - i, Agnus De - - - - - -
- - - - - - - - i, A - gnus De - - - - i, A - gnus
gnus De - - - - - - - - - - - - i, A.gnus De - - - - - -
De - - - - - - i, A - gnus De - - - - - i,

20
A - gnus De - - - i, A - gnus De - - - i,
- gnus De - - - - - - i,
- - - i, A - gnus De - - - - - i, qui tollis
De - - - - - - - - - - i, A - gnus De - - - i,
- i, A - gnus De - - - - - - - - i, A - - gnus De - -
A - gnus De - - - i, A - - gnus De - - i,

qui tol-lis pec-ca - - ta mun - di, qui tol-lis pecca - - - ta
qui tol - - - lis
pecca-ta mun - - - - - - - di, qui tollis
qui tollis pecca - ta mundi, qui tollis pec-cata mun-
- - i, qui tollis pecca-ta mun-di,
qui tollis pecca-ta mun - - - - di,

30
mun. di, qui tollis pec. ca . . . ta mun. di, qui tol.lis pec-
pec . ca . . ta mun . . . di:
pec . . ca . ta mun di, qui tol . lis pec.ca . . . . ta
di, qui tol.lis pec.ca.ta mun-
qui tol . . . lis, qui tol lis pec.ca.ta mun . di, pec-
qui tol lis pec.ca.ta mun . di, qui tol . lis pec.ca-

40
cata mundi: mi . se . re . re no . . bis, mi . . se.re . . . re
mi . . . . se . . . re . . . . re
mun . . . di: mi . se. re.re no . . . . bis,
di: mi . se . re . . . re no . bis, mi . . .
cata mun . . di: mi . se.re . re no . .
ta mun.di: mi . se.re . re no . . . bis,

50
no . bis, mi . se . re . re no . . . bis, mi . se . re . re no . . .
no . . bis, mi . . se . . .
mi . se.re . re no . . . . bis, mi . . se
se.re . re no . . . . bis, mi.se.re re no . . . . . bis
bis, mi . se.re . re no . bis, mi se.re.re no . bis, mi-
mi.se.re . . re nobis, mi.se.re.re no.bis, mi.se.re.re no . . .

Agnus Dei II

CANTUS I — A - - - gnus De - - - i, A - gnus De - i,

CANTUS II — Canon in Subdiapente — A - - - - gnus De - - - -

ALTUS I — A - gnus De - i, A - - - - gnus De - i, A - - - - gnus

ALTUS II — A - - - - gnus De - i A - gnus

ALTUS III — Resolutio — A - - gnus De -

TENOR — A - gnus.... De - - - - - -

BASSUS — A - gnus.... De - i, A - gnus De - -

10
A - gnus De - - - - - - - - i, A - - gnus De - - i,
- i, A - - - - - - - - gnus De - -
De - - - - - - - - i, A - gnus De - - - - -
De - - - i, ... A - gnus De - - - - - - i, A - - gnus De - - -
- - - i, A - - - - - - - gnus....
- i, A - gnus De - i, A - - - - gnus..... De - i,
i, A gnus........ De - - - i, A - - gnus... De - -

20
A - - gnus De - - i, qui tollis pec-ca-ta mundi qui tollis pec
- i, qui tol - lis pec - -
- i A - - gnus De - - - - i, qui tollis pec. ca. ta mun - di,
- i, A - gnus De - - i, qui tollis pec. cata mun - di, qui tollis
De - - i, qui tol - lis
A - - gnus..... De - - i, qui tollis pec - cata
- - - - - - i, qui tollis pec-ca-ta mun - di,

30
-ca ta mun - di, qui tollis pec ca - - - ta mun - - - di:
-ca - - ta pec - ca - - - - - ta mun-di:
qui tollis pec - ca - - - ta mun - di, peccata mun - - di:
pec-ca-ta mun - - - - - di, qui tollis pec - ca - ta mun - -
pec - ca - ta, pec - ca - - - ta
mun - - - di, qui tollis pec-ca-ta mun - - - di: do-
qui tollis peccata mun - di, qui tollis pec - ca - ta mun -

40
do - na nobis pa - - - - cem, do - - - na no - - -
do - na no - - bis pa
do - na no - bis, do - na no - bis pa - cem, do - na no - bis pa -
- - - di: do - na no - bis pa - cem, do - na nobis pa - cem, do - -
mun - di: do - na no - bis
- na no bis pa - cem, do - na no - bis pa - - cem,
- di: do - na no - bis pa - - - - - - -

50
bis pa - cem, do - na no - bis pa - cem, do-na no - bis
cem, do - na no - bis
cem do - na nobis pa - cem, do - na nobis pa - cem,
na no - bis pa - cem, do - na nobis pa - cem,
pa - cem, do - na
do na nobis pa cem, do - na nobis pa - cem, do - na nobis
cem, do - na nobis pa - cem, do - na no - bis pa-

60
pa - cem, do - na nobis pa - cem.
pa - cem, do - na nobis pa - cem.
do - na no - bis pa - cem, do - na no - bis pa - cem.
do - na no - bis pacem, do - na nobis pa - cem.
no - bis pa - cem.
pa - cem, do - na no - bis pa - cem.
cem, do - na no - bis pa - cem.

Mass: Repleatur os meum laude.

Palestrina

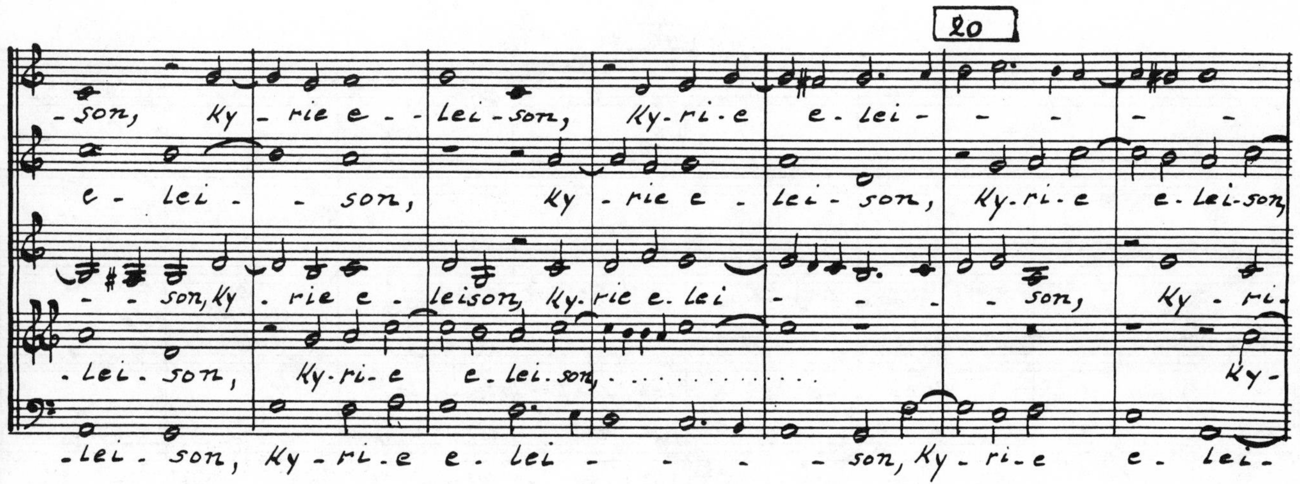

-son, Ky-rie e-lei-son, Ky-rie e-lei- - son, Ky-rie e - - - lei-
Ky-rie e-lei-son, Ky-
-e e-lei - - - - - - - - - son, Ky-
-rie e-lei-son, Ky-rie e-lei - - - - - - - -
- - son, Ky-ri-e e - - lei - - - - - - - - -

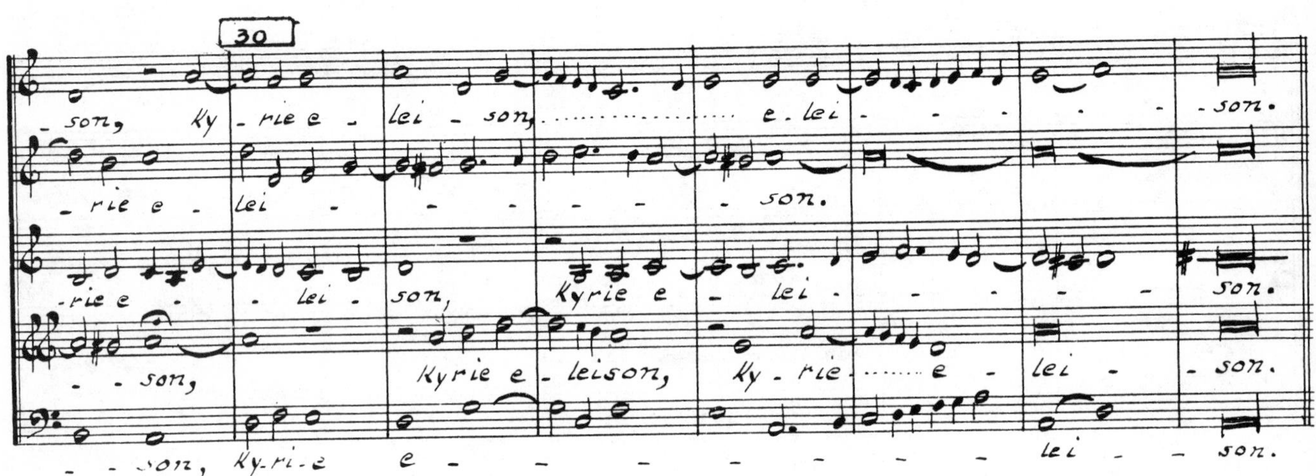
30
-son, Ky-rie e-lei-son, e-lei - - - - -son.
-rie e-lei - - - - - - son.
-rie e - lei-son, Kyrie e-lei - - - - - - son.
- -son, Kyrie e-leison, Ky-rie e-lei - -son.
- -son, Ky-ri-e e - - - - - - - - - - lei - - son.

40
Chri-ste e - - lei - - son, Christe e-
Resolutio
Chri-ste e-lei-
Chri-ste e - - - - lei-son, Chri-ste e-
Canon ad Septimam
Chri-ste e-lei-son Christe e-lei-son,
Chri-ste e-lei-son, Christe e-lei-son, Chri - - ste e-

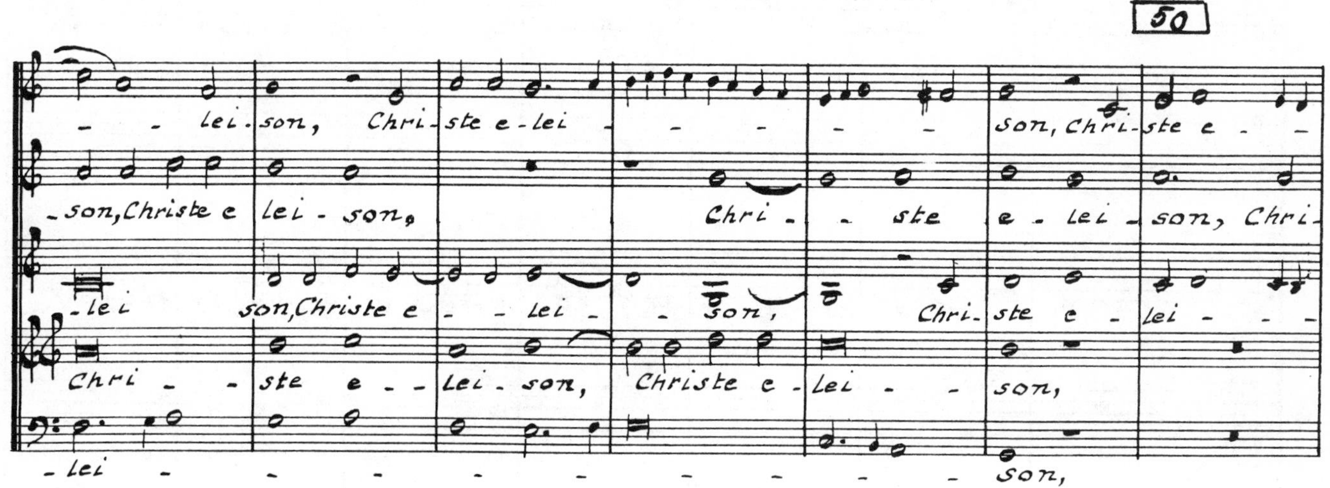
50
- - lei - son, Chri - ste e - lei - - - - - son, Chri - ste e - -
- son, Christe e lei - son, Chri - - ste e - lei - son, Chri -
- lei son, Christe e - - lei - - son, Chri - ste e - lei - - -
Chri - - ste e - - lei - son, Christe e - lei - - son,
- lei - - - - - - - - - - son,

- - lei - son, Christe e - lei - - son, Chri - ste e - lei -
- ste e - lei - - son, Christe e - lei - - - son,
- son, Chri - ste e - - lei - son, Chri - ste e - lei - - - son,
Chri - ste e - lei - - - son,
Christe e - lei - son, Christe e - - - lei - - son, Chri -

60

- son, Christe e - lei - - - - - - - - son.
Christe e - lei - - - - - - son.
Chri - ste e - lei - - - son, Chri - ste e - lei - son.
Christe e - lei - - - - son, Christe e - lei - - - son.
- ste e - lei - - - - son, Chri - ste e - lei - - son,

70
Ky - ri - e .... e - lei - son, e - - - lei-
Resolutio.
Ky - ri - e .... e - lei - son, ...
Canon ad Sextam.
Ky - ri - e .... e - lei - son,

80
- son, Ky - rie e - lei - son, Ky - ri - e .... e - lei - son, Ky - rie e - lei -
Ky - ri - e .... e - lei - son, Ky - ri - e .... e -
...... Ky - ri - e elei - - son, Ky - - ri - e e - - lei - - -
Ky - ri - e .... e - lei - son, Ky - ri - e .... e -
Ky - ri - e .... e - lei - son, Ky - ri - e e - - lei - son,

-son, Ky-rie e-lei - - - - son, Ky- ri-e.........e-lei - - son,
-lei-son, Ky- ri- e....... e- lei-son, Ky- rie e - lei - - son,
- - son, Ky- ri-e e-lei - - son, Ky- ri- e e-
-lei-son, Ky-rie e - lei - son, Ky- ri-
Ky- ri-e.........................e-lei - son, Ky - ri-e.........e-lei-

90
Ky- ri- e e- lei - - son, Ky - ri- e e- lei- - son.
Ky-ri- e....... e- lei - - son.
-lei - - - - son, Ky- ri-e e-leison, Ky- rie....... e - lei - - son.
-e..... e- lei - - son, Ky-ri - e....... e - lei - - son.
- - - - son, Ky-ri-e e - lei - - - - son.

Sanctus
CANTUS
ALTUS (I)
QUINTUS (ALTUS II)
TENOR
BASSUS
Resolutio
Canon ad Tertiam
San - ctus, ... san - - - - ctus, ... San -
San - ctus, ... San - - - ctus, San -
San - -

10
- ctus, San - - - - ctus, San - - ctus, Dominus De - us
- - ctus, San - - ctus Do - minus De - us
San - - ctus, Sanctus, San - - - -
San - - ctus, San - ctus, San - - - - - ctus
- ctus, ... San - - ctus, San - - ctus, San - - ctus Do -

20
Sa - - ba - oth, Do - mi - nus De us .... Sa - - ba - oth. Ple -
Sa - ba - - oth, Dominus De - us Sa - ba - - oth, Do - minus De - us Sa -
ctus Do - minus De - us Sa - ba - - oth.
Dominus De - us Sa - ba - oth. Ple -
- minus De - us, Do - minus Deus Saba - oth, ... Sa - ba - oth ..... Ple -

30
-ni sunt coeli et ter-ra, ple-ni sunt coe-li et ter- - - -
-ba-oth. Ple-ni sunt coe-li et ter-ra, ple-ni sunt coe-li et terra...
Ple-ni sunt coe-li, ple-ni sunt coe-
-ni sunt coe-li, ple-ni sunt coe-li et terra
-ni sunt coe-li et ter-ra, ple-ni sunt coe-li et ter- - - - -

- - ra glori-a tu- - - - - a,..... glori-a tu- -
..... glo-ri-a tu-a, tu- - - - - a, glo-
-li et ter-ra glori-a tu- - - a, glo-ri-a tu-
glo-ri-a tu- - - a, glori-a tu- - - a,
- - ra glo-ri-a.....tu- a, tu- - a, glori-a tu- - a, glo-

40
-a, glo-ri-a tu- - - - a, glo-ri-a tu- - - a.
-ri-a tu- a, tu- - a, glo- - ri-a tu- a, tu- - - - a.
- - a, tu- - - a.
tu- - - - - - - a.
- -ri- - - a tu - a, glo-ri-a tu-a, gloria........tu - a.

Hosanna

CANTUS
Ho. san. na in ex - - cel. sis, ... in
ALTUS
Ho. san.na in ex.cel.sis, ho. sanna in excelsis, ho. sanna in
TENOR (I)
Canon ad secundam.
Ho - san - na in ex - cel -
QUINTUS (Tenor II)
Resolutio
Ho - san - na in ex.
BASSUS
Ho. san. na in excel - -

10
........ex - cel - - - sis, hosanna in excel - sis, hosanna in ex.cel.
ex - cel. - - sis, hosanna in excel - - sis, ho - - sanna
- sis, ... ho . sanna in ex.cel - -
- cel - sis, ... ho - sanna in ex
- . sis, ... ho.sanna in excel - - sis, ... ho.sanna

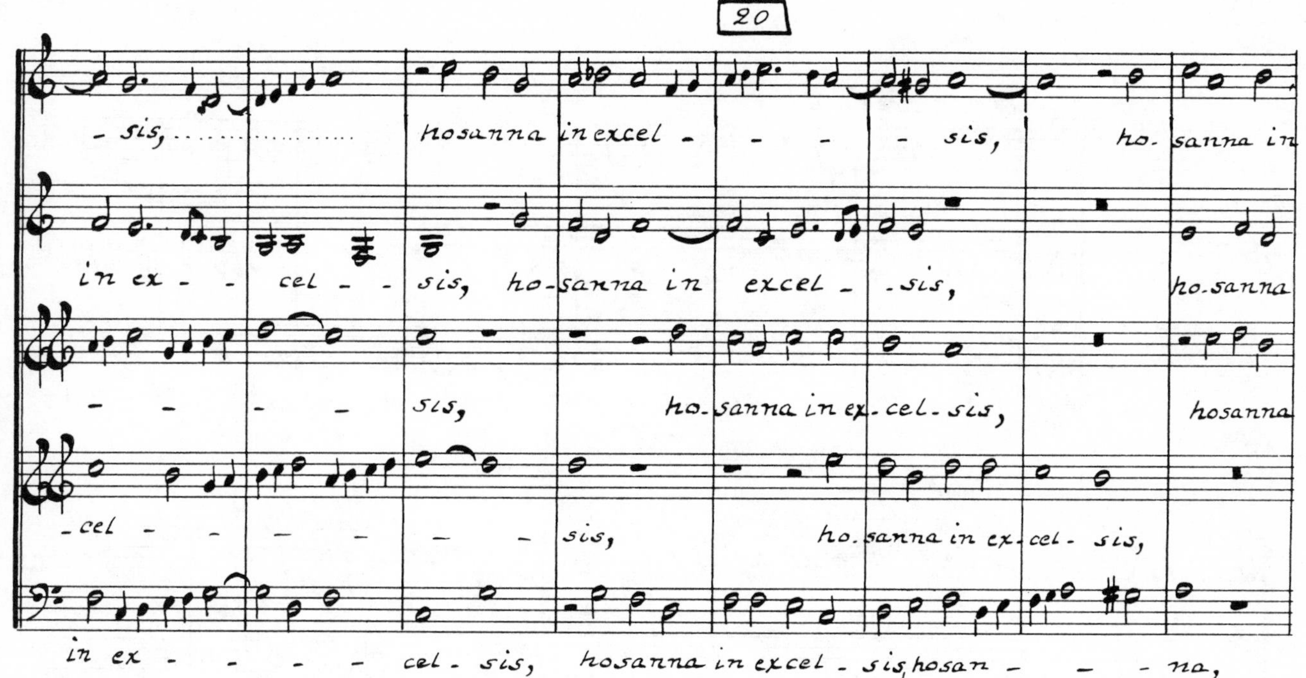
20
- sis, ... hosanna in excel - - - - - sis, ho- sanna in
in ex - - cel - - sis, ho- sanna in excel - - sis, ho-sanna
- - - - sis, ho- sanna in ex- cel- sis, hosanna
- cel - - - - - - sis, ho- sanna in ex- cel- sis,
in ex - - - - - cel - sis, hosanna in excel - sis, hosan - - - na,

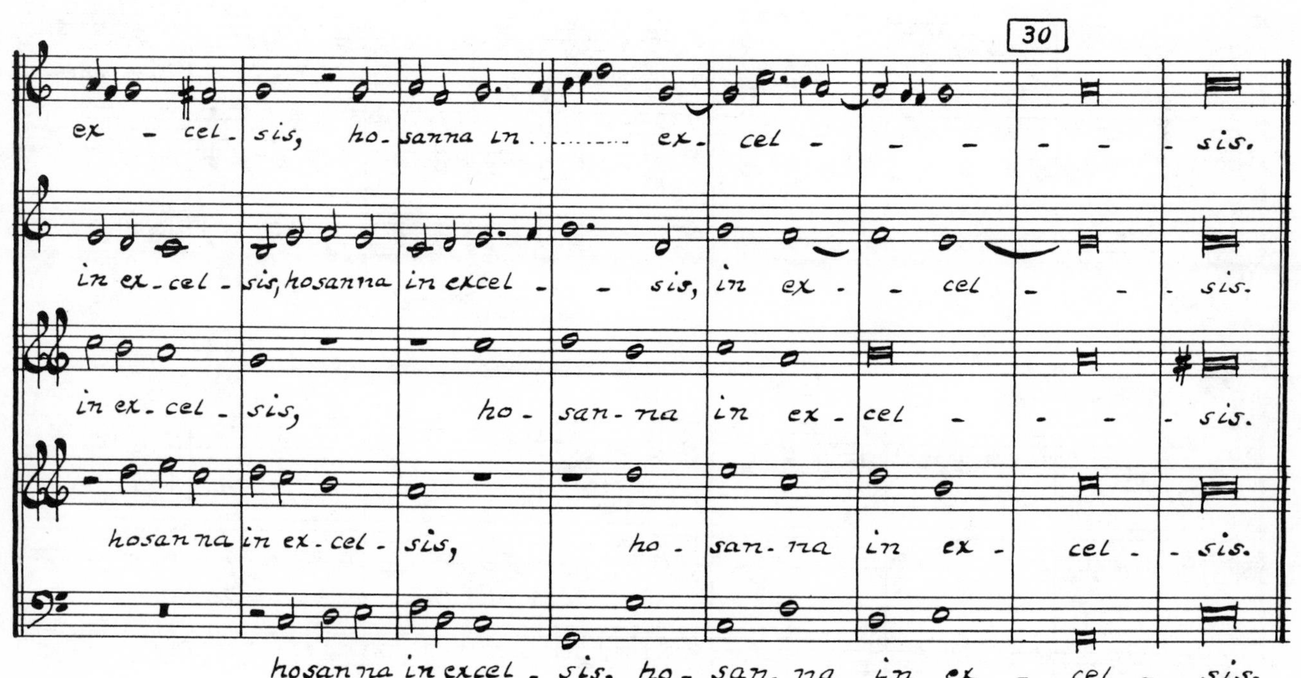
30
ex - cel - sis, ho- sanna in .... ex- cel - - - - - - sis.
in ex- cel - sis, hosanna in excel - - sis, in ex - - cel - - - sis.
in ex- cel - sis, ho - san- na in ex - cel - - - - sis.
hosanna in ex- cel - sis, ho - san- na in ex - cel - - sis.
hosanna in excel - sis, ho - san- na in ex - cel - sis.

Benedictus
CANTUS
ALTUS
TENOR(I)
Be - nedictus qui ve -
Be - nedictus qui ve - - - - - -
Be - ne-dictus qui ve - - nit, be - - ne-di - ctus qui...

10
- - - - - - - - - nit, be - ne-dictus qui ve -
- - - - - - - - nit, be - ne-dictus qui ve - -
.... ve - nit, be - ne-dictus qui......... ve - - - - - -

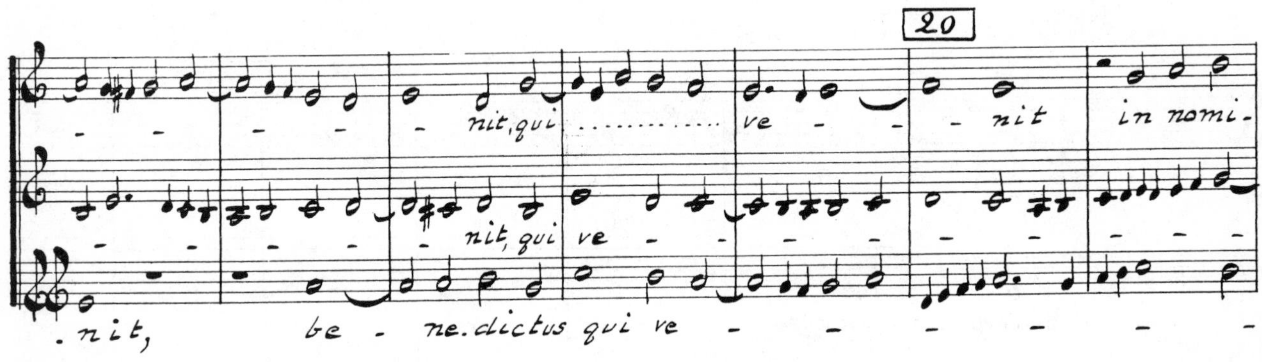
20
- - - - - - nit, qui .... ve - - - nit in nomi-
- - - - - nit, qui ve - - - - - - - - - -
-nit, be - ne-dictus qui ve - - - - - - -

-ne .... Do - - mi-ni, in no-mi-
- -nit...... in nomi-ne............Do - - mi-
- - nit in nomi-ne.......................Do - - - mi-

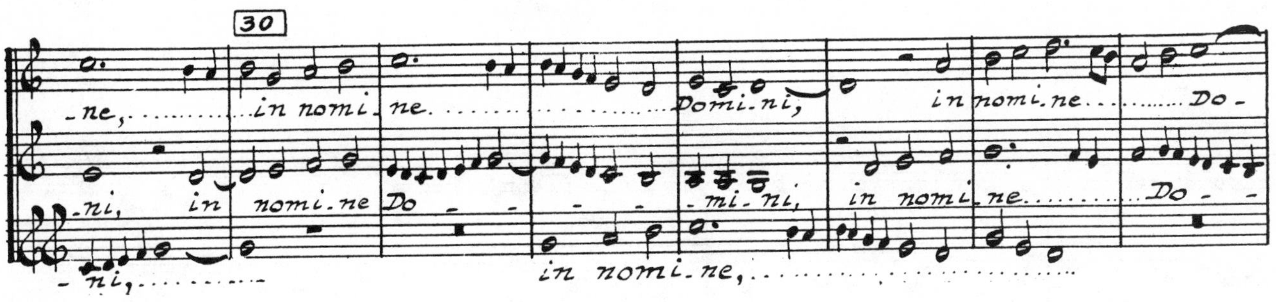
30
-ne, in nomine Domini, in nomine Do-
-ni, in nomine Do - - - - mini, in nomine Do-
-ni, in nomine,

40
- - - - mi-ni, in nomine Do-mi-ni.
- - - - mini, in nomine Do-mi-ni.
in nomi-ne in nomine Domine in nomi-ne Do-mi-ni.
Hosanna ut supra.

Agnus Dei. I.

CANTUS
ALTUS
TENOR(I)
QUINTUS TENOR(II)
BASSUS
Canon ad unisonam
Resolutio
A - gnus De - - - - i, qui tol-lis
A - gnus De - - - - i,
A - gnus De - i, A-gnus De - i, qui
A - gnus De - - i,
A - gnus De - i A -

10
pec-ca-ta mun-di, A - gnus De-i, qui tol-lis pec-
A - gnus De - i, qui tollis pec-ca-ta
tollis pec-ca - - ta mun - - - di:
A - gnus De - i, qui
-gnus De - i, qui tollis pec-ca-ta mun - - - di, pec-

20
-ca-ta mun - - - di, ... mun - - - di: mi-se-re-re no-
mun - - di: mi-se-re-re no - bis, mi-se - re-re no - bis, mi-
mi-se-re-re no - - bis, no - bis,... mi-se-re-re..........
tol-lis pec-ca - - - ta mun - - - - - - -
-ca - ta mun - di: mise-re-re no - - bis,......

- - - - bis, no - - - bis, mi-se-re-re no - - - -
-se - re - - re...... no - bis, mi-se-re - re no-bis, no - - -
no - bis, mi-se-re-re.................. no - - - bis, mi-se-re
- - - - di:
mi-se-re - - re no - - bis, mi - se-re-

30
- - bis, mi-se-re - re no - - - - - bis,...... mi-
- - bis, mi-se-re - re no - bis, mi-se-re-re ....
- re no - - - - - bis, mise-re - re nobis, mi-se-re - - -
mi - se - re - - re no - - -
- - re no - bis, mi - se-re-re no-bis, ...

40
-sere-re .... no-bis, mi-se-re - re no - - - bis.
no - bis, mi-se-re - re, mi-se-re-re no - - bis.
-re no - bis, mi-se-re - - - re no - - - - bis.
- bis, no - - bis.
mi-se-re - re, misere - re no - - - - bis.

Agnus Dei. II

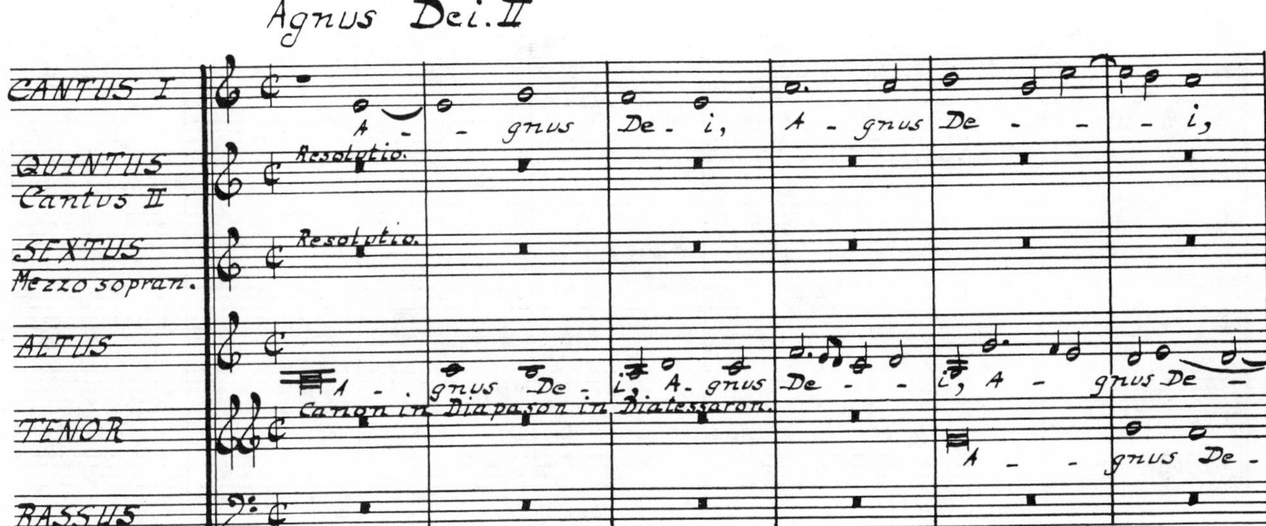
CANTUS I
QUINTUS
Cantus II
SEXTUS
Mezzo sopran.
ALTUS
TENOR
BASSUS
A - gnus De - i, A - gnus De - - i,
Resolutio.
Resolutio.
A - gnus De - i, A - gnus De - - i, A - gnus De -
Canon in Diapason in Diatessaron.
A - - gnus De -

10
A - - - - - gnus De - - - - i,
A - - gnus De - i, A - gnus De - - -
A - - gnus De - i, A -
- - - i, A - - - - - gnus...... De - - -
- i, A - gnus De - - - - - i,
A - gnus De - i, A - - gnus De - i, A - gnus De - - - i,

20
qui tollis pec - ca - ta mun - - di, qui - tol - lis pec - ca -
qui tollis pec - ca - -
-gnus De - - - - - i, qui
- - - - - - - - - - i, ... qui tol - lis pecca -
qui tollis pec - ca - - ta mun - - di,
qui tollis pec - ca - - ta mun - di, qui....

- ta mun - - - di, qui tollis pec - - ca - ta mun - di, qui
- ta mun - - di, qui tollis pec -
tollis pec - ca - - ta mun - - - di,
- - ta, pecca - ta mun - - di, qui tol - lis pec - ca - - ta mundi, qui
qui tollis pec - ca - - ta .... mun - di, mun - - di:
.....tollis pec - ca - ta mun - - di, qui tol - lis pec - ca - ta .... mun -

30
tol - lis pec - cata mun - di, qui tol - lis pec - ca - ta .... mun - di:
- ca - ta .... mun - di, mun - - di:
qui tol - lis pec - ca - ta .... mun - di, mun - - di:
tol - lis pec - ca - ta mun - - di, pec - ca - ta mun - di: do - na
do - na no -
- - di, ... mun - - di, pec - ca - ta mun - di: do -

40
do - na no - bis pa - cem, do - na no - bis pa - cem, do - - -
do - na no - bis pa - cem, pa - - cem
do - na no - bis pa -
no - bis pa - cem, do - na nobis pa - cem, do -
- bis pa - cem, pa - - cem,
- na no - bis, do - na nobis pa - cem, do - na no - bis pa - cem,

- na no - bis pa - cem, pa - cem, do - na no - bis pa - cem,
pa - - -
- cem, pa - - cem,
- na no - bis pa - - - cem, do - na no - bis pa -
pa - - - cem, do na nobis pa - cem, do -
do - na no - bis pa - cem, do - na nobis pa - cem, pa - - cem,

50
do - na no - bis pa - - - cem.
- cem, do - na nobis pa - cem
pa - - - cem.
cem, do - na no - bis pa - - - - - cem.
- na no - bis pa - cem, dona no - bis pa - - cem.
do - na no - bis pa - - cem, pa - cem.

SOURCES, COMMENTARY, AND TRANSLATIONS

GREGORIAN CHANT

Gregorian chant, or plain song, is the name of unisonous ecclesiastical art music in use in the Christian Church of the West before the development of harmony, written on scales derived from the Greek modes.

The modes used in plain song were limited, quite early, to four authentic, (Dorian, Phrygian, Lydian, and Mixolydian), and four plagal (Hypodorian, Hypophrygian, Hypolydian, and Hypomixolydian) modes.

This modal system is different from that of the original Greek modes, due to some misunderstanding of the latter.

There are two main collections of Gregorian chant: the Gradual* and the Antiphonal. In the Gradual the chief ancient pieces are: the Introit, or Antiphona ad introitum, at the beginning of the service; the Gradual, with Alleluia or tract, which precede the Gospel; the Offertory which accompanies the preparation of the oblations; the Communion or antiphona ad Communionem which accompanies the partaking of the Sacrament.

In the parallel collection of music, the Antiphonal, we find the Responds which form musical interludes between the lessons and the Antiphons which form an integral part of the Psalmody. This collection is used mainly in the monasteries for the singing of the Office.

In both collections the modes are indicated by the numbers one to eight.

---

*The most important parts of the Gradual and Antiphonal are available in modern notation (Liber Usualis).

The relation of plain song to measured music may be expressed thus: plain song is analogous to prose, and measured music, with its definite, generally regular, subdivisions of time, is analogous to poetry, with its definite subdivisions of metre.

Explanation of signs found in Gregorian chant:

Ictus. The rhythmical ictus is an alighting or resting place sought by the rhythm at intervals of every two or three (eighth) notes. It does not mean accent or stress. The rhythm is one of the simplest, i.e., two or three eighth notes, their order of succession free.

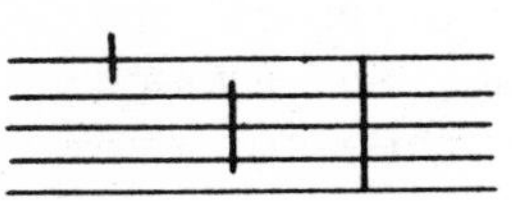

Musical punctuation, in general corresponding to comma, semicolon, period.

^

Pressus, a neum meaning a compact strong sound of double value, demanding, in many cases, some degree of acceleration on the preceding notes.

Distropha and tristropha, meaning a twice or thrice repeated vocal pulsation, very rapid in character, like a hand tapping (according to ancient authority).

V.

Verse (from the psalms).

℟

Back to response.

i ii iij

i, ii repeated; iij to be sung three times.

———

Episema, meaning holding.

e u o u a e

Saeculorum Amen (end of Gloria Patri).

*

Asterisk meaning division of the choir according to previous agreement.

Quilisma. The note or the group of notes immediately preceding the note below or above this sign must be prolonged. It appeared in the old notation as a jagged neume.

The above signs are all taken from the modern notation in Liber Usualis.

Page

1. Kyrie (sung after Introit). Recorded by The Pius X School. 1
See translation of mass.

2. Alleluia. Recorded by the Solesmes Monks.
Alleluia. V. The just shall spring as the lily; and shall flourish forever before the Lord. Alleluia. 1

3. Passer. Transposed chant, in which the first part belongs to the third tone and ends with a psalm cadence in the third tone; the second part is in the first tone. Notice the attempt at imitation of the cooing of the turtledove. 2

The sparrow hath found herself a house, and the turtle a nest, where she may lay her young ones: thy altars, O Lord of hosts, my King, and my God: blessed are they that dwell in thy house, they shall praise thee for ever and ever.

4. Ad te levavi. Recorded by the Solesmes Monks. 2
To thee have I lifted up my soul. In thee, O my God, I put my trust: let me not be ashamed. Neither let my enemies laugh at me: for none of them that wait on thee shall be confounded.

5. Kyrie. In this ancient chant we find the old dominant b. Because of the frequent modification of b to b flat due to the tritone the dominant was later changed to c. 2

6. Sanctus. In this chant we find both the old and the new dominant. 3
For translation, see mass.

7. Kyrie. Dominant on c only. 3

8. Alleluia. With modulation 3
Alleluia. V. Come, O Lord, and do not delay; forgive the sins of thy people Israel. Alleluia.

9. Response. Recorded by the Solesmes Monks. 4
Behold how the Just dieth, and none taketh it to heart: and just men are taken off, and no one considereth: the Just is taken away from the face of iniquity: and his memory shall be in peace. V. He was dumb like the lamb before his shearer, and opened not His mouth: He was taken away from distress, and from judgment. R.

10. Sanctus. Recorded by The Pius X School. 5

11. Agnus Dei. Recorded by The Pius X School. 5

12. Antiphon. In the pure Lydian mode. 5
Behold, the Lord will come, and with Him all His saints: and on that day there will be a great light, alleluia.

Page

13. Gradual. The mode is mixed, i.e., it has both b and b flat. With modulation 6
Princes sat, and spoke against me: and the wicked persecuted me: help me, O Lord, my God: Save me for thy mercy's sake.

14. Gradual. Benedictus. In the Lydian mode (mixed). 6

15. Communion. Recorded by the Solesmes Monks. 7
Christ our Pasch is immolated, alleluia: therefore let us feast with the unleavened bread of sincerity and truth. Alleluia, alleluia, alleluia.

16. Antiphon.
Thou shalt sprinkle me with hyssop, O Lord, and I shall be cleansed; thou 7
shalt wash me, and I shall be made whiter than snow. Ps.50. Have mercy on me, O God, according to thy great mercy. V. Glory be to the Father, and to the Son, and to the Holy Ghost. As it was in the beginning, is now, and ever shall be, world without end. Amen.

17. Gradual. Recorded by the Solesmes Monks. 8
Thou, O Lord, that sittest upon the Cherubim, stir up thy might, and come. V. Give ear, O thou that rulest Israel: thou that leadest Joseph like a sheep.

18. Offertory. Recorded by the Solesmes Monks. 8
Moses prayed in the sight of the Lord his God, and said: Why, O Lord, is thy indignation enkindled against thy people, Let the anger of thy mind cease; remember Abraham, Isaac, and Jacob, to whom thou didst swear to give a land flowing with milk and honey: and the Lord was appeased from doing the evil, which he had spoken of doing against his people.

19. Introit. Recorded by the Solesmes Monks. 9
The Spirit of the Lord hath filled the whole earth, alleluia; and that which containeth all things hath knowledge of the voice, alleluia, alleluia, alleluia. Ps. 67. Let God arise, and let his enemies be scattered; and let them that hate him, flee from before his face. V. Glory.

Orlandus Lassus (1532-94).

Cantiones duarum vocum. In all the modes used in ecclesiastical style.
Texts from the Vulgate: 10

2-1. Eccl. 14:22.
Blessed is the man that shall continue in wisdom, and that shall meditate in his justice, and in his mind shall think of the all seeing eye of God.

2-2. Proverbs 3: 13,14. 12
Blessed is the man that findeth wisdom and is rich in prudence: The purchasing thereof is better than the merchandise of silver, and her fruit than the chiefest and purest gold.

Page

2-3. I Cor. 2:9. 14
That eye hath not seen, nor ear heard, neither hath it entered into the heart of man, what things God hath prepared for them that love God.

2-4. Eccl. 39:6. 16
He will give his heart to resort early to the Lord that made him, and he will pray in the sight of the most high.

2-5. Proverbs 10: 28,29. 18
The expectation of the just is joy; but the hope of the wicked shall perish. The strength of the upright is the way of the Lord: and fear to them that work evil.

2-6. John 8:12. 20
He that followeth me, walketh not in darkness but shall have the light of life, sayeth the Lord.

2-7. Book of Wisdom 10:19. 22
The just took the spoils of the wicked, and they sung to thy holy name, O Lord, and they praised with one accord thy victorious hand.

2-8. This is part of the responsory for Lesson VI in Matins for the Feast of All Saints, Nov. 1. 24
My holy people, who in this world have known only toil and strife, I shall grant to you the reward for all your labors.

2-9. Matthew 16:24. 26
If any man will come after me, let him deny himself, and take up his cross, and follow me, sayeth the Lord.

2-10. Matthew 25:23. 28
Well done, good and faithful servant: because thou hast been faithful over a few things I will place thee over many things: enter thou into the joy of thy Lord.

2-11. Book of Wisdom 3:7. Matt. 13:43. 30
The just shall shine, and shall run to and fro like sparks among the reeds.

2-12. Motet in honor of the Blessed Virgin Mary. 32
As a rose among thorns even to them its beauty lends,
So the Virgin Mary casts her grace and charm
Over all her progeny. For from her has sprung
The Flower, whose fragrance is the gift of life.

Translation of the text of the Mass:
Kyrie eleison, Christe eleison, Kyrie eleison.
Lord, have mercy. Christ, have mercy. Lord, have mercy.

Gloria: Glory be to God on high (intoned by the priest).
Choir: And on earth peace to men of good will. We praise thee; we bless thee; We adore thee; we glorify thee. We give thee thanks for thy great glory, O Lord, heavenly King. God the Father Almighty. O Lord Jesus Christ, the only-begotten Son: O Lord God, Lamb of God, Son of the Father, who taketh away the sins of the world, have mercy on us: who taketh away the sins of the world, receive our prayers: who sitteth at the right hand of the Father, have mercy on us. For thou only art holy: thou only art Lord: thou only, O Jesus Christ, are most high, together with the Holy Ghost, in the glory of God the Father, Amen.

Credo: I believe in one God (intoned by the priest).
Choir: The Father Almighty, maker of heaven and earth, and of all things visible and invisible. And in one Lord Jesus Christ, the only begotten Son of God, born of the Father before all ages; God of God, light of light, true God of true God; begotten not made; consubstantial with the Father; by whom all things were made. Who for us men, and for our salvation, came down from heaven; and was incarnate by the Holy Ghost, of the Virgin Mary; and was made man. He was crucified also for us, suffered under Pontius Pilate, and was buried. And the third day he rose again according to the scriptures; and ascended into heaven. He sitteth at the right hand of the Father; and he shall come again with glory to judge the living and the dead; and his kingdom shall have no end, and in the Holy Ghost, the Lord and giver of life, who proceedeth from the Father and the Son, who together with the Father and the Son is adored and glorified; who spoke by the prophets. And one holy catholic and apostolic church. I confess one baptism for the remission of sins. And I await the resurrection of the dead, and the life of the world to come. Amen.

Sanctus: Holy, holy, holy, Lord God of hosts. Heaven and earth are full of thy glory. Hosanna in the highest.
Benedictus: Blessed is he that cometh in the name of the Lord.

Agnus Dei I: Lamb of God, who takest away the sins of the world, have mercy on us.
Agnus Dei II: Lamb of God, who takest away the sins of the world, grant us peace.

Page

4-1 De Feria 124
In the Phrygian mode. For ferial days (a ferial day is one on which no feast of the Lord or a saint is observed). In this kind of mass the Gloria and the Credo are omitted.

4-2 Dies Sanctificatus 129
In the Mixolydian mode. On the motet of the same name.

4-3 Gabriel Archangelus 132
In the Aeolian mode. On a motet by Verdelot.

4-4 Sine nomine. 134
In the Hypophrygian mode. Thematic origin unknown.

4-5 Dies Sanctificatus 137
In the Mixolydian mode. A Christmas motet.
The sacred day has dawned upon us,
Come ye people and praise God,
Because this day a great light has fallen upon the earth.
(Psalm 117:24): This is the day that the Lord hath made -
let us rejoice and be glad in it.

4-6 In Festo Transfigurationes Domini: On the Gregorian hymn. 141
Quicumque Christum Quaeritis (see Liber Usualis, page 1465.)
In the Phrygian mode.

4-7 Magnificat. In the Lydian mode. 146
There are two Magnificats in each of the eight modes. This one has been selected because it is one of the few examples of the use of the pure Lydian mode. Notice the invariable final cadence on A. The composition is fugal throughout. The following Gregorian chant is intoned at the beginning:

1. Magnificat a - ni - ma me-a Do- mi-num

The polyphonic treatment alternates with the chant according to the numbers.

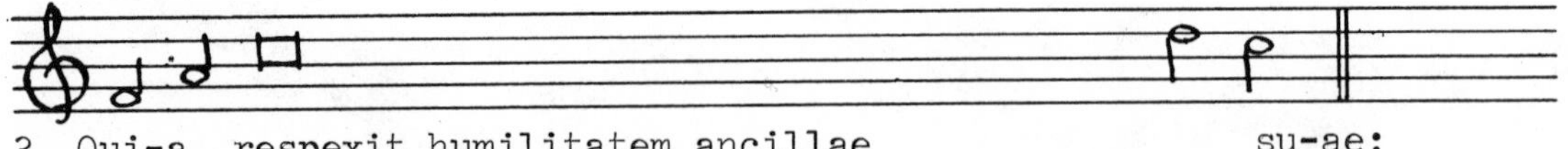

3. Qui-a respexit humilitatem ancillae su-ae:
5. Et mi-sericor- dia ejus a progenie in pro-geni-es
7. De- po-suit potentes de se-de,
9. Sus-ce-pit Israel puerus su-um,
11. Glo-ri-a Patri, et Fili-o,

Page

3. ecce enim ex hoc beatam me dicent omnes gene -ra -ti -o -nes
5. ti - - - - - - - - - mentibus e-um.
7. et exal- - - - - - - - ta -vit humiles.
9. recordatus miseri - - - - cor-diae su-ae.
11. et Spi - - - - - - - - ri-tui sancte.

1. My soul doth magnify the Lord:
2. And my spirit hath rejoiced in God, my Savior.
3. For He hath regarded the lowliness of His handmaid: for behold, from henceforth, all generations shall call me blessed.
4. For He that is mighty, hath done great things to me: and holy is His name.
5. And His mercy is from generation to generations: unto them that fear Him.
6. He hath shown might in his arm: He hath scattered the proud in the conceit of their hearts.
7. He hath put down the mighty from their seat: and exalted the humble.
8. He hath filled the hungry with good things: and the rich He hath sent empty away.
9. He hath helpen Israel His servant: being mindful of His mercy.
10. As He spoke to our fathers: to Abraham and to His seed forever.
11. Glory be to the Father, to the Son, and to the Holy Ghost:
12. As it was in the beginning, is now, and ever shall be, world without end, Amen.

4-8, 5-1 Sanctorum Meritis 157, 158
In the Phrygian mode. On the Gregorian Hymn of the same name (see Liber usualis, p. 963).

5-2 Petra Sancta 162
In the Aeolian mode. Thematic origin unknown.

5-3, 5-4 Vestiva i Colli. 168, 173
In the Dorian mode. On his own madrigal of the same name.

5-5 Alleluia Tulerunt Dominum. 182
In the Mixolydian mode.
They have taken away my Lord, and I know not where they have laid him. If thou hast taken him away, tell me and I will take him away. (Mary Magdalen, following the resurrection.)
Taken from John 20:13,15 (last portion of each verse)

5-6 In Dominicis Quadragesima: Vesper hymn on the Gregorian theme . . 190
"Ad preces nostras." Only the two last movements are used in this book.
In the Aeolian mode. In the last movement the soprano and the second tenor form a canon at the octave.
Grant to us a fountain of tears, the potent strength that comes from fasting; destroy with thy might (literally "sword") our thousand carnal vices.
Glory be to God, the Father Eternal, and to thee, eternally begotten Son, with whom the Holy Spirit, (in all things) equal, reigneth forever.

Page

5-7 Laudate Dominum:. 193
In the Ionian mode.

5-8 Improperium 197
In the Ionian mode.
My heart hath expected reproach and misery; and I looked for one that could grieve together with Me, but there was none: I sought for one that would comfort Me, and I found none; and they gave me gall for my food, and in My thirst they gave Me vinegar to drink.

5-9 Exaltabo Te 202
In the Ionian mode.
I will exalt Thee. O Lord. for Thou hast upheld me,
and hast not made mine enemies to rejoice over me:
O Lord, I have cried to Thee, and Thou hast healed me.
(Translation from the St. Andrew missal)

5-10 Litany of the Blessed Virgin Mary 207

Lord have mercy on us
Christ hear us
Christ graciously hear us
God the Father of heaven, have mercy on us
Holy Trinity, one God, have mercy on us.

Holy Mary, — Pray for us
Holy Virgin of virgins
Mother of Christ
Mother most chaste
Mother most amiable
Mother most faithful
Virgin most merciful
Refuge of sinners
Comfortress of the afflicted

(Same response after such invocation down to the "Agnus Dei")

Queen of Angels
Queen of all Saints

Lamb of God, who takest away the sins of the world, have mercy on us.

Page

Masses:

Ad Fugam 214

In the Mixolydian mode. In this mass Palestrina shows his mastery of the contrapuntal devices of the Netherland school. Canonic throughout, the Kyrie and the Hosanna show two pairs of canons; the Benedictus a canon "trinitas in unitate," i.e., three in one, and the five part Agnus Dei the three upper voices are in three part canon, while the two lower voices form a canon in two parts.

L'Homme Armé. 220

In the Mixolydian mode. L'Homme Arme, an old French Chanson used as canto fermo by a number of 15th and 16th century masters in the composition of a mass called Missa L'Homme Arme, the purpose of which was to show their skill and ingenuity in the use of contrapuntal devices.

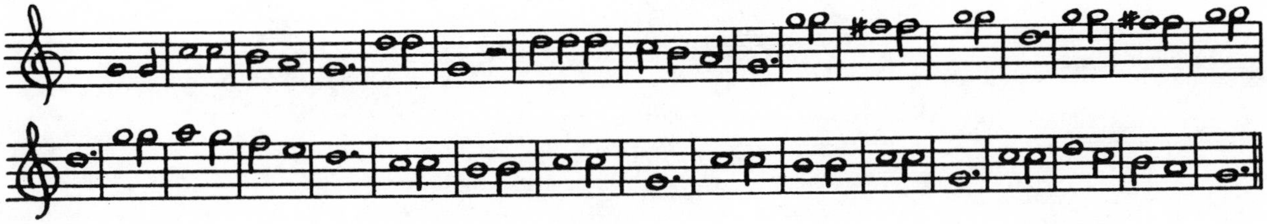

The above theme while not fully agreeing with the canti fermi used by the composers previous to Palestrina, may be accepted as the standard form. It is the version resulting from joining the phrases as they appear in the mass by Palestrina.

There are two editions of this mass: 1570 and 1599; the first, in triple time, and the second, in $\frac{4}{2}$ time. The curious fact about these two editions is that by changing the triple time of the first edition to $\frac{4}{2}$ time by rebarring it the result will be that of the 1599 edition with every important cadence correctly placed.

Ut Re Mi Fa Sol La. 250

In the Ionian mode. Also called the Hexachord Mass. Two forms of the Guidonian hexachord are used; on C (hexachordum naturale), and on G (hexachordum durum). The hexachord on F (hexachordum molle) is not used on account of its modulating properties.

Repleatur es meum laude 279

In the Phrygian mode. A great example of the canonic art, in all possible intervals. (The Gloria, in canon at the fourth, and the Credo, in canon at the fifth, are omitted in this book, since there are numerous other examples of imitation in these intervals.)